TEACH THEM ALL TO READ

Theory, Methods, and Materials
for Teaching the Disadvantaged

TEACH THEM
ALL TO READ

*Theory, Methods, and Materials
for Teaching the Disadvantaged*

S. Alan Cohen

RANDOM HOUSE
New York

To my wife, Rita,
who worked as hard
on this book
as I did.

Preface

A primary goal of this book is to influence the teaching of reading to children caught in the poverty pockets of urban and rural slums. A secondary goal is to provide more effective techniques for the teaching of reading to *all* children. This book is directed, therefore, to all teachers of reading and to all teachers of disadvantaged children.

Education alone cannot solve the debilitating effects of poverty and second class citizenship. But education can contribute significantly to the amelioration of these disadvantages. As a result of their unique responsibility to teach children how to read and write, educators can help to bring about social change. If we can increase the quality and quantity of reading and writing among socially disadvantaged youth, we can better prepare them to cope with the demands of a highly technological society.

It is folly to suggest that minority groups living in a state of poverty and illiteracy can be free to *be* as they choose to *be*. Choice implies the *power* to choose. In this country, members of disadvantaged minority groups cannot choose to *be* as long as they meet the dominant culture on unequal ground. Education must give these disadvantaged youth the literacy skills necessary to gain power in American culture. With that power they can choose values, mores, and behaviors to whatever degree modern man has free choice. Without this power, poverty populations are victimized by the dominant culture. We must teach the children of the poor to read and write effectively. Whatever more we can do, we must not do less.

This book describes materials and methods used in experimental programs that I have conducted in educational projects involving black, Puerto Rican, and white children and youth. According to the school's expectations, most of these children were academically retarded.

Viewing this manuscript in retrospect, the strength of it derives largely from two years of work as Director of Reading and Materials Development for Mobilization For Youth (MFY) on New York City's Lower East Side. Mobilization For Youth was the first large-scale experiment in the Kennedy-Johnson War on Poverty. It brought together a creative group of educators who pioneered a number of methods that are now commonplace in education for disadvantaged children and youth. At that time, Dr. Abraham Tannenbaum was MFY's Director of Education; he is now at Teachers College, Columbia University in New York City. Dr. Harry Passow wrote MFY's education proposal and was educational consultant throughout my tenure at MFY; he, too, is now at Teachers College. Marilyn Gibbons was Director of MFY's Junior High Reading Clinic. Dr. Anna Harris directed the Elementary Reading Clinic and is now head of reading for the Mt. Vernon, N.Y., school system. Hannah Levin was MFY's Assistant Director of Education. Dr. Robert Cloward, now at Rhode Island College, Providence, was the Director of Educational Research.

Some of the material reported in this book came from MFY's 1964 Experimental Summer Reading School. Larry Brody, Director of MFY's Curriculum Center and principal of the Experimental Summer School, shielded me from the drudgery of permits, attendance, recordkeeping, and other administrative duties. He tolerated my inconsistencies with tact and restraint beyond the call of duty. Al Deering, Coordinator of MFY's Laboratory School and Director of the Homework Helpers programs, aided in more projects than I can remember. He also compensated for my low frustration level in dealing with the politics of the large city schools. Dr. Barbara Berger helped me in a most difficult assignment—the perceptual-motor investigation of second- and third-graders. Dr. Berger's report is the basis of Chapter Six. Of particular pride to me was the performance of my Materials Development Unit. Carol Grosberg, Lois Kalb, Elaine Waldman, and Herb Rabb formed the core of that staff.

Officially, the MFY Education Division was unable to affect the New York City schools to the extent of the knowledge and skills it accumulated. The rigidity of a large city school system, the unjust and disgraceful attack upon MFY in 1964 by newspapers and public leaders, and the concomitant lack of support by educational and political leaders made the implementation of official changes impossible. However, the spread of knowledge and techniques gained in MFY work through classroom teachers who worked in the programs is much greater than most people realize. If we add the effect of staff members who have moved to other educational endeavors, MFY's role in the War on Poverty grows to its true proportions.

I would like to think that whatever value this book has is a tribute to MFY in its early, dynamic, and precarious stage under the leadership of its three directors: Jim McCarthy, George Brager, and Richard Cloward. They dared to pioneer a real war on poverty. To whatever extent MFY and the national poverty program have since been diluted may be testimony to the potential success of MFY's early phase under this leadership.

Other people deserve equal praise for their contributions to the various projects from which this book draws data. Vivian Gaman, Nick Mamola, Harry Milner, Joel Sperber, Jerry Skapoff, and hundreds of other creative teachers throughout the country have contributed to the development of materials and methods.

One person must remain unnamed. He is the principal of an urban junior high school populated by Puerto Rican, black, and white lower class underachievers. Faced with a declining achievement curve, an increasing delinquency curve, and an obstinate, politic-ridden board of education, this principal found foundation money to help his desperate pupils. Without official sanction from his superiors (in two cases, against the wishes of immediate superiors), he gave me the freedom to implement radical curriculum changes. He weathered teacher and parent pressures, as well as professional harassment, to see the project through to a successful conclusion. Such courage and dedication are rare in any profession, but most rare, perhaps, among school administrators.

I have written this book for professionals. Therefore, my analyses of people, programs, and materials have been candid. In every case, my conclusions were based *at least* upon my observations verified by the perceptions of my staff and *at most* by statistical data.

This book is, in one respect, too early. The data are scanty, so the conclusions are tentative. On the other hand, it may be too late. We have allowed the problem of poverty to accelerate beyond our present abilities to solve it. With the increase of federal funds, money is pouring forth faster than professionals know how to spend it.

The children we have been studying and working with are mostly lower class Puerto Ricans, blacks, Chinese, and what we affectionately call "white and others." Their learning problems know no bounds of race, religion, or subculture. Their frustrations, desires, and misbehaviors are not different from what each one of us experienced at their age. They deserve much more than we now can give them. In the hope that we soon will meet their educational needs, I am willing to expose myself to failure or success in the open market of educational experimentation. I do so, knowing that time is running out—that their unemployment is increasing, their social problems multiplying, and their childhood frustrations maturing into adult discontents. On behalf of these children, I request that educators seriously consider the conclusions and recommendations of this book.

S.A.C.

Contents

Chapter One **A Point of View**   3

Education and the War on Poverty   3
Education's Role in the War on Poverty:
    Reading's Role in Education   5
The Breakthrough in Reading Instruction
    for Disadvantaged Children   7
Lower Class Children Compared with Middle
    Class Children   8

Chapter Two **Products of Poverty**   13

Who Are the Socially Disadvantaged?   14
The Difference Between "Culturally Deprived"
    and "Socially Disadvantaged"   17
Life Styles of Disadvantaged People   19
Environmental Opportunity and Learning   25

Chapter Three **Intelligence and Learning**   32

Intelligence   32
Model Building   38
Four Models   40

Chapter Four **Diagnosing Reading Disabilities**   56

The Controversy over Standardized Tests   56
Three Uses of Tests   57
Seven Ways Not to Use Tests   60
Tests to Meet the Three Priorities for
    Disadvantaged Children   61

Reading Disability Patterns in Disadvantaged
  Urban Children   70

Chapter Five   Problem of Visual Perception   77

What Is Perceptual Development?   78
A Definition of Visual Perception Dysfunction   80
Behaviors Found in Perceptually Dysfunctioning
  Retarded Readers   81
Perceptually Dysfunctioning Children Can Learn
  to Read   96

Chapter Six   Solutions for Visual Perception   101

Visual Perceptual Training   103
A Program in Visual Perceptual Training   105

Chapter Seven   The Role of Preschool   122

Effectiveness of Kindergarten Programs   123
A Misassumption About Child Development   125
A Realistic Goal for Preschool Education   126
Guidelines for Building Preschool Curriculums   127

Chapter Eight   Teaching Learning Readiness   132

Teaching Control   132
Teaching Routine   134
Teaching Physiological Readiness   135
Teaching Language and Concept Development   141

Chapter Nine   Teaching Reading Readiness   156

Present Methods of Assessing Reading Readiness   156
A List of Basic Reading Readiness Skills and Perceptions   160

Chapter Ten   **Reading in Elementary Schools**   181

Some Basic Problems in Teaching Beginning Reading   182
Developing Reading Skills in Five Levels   187
An Elementary School Reading Program   214

Chapter Eleven   **Skills Centers**   224

A History of Skills Centers   225
An Example of Skills Centers   226
Principles Underlying Skills Centers   230
Operation of Skills Centers   234

Chapter Twelve   **Reading in Content Areas**   249

Some Problems and Solutions   250
Reading in Content Areas for High Achievers   255
Paperbacks—One Key to Teaching Reading Through
   Content Areas   259

Appendix   **Materials for Teaching Reading**   275

Index   321

TEACH THEM ALL TO READ

Chapter One

A Point of View

Education and the War on Poverty

The Kennedy-Johnson four-year War on Poverty has changed the attitudes and aspirations of disadvantaged minority groups. America's ten million blacks are more impatient than they have ever been, and this dissatisfaction is shared by millions of other underprivileged minorities. Ominous signs of this discontent have been especially apparent during recent summers, and, as this discontent erupts into riots, society's favorite scapegoat—the school—is blamed. In this particular instance, however, the school *is* at fault, for the War on Poverty has laid bare the impotence of American schools. Thrust suddenly from a state of impoverishment and low social priority to affluence and high domestic priority, the school has demonstrated its inability to assume social leadership as defined by John Dewey. Why? One reason is a lack of brainpower, the result of the traditional shortage of funds in the field of education. Before the War on Poverty, other social institutions had the money and the brainpower; now, however, the emphasis on the growing importance of education has given the school a sudden and significant increase in financial resources.

This sudden surge of wealth has brought behavioral, social, and physical scientists into the field of education. But these scientists exhibit a naiveté like that of educational progressivists of the 1930s and 1940s. The situation will change if funds continue to be available, but years of research are still necessary in order to weld together esoteric theories and the harsh realities of everyday classrooms.

For example, in the teaching of reading, naive attempts at direct applications of linguistic theory to beginning reading instruction are reminiscent of the nineteenth-century McGuffey readers. The literary content of these readers is no less contrived and artificial than the twentieth-century adventures of Dick, Sally, and Spot. The assumption that a "linguistic" approach to beginning reading is the best way for children to learn to read is as faulty as the opposing view that favors the "sight" method. Neither assumption recognizes everyday classroom reality—that linguistic approaches are best for some children and not for others—that some teachers who tend to do certain things in the classroom are effective regardless of the linguistic versus sight controversy. The gulf between these competent linguists, who are usually armchair reading researchers, and the realities of how children actually learn in classrooms is as wide as the universe that separates colleges of education from P.S. 102 in Harlem.

Because schools now have the money to spend, a host of industrial giants have crashed the education market. But the danger is that money, corporation profits, and high-pressure marketing techniques will distort the methods and goals of learning. The goals of big business and the goals of education are not inherently the same. For example, a $3 million computerized learning installation in New York City in 1968 may be good for corporation profits but may not change the illiteracy problem in Bedford-Stuyvesant. In 1978, the situation may be different, but right now $3 million could buy more than 1.5 million colorful storybooks for kindergarten and first-grade classrooms, which *could* make a difference in reading achievement in Bedford-Stuyvesant. Therefore, although money and raw brainpower will eventually enhance the education of disadvantaged children with new methods and materials, at present the best solution to severe reading retardation among these children is to depend more on the know-how that is available than on Ph.D.s in linguistics and federal pork barrels.

Education's Role in the War on Poverty: Reading's Role in Education

Social change is easier to write about than to engineer. The War on Poverty has at least shown us the truth of that statement. Looking across the social scientific spectrum, the certainty of one fact is apparent—no *single* approach will win the war. The problem is economic, political, moral, and educational. Of these four aspects of social change, where could the first breakthrough occur? Five years of research seem to indicate that the answer lies in education.

Moral change seems unlikely. In Western society, religion purports to be the guardian of man's moral sense. But religious institutions have long ago committed themselves to self-preservation first and to moral and religious matters second. A brief and exhilarating upsurge of man's religious sense in a moral frame of reference launched Dr. Martin Luther King's nonviolent revolution, but it soon fizzled out when it moved into the "liberal" North.

Then community action groups began operating in political areas. This led directly to problems of economics. Community programs upset local political applecarts by jeopardizing political-business "arrangements" for spending public funds. Such a threat to the established order cannot be tolerated by the power structure, so the U.S. Office of Economic Opportunity's community action program was dissolved. This was the issue, for example, behind Mobilization For Youth's demise, because that first experiment to combat poverty on New York City's Lower East Side was essentially a community action program.

What about education? Early in the War on Poverty, the school's first impulse was to remain uninvolved. Unfortunately, this position was not sustained for long. The school traditionally has served as scapegoat for domestic unrest, so the civil rights movement, which prefaced the War on Poverty, chose the schoolhouse as its main battlefield. Other social institutions, such as the family, the church, law-enforcement agencies, social welfare agencies, and state and federal legislatures, have always tried to blame the school for the problems of society, and, amusingly, the school has usually accepted this blame. The school has always served the useful purpose of relieving other social institutions of responsibility. If highway accidents increase, the school's driver training program is criticized. A Russian spaceship is launched, and the school science program is attacked. Venereal disease rates rise, and the school must assume responsibility for sex education. Skirts get shorter, hair gets longer, and the school becomes the guardian of bare thighs and clean scalps. Juvenile delinquency rates climb, and the school is told to increase homework assignments in order to keep kids off the streets. Finally, social immorality breeds segregated societies, and the schools are again the scapegoat.

The tragedy of this situation is that, while the school continues to accept the responsibilities of other social institutions, many educators are no longer clear about the nature of the social function of their own institution. For example, when the black community cries out about the low reading achievement of its children, the school refuses to accept this responsibility. Instead, educators respond with long dissertations on the psychosocial factors of home, community, family structure, and so on, as determinants of low reading achievement. How ironic, indeed; for having finally taken a stand, they stand the wrong way on the most crucial school issue—literacy.

What is the school's first responsibility in the War on Poverty? This book offers a very specific answer: The chief aim of the school is to promote literacy. Although the school may share certain social and moral problems with other institutions, none of these has the unique job of increasing the quantity and quality of learning to read, write, and do arithmetic. Thus, the school must give priority to its *raison d'être*. Of course, other social institutions are expected to help, but even if they do not, the school is not relieved of its responsibilities. If children cannot read, the school should rightly be blamed, and similarly, if immorality increases, the family and church are at fault.

Now let us return to the original problem of social change and the War on Poverty. What if the school reevaluated its list of priorities and, as a result, marshaled its forces to concentrate on literacy? Imagine, for example, the ultimate result if we were to teach 90 percent of Harlem's children to read, write, and do arithmetic adequately. At this stage of the War on Poverty, could any other profession make such a singularly powerful contribution toward the alleviation of poverty?

The Breakthrough in Reading Instruction
for Disadvantaged Children

No breakthrough in reading achievement of disadvantaged children will occur as long as educators assume that the psycho-social and psychophysical conditions of disadvantaged children preclude their learning to read. My position is precisely the opposite and is based on work with both disadvantaged and advantaged children. It is true that disadvantaged children, as a group, manifest certain negative psychosocial, psychophysical, and cognitive factors to a greater degree than do more advantaged children. (The first five chapters of this book describe these factors as they influence the learning of reading.) But the presence of these conditions does not preclude children's learning to read. (The second half of this book presents methods and materials that have taught disadvantaged children to read in spite of these environmentally determined conditions.)

The breakthrough in the teaching of reading to disadvantaged children will come if we concentrate on the methodology of teaching, rather than on the causes of the "disadvantaged" condition. This point of view is not popular, but it is the best conclusion that can be drawn from experience with all types of children. For example, to know that Johnnie was dropped on his head at two months of age, that his father does not live at home, that his mother is a prostitute, and that his big brother beats him daily does not suggest the most efficient way to teach him to read. To begin with, the school is severely limited in any attempt to directly influence these factors. Second, nothing in these factors automatically precludes Johnnie's learning to read; in fact, Johnnie might even find security and ego fulfillment in school achievement. Third, the best method of promoting such achievement may derive from general laws of learning, not from knowledge of Johnnie's environmental conditions. Such knowledge of the child's environment is occasionally helpful, particularly for social scientists who are seeking methods of preventing the disadvantaged condition, but general laws of learning that underlie methods of teaching reading are usually the most efficient guides to success in teaching already disadvantaged children and youth. Children's specific behaviors, regardless of etiology, are the cues to methods of changing present behaviors, and this is as true for children from Scarsdale as it is for children from Watts.

Lower Class Children Compared with Middle Class Children

In general, lower class children are more dependent upon the school in learning to read, write, and do arithmetic than are middle class children. Middle class children are "smarter" only in the sense that they are better prepared to read at the outset of their education and so sustained in that preparation by their home environments and by their teachers' expectations that the current poor or mediocre materials and methods are sufficient. The *same* methods and materials will not teach most lower class children to read and write. Less adequate methods and materials certainly will do worse. Why? Because lower class children come to school with less preparation to read. But research indicates that learning set, or readiness, is learned; and if it is learned, it can be taught. Perceptual dysfunctions and cognitive deficits add up to low IQs. But perception and cognition, as they are measured, are learned behaviors. Thus, much of what is termed the intelligence quotient (IQ) is learned, not innate.

Our job as educators, then, is to increase the quantity and quality of classroom techniques for teaching disadvantaged children. The rigidity of current pedagogy is not caused by a lack of available knowledge, but by a lack of courage and commitment to apply this knowledge. Most school systems serving disadvantaged children appear to be more committed to maintaining the status quo than to applying the gains of the past fifty years to the classroom. Closing the gap is usually irrelevant to the day-by-day priority list of most schools that are involved in the education of disadvantaged children. For example, some schools appear more concerned with maintaining segregation than with tampering with the quality and quantity of learning. Similar conditions prevail in schools where the principal's major effort is to prevent blacks from filling administrative positions. Many schools spend more energy circumventing federal strategies to mix blacks and whites in classrooms than they do on breaking down the old system of statewide textbook adoptions—a change that would affect the quality of reading instruction.

This situation is just as true of teacher-training institutions. For example, these colleges still train prospective teachers to write lesson plans in which "motivation" is separate from the body of a lesson, a practice totally inconsistent with research in learning. Many colleges are still largely staffed by either well-trained academicians who are ignorant of classroom realities or former classroom teachers who are ignorant of learning theory. In spite of increased federal and foundation commitments, neither course content nor pedagogy has been significantly changed in the curriculums of teacher-training institutions. As a result, these colleges continue to produce poorly trained professionals and supervising "specialists" who spout outdated generalities concerning, for example, "individualized instruction," but who are unable to connect knowledge and practice in the classroom. The educational revolution will occur when the gap is closed in the teacher-training college as well as in the grade school.

Some erroneous practices, however, must be eliminated from education if we are to be successful. First of all, many schools hold to the myth that a mental age of 6 or 6.5 is a reliable guide for beginning reading. But correlations between IQ and reading success in early grades are too low to use mental age as a guide for individual predictions. Nor can chronological age be used as a reliable guide. Neither mental nor chronological age should be used as determinants of when and what to teach as reading readiness.

A second myth involves the belief that a child should indicate readiness to learn to read before we begin to teach him (see pp. 125–126). Teaching young children words, letter sounds, alphabet, even beginning phonics will not injure either their psyches or their bodies. We teach children to throw and catch, to play certain games, and to behave in certain ways. There is no reason to withhold the teaching of readiness and beginning reading *if the methods and conditions are consonant with the developmental stage of the child.* Certainly the teaching of anything from toilet training to playing with blocks can be injurious to a child when the demands are beyond his abilities. In addition, too much of a demand on the child can be injurious to later development in that skill if the child develops early, deep-seated negative attitudes toward the skill being taught. The problem, therefore, is not the skill, but the method by which it is taught.

Furthermore, the favorite offense of those who oppose early reading instruction, that we should "let children be children," is equally absurd. This statement reflects personal biases that are not universal. It implies that reading children's books before seven years of age is adult and that teaching letters, sounds, and related activities are robbing children of their childhood. Reading or reading activities are not peculiarly adult. A three- or four-year-old reading a picture book, sounding out words, playing with letters, playing rhyming games, enjoying visual discrimination of letter games, tracing letters or words, and even working in certain types of reading workbooks is enjoying his childhood status. These are childhood activities, just as such pastimes as "Simon Says" and playing with blocks (see Chapter 7 for a more extended discussion).

A third myth still in evidence is that emotionally disturbed children cannot learn to read. Of course, psychotic children are more difficult to teach, whether we are trying to teach them to read or to ride a bicycle. Unless the psychosis has some unusual connection with reading, however, there should be no more difficulty in teaching such children reading than in teaching them any other skill that involves interpersonal activity. Emotionally disturbed children may or may not be easy to teach depending upon the nature of the disturbance; the point is that with such children, learning to read enjoys the same status as learning anything else. If an emotionally disturbed child has trouble with his interpersonal relationships, then he may also have difficulty learning to read. For example, evidence indicates that when reading instruction is automated (removing the interpersonal factor), schizophrenic children do learn to read (Chapter 8 includes a further discussion of this myth).

These three myths have particular relevance to socially disadvantaged children. The myth that a mental age of 6.5 is necessary for beginning reading instruction would seriously delay that instruction for most black, Puerto Rican, Appalachian white, and other lower socioeconomic status children. In general, their performances on IQ tests are poor compared to the test norms. Perhaps 50 percent of these children would not receive formal instruction until they were actually seven or eight years old. Considering, among other factors, the realities of cultural demands in American society, this is obviously too late to begin reading instruction. The myth that we should wait for children to become ready would be impossible to implement in many city slum areas, because in these areas most children will never become ready. If the home does not teach reading readiness incidentally, then the school must teach it purposely. If the school teaches it purposely, it must make sure that it reaches children who need it. Skin color, minority status, and low economic status should not be sufficient criteria for assuming that a particular child needs reading readiness training. Ability to perform the reading readiness skills is the only acceptable criterion for deciding whether or not a child should receive reading readiness training.

The myth that we cannot teach disadvantaged children to read until we solve their psychosocial problems is therefore both untrue and impractical. The schools cannot begin to solve the psychosocial problems of deprived children. Solving this problem is essentially the purpose of the entire War on Poverty, of which education is only one part. At this stage, the war has been markedly unsuccessful in changing the psychosocial conditions of most disadvantaged people. If we wait for changes, we will never get around to teaching disadvantaged children to read in our lifetimes. Furthermore, literacy is one major prerequisite to affecting psychosocial change; *it must come before, not after, the fact.*

These myths sustain the fifty-year gap between know-how and practice. On the other hand, that know-how consists of some familiar landmarks. Thus, readers seeking dramatically new methods for teaching reading may be disappointed in this book. Many of the methods and materials that work well with disadvantaged children are not as new as they are intensive, thorough, sequential, and of very high quality. Because there are more similarities than differences between disadvantaged and advantaged children, the basic principles of teaching reading can apply to both. But, unless we apply these familiar principles, the educational breakthrough may never come and the social revolution that depends upon it will not occur. What may occur, instead, is the development of a more mechanized, more efficient structure to maintain the status quo—a computerized technological monster called "education."

Chapter Two

Products of Poverty

Introduction

Linked to race and color, poverty infests every American community. Yet, how ironic that in the middle of the twentieth century, with such high population mobility and unprecedented mass communications media, the effects of poverty are functionally invisible to most middle class Americans. The 1967 and 1968 summer riots were actually shocking to them. But the inability or refusal to be aware of the disadvantaged condition, not the *denial* of poverty, is the factor that separated these classes and prevented middle class people from recognizing that the riots were actually less shocking than the desperate predicament of the victims of poverty and discrimination. The conditions of poverty deny lower class minority group members the opportunity to participate fully in the mainstream of American culture and place their children at a severe disadvantage when they enter the classroom, for the school, as a middle class establishment, is culturally oriented toward the advantaged child.

The following sections describe the extent, intensity, and effects of poverty, the types of psychosocial and educational problems that derive from it, and the types of people that are born into and remain in it. Specifically, the statistics of poverty, definitions of "culturally deprived" and "socially disadvantaged," life styles of disadvantaged people, language characteristics of lower socioeconomic class people, and problems of environmental opportunity and learning are presented. Finally, as an example of their predicament in the school, the report of a study of reading achievement in one population typical of urban slum children is presented.

Who Are the Socially Disadvantaged?

There are 34 million Americans living in poverty. Another 32 million live in marked deprivation. These 66 million Americans are not starving, but they go to sleep hungry every night. They are "fat with hunger, for that is what cheap food does," says Michael Harrington in his provocative book, *The Other America*. [1] That is not all that "cheap food" does. Along with substandard housing and clothing, poor diet incapacitates them and endangers their already tenuous employability. [2] For example, 17.6 percent of adults over seventeen years of age from families with annual incomes under $2,000 are limited in their employability by chronic ailments. As a comparison, only 4 percent in families with annual incomes of $7,000 or more have this limitation.

More shocking, perhaps, are federal statistics that show a 17 percent higher infant mortality rate in low income states compared to the rest of the United States. Nonwhites, over 65 percent of whom are poor, have a maternity death rate four times higher than whites. The incidence of heart disease is three times higher; orthopedic impairment and high blood pressure are four times as frequent; arthritis, five times as prevalent; mental and nervous conditions and visual impairment, more than six times as frequent in middle-aged men earning less than $2,000 per year compared to those earning $7,000 or more. [3] If we eliminate the 8 million of these people who are over sixty-five years of age, we are left with about 25 percent of the nation's population living in poverty or deprivation. That figure does not represent equal amounts of various subcultures. Within that 25 percent are disproportionately high numbers of blacks, Puerto Ricans, Mexican Americans, and American Indians; the other groups are Southern rural whites, migrant farm workers, and Appalachian whites. And not one section of the United States is free from poverty pockets.

The average age of the poor is lower than the middle class population: 33 percent are under eighteen years of age, compared with about 25 percent of the middle class. They have larger families, which means that they send more children per family to elementary school than do middle class families. The increase in their numbers in turn only aggravates their situation. In 1963, 36.9 percent of all American families received only 14.6 percent of the total national family income. Although just 5.4 percent of American families are affluent, this small group receives almost 17 percent of the total national family income. [4] Nonwhites account for approximately 12.5 percent of the American population, but they comprise over 25 percent of the poverty population. In 1961, the total annual monetary income of over 60 percent of black families was below $4,000, the figure cited by the United States government as a modest, but adequate, income for *childless* families (husband and wife only). Only 28 percent of white families were included in a comparable category. According to the Bureau of the Census, 1961, 20 percent of the white and 50 percent of the nonwhite families earned under $3,000 per year. When a $1,500 or less annual income is used as a category of family income, 24 percent of the nonwhites qualify compared to 7 percent of the whites.

The economic poverty of so many of the minority families makes them natural candidates for problems in every area of life— physical, mental, and social—and their living quarters, the ghetto that drains public resources. For example, delinquency has doubled in the past decade in New York City. In 1964, Secretary of Labor Willard Wirtz announced that on a nationwide level an "outlaw pack" of 350,000 young men will be permanently unemployed at a cost of $1,000 each year per person. [3] In 1960, 68 percent of youth between seven and twenty years of age living in Manhattan had juvenile delinquency records.

According to the Selective Service report of 1963, 50 percent of the young men taking preinduction tests failed because of physical or intellectual deficiencies. Most of these came from low-income families. Mississippi, with the lowest average family income, sent only three out of ten men who applied into the armed services; almost seven out of ten who applied flunked the mental exam. Eight out of ten rejectees were school dropouts. Compared to all eighteen-year-olds, draft rejectees have doubled the national unemployment rate. In October 1965, the Selective Service lowered its intellectual requirements to the 15th percentile on the induction intellectual exam.

About 36 percent of the American population has eight years or less of formal education. About 7 to 10 percent of those are illiterate (reading at fourth grade level or below). In one study of 680 able-bodied men and women on relief in Chicago, over 50 percent were illiterate. In 1962, President Kennedy estimated that 7.5 million youngsters would drop out of school during this decade, and most of these dropouts will be retarded readers. When we investigate the backgrounds of juvenile delinquents, we find 95 percent of seventeen-year-olds, 85 percent of sixteen-year-olds, and 50 percent of fifteen-year-olds are school dropouts. Most of them come from families earning less than $4,000 per year.

Over 60 percent of all American children come from blue collar homes. As a group, these children earn lower mean intelligence test scores than do children of parents in the managerial and professional classes. Their mean "highest grade attended in school" is lower, as are school achievement scores, compared to children from white collar families. Socially disadvantaged children come from this group, but they constitute probably its lower 20 percent. The majority of blue collar children, for all intents and purposes, are academically and culturally indistinguishable from children of white collar workers. Many of them move quickly from blue to white collar status as a result of accelerated economic mobility—their fathers earn salaries that allow them the comforts and stresses of suburbia. This group of 40 to 45 percent participates in America's mass core culture; they are not disadvantaged because they do not suffer social and economic discrimination at the hands of the power culture. Children in the lower 20 percent of the blue collar class usually come from a rural background. They are white as well as black and have migrated to industrial centers, usually in the North. They are Puerto Rican and Mexican American; often, they are children of Eastern and Southern European immigrants a generation or less removed from their homeland.

The socially disadvantaged, then, are those who are economically in difficulty; whose economic difficulties increase because poor diet, clothing, and shelter make them physically unable to hold a job; whose education is at best minimal because they come from homes in which most energy is devoted to sheer survival and so are not prepared to enter a middle class school system that depends for its success upon prior training by the family; who are, therefore, unable to take advantage of whatever opportunities are available to them—training through service in the army, for example—that might help them to share even the material advantages of the mass core culture. They are the black, the Indian, the Puerto Rican, the Appalachian white, the "poor family" of a small town. They are found in almost every community in the United States.

The Difference Between "Culturally Deprived" and "Socially Disadvantaged"

A Puerto Rican child from East Harlem does not lack a culture. Any teacher working with him can attest to his rich, complex, deeply imbedded cultural inheritance. What he lacks are the cultural qualities measured by, for example, standardized intelligence tests—qualities common to middle class children for whom the school's curriculum is constructed. Only when we establish the power culture of the American middle and upper class as the criterion for a value judgment can the Puerto Rican child from East Harlem be considered as being *culturally deprived.*

Being so deprived, he finds living in the power culture's society more strenuous and hazardous than does the middle class child. Why? *Because his degrees of freedom to choose alternative behaviors in that culture are severely constricted.* For example, Juan is a nine-year-old Mexican American with limited verbal facility in English. He was infuriated one day by his teacher, who had mistakenly chastised him for someone else's misbehavior. A middle class youngster's alternatives would have included verbally explaining the incident, crying, telling mother so that she would talk with the teacher, screaming invectives, or striking out aggressively. Juan's alternatives were limited to the latter two. Strong little Mexican boys do not cry. Mother would not dare approach the school, and chances are that if she did, she would blame Juan and not the teacher. Juan's limited facility in English tended to make him "nonverbal," especially at the height of emotion. So Juan screamed Spanish invectives and struck the boy who had misbehaved.

Culturally deprived youngsters cannot succeed as easily in a verbal culture when they must function as if they were nonverbal. They cannot achieve optimally in a school program that assumes patterns of visual and auditory development that they have not yet acquired. They cannot be electrical engineers if they cannot read. When these cultural deprivations are accentuated by concomitant or resultant factors of language patterns, economic oppression, and racial prejudice, the culturally different children of lower socioeconomic minorities operate at a severe disadvantage. They are *socially disadvantaged*. Even the rationalization of well-intentioned writers who admire cultural styles of disadvantaged minorities and who advocate explicitly or implicitly that they be left untainted by the power culture cannot eradicate this fact. The disadvantaged lack the skills necessary to make free choices of alternatives controlling their destinies. They are less free than I am—and that is a severe disadvantage, for I, too, have delimited alternatives.

The disadvantaged predicament is linked to both subcultural differences of minority group people and to the power culture's refusal to adjust to these differences. That refusal is symbolized by the term culturally *deprived,* which many educators use to describe culturally *different* children. The term *deprived* is part of the power culture's strategy to change the minority subculture. To advocate that the deprived subculture remain untainted is just as impractical as to advocate that the power culture change to conform to the subculture's demands. Both are unacceptable extremes. What the school must seek is an accommodation by both sides—minority group members learning to cope successfully with the school's (power culture's) demands, and the school adjusting, enjoying, and assimilating the unique features of the minority subculture. This, of course, can only be done when the different cultures confront each other with equal power—that is, when the subculture community has a share in determining the cultural climate (mores, goals, and methods) *equal* to the school's share.

Life Styles of Disadvantaged People

The portraits of lower class life styles that abound in current literature on poverty often feed stereotypes that impede our attempts to educate the children of the poor. For example, some writers reason that because the slum child's parents are unemployed, his meals irregular, and his future uncertain, the child lives in the present, looks for trouble, and acts on impulse. Such logic is absurd. Other writers reason that from poverty, insecurity, and discrimination come characteristics of open hostility, pride in physical strength, distrust of schooling, impulsive behavior, emphasis on the now and the concrete, antagonism to authority, and loyalty to one's peers. However, this same list of characteristics also describes high schoolers from any suburban middle class community. These are characteristics of adolescence, not socioeconomic class.

Although Riessman in *The Culturally Deprived Child* [5] includes such stereotypes, he also accurately portrays some characteristics of the children and parents we observe in urban slums. These characteristics are neither universal nor unique to this population, but they do offer persons with middle class teacher-training backgrounds some idea of life styles of lower class children and adults. For example, Riessman's characteristics, adapted below, appear to be valid, at least for the Puerto Rican and black children in urban slums of the Northeast.

1. In such areas as morality, punishment, customs, diet, and education, the lower class individual has intense convictions that he tenaciously preserves. In all these areas he is a traditionalist.
2. He is more superstitious and, to an extent, more religious than his middle class neighbor.
3. At this time, he feels strongly alienated from the mainstream of American life. The black and Puerto Rican adolescent displays a sense of futility and helplessness not encountered with other groups of adolescents.
4. He tends to see issues as good or bad, right or wrong. Moderation and balance are middle class luxuries.
5. He suffers severe self-denigration that he covers with a thin veneer of superiority: "Not *I*, but *they* are the causes of my

misfortunes." Although this appraisal is often accurate, it also serves as a convenient rationalization for expressing his aggressions.

6. Security, rather than progress, is his vocational goal. "Getting by," rather than "getting ahead," is more consistent with the realities of his condition. [This situation is illustrated quite well by an incident that occurred at Mobilization For Youth. Indigenous workers were hired in many of MFY's poverty projects, and one such worker refused a promotion to supervisor, which would have meant a substantial salary increase, because she would have lost the job security of her original position. That position was protected by an employee's union which did not cover supervisors.]

7. Perhaps as a result of the first and fourth characteristics, his responses to public opinion polls tend to be "right of center" on issues of civil liberties and foreign policy.

8. He is politically apathetic. In spite of massive efforts to register southern blacks and other lower class minority groups, they still tend not to vote. Getting the lower class citizen to the poll booth is a strenuous task—and his not voting perpetuates his difficulties. Because he does not wield political pressure at the polls, his legislators conveniently forget him. As a result, welfare legislation so far has actually passed over the poor to serve unionized labor, and upper-lower and lower-middle class workers. [For example, about 80 percent of federal funds under the Elementary and Secondary Education Act, Title I, for educating disadvantaged children is spent on professional salaries, and this expenditure has not led to a substantial rise in the reading achievement of disadvantaged children.]

9. He appears to demand strong authority figures. [In one experimental education program for school dropouts, for example, nineteen-year-olds insisted that we explain the chain of command in a staff consisting of a director who taught, two teachers who directed, and a consultant who also did both. "But who is the boss?" they demanded to know.]

10. He tends to perceive "intellectuals" as possessing abilities in all fields. [For example, lower class children often expect the teacher to be knowledgeable and skilled in such fields as medicine and law.]

Some experts list other characteristics, but these do not appear representative of most lower class people. For example, one such characteristic is that many are "anti-intellectual," but there is no evidence that most Puerto Ricans in East Harlem dislike "eggheads." Riessman claims that culturally deprived people appear to learn in a more physical or motoric fashion. As evidence, he cites religion, where lower class people tend to enjoy physical means of expressing emotion: They clap hands, sing, and dance, rather than listen to sermons. Certainly, the Puerto Rican Pentecostal church uses music and movement, but there are also sermons. In fact, many Puerto Ricans attend the same churches as their white neighbors, as do northern blacks. Hymns are also sung in the churches of middle class citizens from across the tracks, although perhaps with less vigor. Other writers have described the disadvantaged boy's emphasis on masculinity as a result of the patriarchal culture in which father is boss by virtue of a strong right arm. They describe the shift in the black family structure from father to mother as a change of roles in which the latter assumes the masculine role of the former. Perhaps a better explanation of the disadvantaged boy's overemphasis on masculine show of force is the fact that he must defend his status. Puerto Ricans living in New York City are just beginning a role shift. Traditionally, the father is the authority, but in an uprooted Puerto Rican family in which the father can no longer find employment to support his family, mother takes over and threatens the masculine role. Boys seem to resort to physical force in response to this traumatic cultural change. The phenomenon, therefore, is less a reflection of the child's model and more a reaction formation.

The most important similarities among members of a group are observed in the dynamics of personality and learning. The psychology of human behavior is, in the main, the same for all children, regardless of where they live. When dealing with children, these universal principles of behavior are far more important to the classroom teacher than the generalities listed above. All children, for example, like praise. They want love. They need to be successful. Especially in the early grades, no convincing evidence exists to indicate that lower class children lack or have a greater abundance of particular psychodynamic factors. There were no indications of higher incidences of neuroses in prekindergarten disadvantaged children compared to middle class children among those observed in every major section of the country during the first year of Operation Headstart. Differences in learned factors of readiness existed, but no differences in emotional stability seemed apparent. It should be remembered, however, that one or two years of school frustration and failure, coupled with other environmental conditions, can create a very different child two or three years later.

A Comparison of Language Factors in Middle and Lower Class Children

One reason the disadvantaged child manifests cultural deprivation is his tendency to use *restricted* language instead of *elaborated* language. "Restricted," "elaborated," and "language" are used here in a technical sense, as described by Bernstein, [6, 7, 8] in his studies of the communicative processes of various socioeconomic classes in England.

Bernstein describes restricted language as consisting of short, grammatically simple sentences that stress the active voice. Syntax is poor. Not only do speakers of restricted language tend to use repetitive conjunctions such as *and, so, then,* but they avoid subordination in their expressive patterns so that dominant subjects are rarely broken down into subordinate categories. Informational content appears to be dislocated because a subject is not held through a speech sequence of reasonable length. Adjectives and adverbs are scarce, but personal pronouns are overabundant, except for the first person, which is cautiously avoided. Conclusions are usually restated minor premises leading to categorical statements. Restrictive language speakers resort to "sympathetic circularity," which is Bernstein's label for such statements as "You see?" or "You know?" This technique is used to reinforce a previous speech sequence. The lower class speaker tends to repeat and repeat particular idiomatic expressions. Over all, his meaning is usually implicit.

Elaborated language, on the other hand, is characterized by traditionally accurate grammar, with the use of standard syntax to regulate expression. Linguistic stress, as well as logical modifications, are mediated by complexities of grammatical construction.

Elaborated language uses a wider range of conjunctions and subordinate clauses. Not only logical relationships, but temporal and spatial contiguity are manipulated by frequent use of prepositions. Contrasted to restricted language patterns, there is frequent use of the pronoun "I." Many more adjectives and adverbs exist in elaborated language patterns. By manipulating structures and relationships within and between sentences, categorical statements are avoided. Rather than repeated idioms, expressive symbols are used to discriminate between meanings within speech sequences. Elaborated speech patterns avoid diffuse generalized expressions by using more specific language.

Elaborated language patterns, which should be learned in the home, are the accepted patterns of the American school. The problem of the child who tends to use a more restricted language pattern is not simply one of the school being oriented to elaborated language; it is also the problem of the school being *disoriented* to restricted language. Professionals err when they assume that restricted language patterns are simple forms of elaborated patterns and that conditioning to elaborate language makes teachers able to operate with restricted language. These patterns differ in *kind*, not in *degree*. Language in this technical sense refers to the total process of conceptualization, experience, and affect, as well as to the spoken word. It is untrue to assume that these two different language styles discriminate social class. Bernstein himself has modified his earlier position, and now recognizes that middle class people also use restricted language in many social contexts. Conversely, evidence is accumulating to show that lower class children have latent elaborated language patterns that they tend to use less often than middle class children. Nevertheless, the tendency is for schools to demand elaborated language patterns from all children and to perceive ghetto children as responding to this demand with restricted patterns. A predicament often results in which the lower class child and the middle class teacher confront one another with different conceptualizations and experiences. A communication breakdown can occur, but unlike most breakdowns where both parties to the communicative process suffer, this breakdown deals penalties to only one party—the lower class child.

We have seen how environment affects the social, physical, and economic conditions of poor children. The following section illustrates how family language patterns further affect the school child when those patterns are restricted. There is evidence of inferior auditory and visual discrimination and inferior general visual perception development among lower class children. Evidence of inferior judgments concerning time and numbers, especially number sequence, also exists. In short, children from a disadvantaged background appear to lack basic concepts and skills assumed to be found in children from more advantaged environments. So far the evidence suggests not physiology or heredity but lack of learning— and, most likely, lack of opportunity to learn—as the major cause of these conditions.

The Family's Effect upon Language and Thought Processes

Havighurst [9] illustrates the effect of family upon thought processes by describing two scenes, one typical of the middle class home and the other of the lower class home. The illustrations are based on field studies by Hess at the University of Chicago. [10] In the latter, the toddler sits on the kitchen floor banging pots and pans with great delight. The telephone rings (an "affluent" lower class home). Mother says, sharply or not, depending on her mood, "Shut up!" She may communicate the same message with a raised hand or the toe of her foot. In contrast, the middle class mother says, "Stop, until mother finishes on the phone," or "Quiet, while mother tries to hear on the phone," or "You must be quiet while mother is on the phone, because she cannot hear." Even if she is in a bad mood, "Shut up!" will likely be followed by a reason, condition, or concept of time ("until," "while," and so forth).

Just in sheer number of oral-aural symbols, the middle class mother has offered the child more language experience than has the lower class mother. Both may be offering as much love, but the second mother offers a highly verbal style of implying cause and effect, time sequence, reason, or explanation. These are cognitive processes the child learns to expect from birth; they become the processes he tends to emulate. This incidental familial learning is slow and potent, more potent than most types of formal learning designed by sophisticated educators. It occurs in the first two or three years of life and is almost irrevocably imbedded (or not imbedded) in the child by the time he begins nursery school, certainly by the time he starts kindergarten or first grade.

If this analysis is correct, those concerned with compensatory education for disadvantaged children should take a realistic view of the problem. Can we compensate for lack of certain language and cognitive stimuli that the middle class family offers its infants and toddlers? Can we compensate for lack of parent models who read for information and occasionally for delight? The middle class child usually has the chance to be fascinated by the colors, pictures, and sounds of *Cat in the Hat* long before his teacher reads it to him in first grade. Middle class parents have conversations with a child that answer his questions and encourage him to ask more; that extend his vocabulary beyond nouns and verbs; that extend his concepts to connotation rather than mere denotation; that help him establish grades of differences, qualities of things; that offer the child an opportunity to explain his point of view. These parents provide trips to interesting places and games and puzzles that teach size, shape, and color. Most important, perhaps, the middle class home offers these opportunities at the crucial stage of development, [11, 10] long before the child enters school. Many socially disadvantaged children miss these opportunities, and there is real question of how much can be supplied formally in the school rather than informally in the home. The school becomes involved at a later and less optimal stage of development, under severe limitations of space, time, money, and know-how in compensatory education programs.

Environmental Opportunity and Learning

In one generation, the measured IQ of black children in Philadelphia and Chicago jumped 10 points. [12] In states that have higher mean family incomes, higher socioeconomic levels, and more cultural opportunities, children score better on educational tests than those in poorer states. Thus, for example, the percentage of blacks in Illinois and New York City passing the Selective Service mental tests exceeded the percentage of whites who passed it from every southern and border state, with the exception of Missouri. [13] Thirty years ago Klineberg showed how IQs of black children born in the South improved steadily with length of residence in the Northeast. [14] Perhaps more important to us is the reverse, that *lack of opportunity has a cumulative effect.* Deficits of disadvantaged children in grade 1 become more marked through the grades. Deutsch calls this the "cumulative deficit phenomenon." [15] How much of an effect does this deficit have on school achievement?

Reading Achievement Scores of Disadvantaged Children

Perhaps the reading achievement scores of one school district in Manhattan can best illustrate the effect of the cumulative deficit phenomenon that manifests itself in slum schools. This district has a school population slightly over 20,000 children. Economic and cultural deprivation in this district is not as bad as in the slums of Washington, D.C., or of Bedford-Stuyvesant in Brooklyn, but it is an excellent example of a poverty pocket. About 56 percent of the people live in slum tenements, and 32 percent in public housing facilities; the ethnic distribution is as shown in Table 1.

Table 1   **Ethnic Distribution of School and Total Population of a New York Slum**

	Black	Puerto Rican	White and Other
Total population	12%	30%	58%
School population	19	55	26

Sources: Total population figures, Demographic Studies, Research Department, Mobilization For Youth, 1963. Other, Institute of Public Administration, *The Administration of Services to Children and Youth in New York City* (New York: Research Center, Columbia University School of Social Work, 1964).

The superintendent of this city district claimed that five or six first-grade pupils out of 30 per classroom in a particular slum school might be below grade level at the end of the year. When we gave individually administered reading tests to all 150 first-graders in the school at the end of the year, only ten children read on grade level. Everyone else in the five classrooms was already below grade level on every subtest of the *Durrell Analysis of Reading Difficulty* [16] battery except on the listening comprehension subtests. Most of the children tended to be on or above grade level on the latter test, which indicated that, if someone had taught them to "bust the written code," their comprehension abilities would have been adequate for reading.

Assuming that the school system's report of reading retardation tends to be conservative, consider the figures reported by the superintendent, which are presented in Table 2. About 75 percent of the sixth-grade population is shown to be retarded in reading. The figures in Table 2 are from an unpublished memo sent by the school superintendent to the principals of the district under discussion two years after the figures in Table 3 were published by Mobilization For Youth and Columbia University.

Table **2   Reading Achievement of 2202 Sixth-Graders in 21 Schools of a New York Slum***

On or above grade	26%
One year retarded	12
Two years retarded	22
More than two years retarded	40

* Subjects were tested at grade 0.0 on the *Metropolitan Achievement Tests.*

Two years earlier, an impartial outside agency under government and foundation funding surveyed the same population. At this time the tests, involving grades 3 and 8, were administered by trained personnel detached from the schools. Data are presented in Table 3.

Table 3 shows that 90 percent of the Puerto Rican children in grade 3 are already retarded in reading and therefore below grade level. About 83 percent of the black children are reported below grade level; they account for about 18 percent of the school population. As much as 45 percent of the white and "other" population scored below grade level. Non-English-speaking children were not included in the data (roughly 78 percent of this population is below grade level in reading).

An analysis of the "Total Number" column in Table 3 shows a significant drop in pupil population by grade 8.5. The dropout

Table **3** **Percentage Distribution by Ethnic Group of Reading Retardation of All Children in Two Grades of a New York Slum**

GRADE, ETHNIC GROUP, RACE	TOTAL NUMBER	OVER 3 YEARS	2.5 TO 3.0	2.0 TO 2.5	1.5 TO 2.0	1.0 TO 1.5	0.5 TO 1.0	0.1 TO 0.5	AT GRADE LEVEL OR ABOVE
					*Degree of Reading Retardation**				
Grade 3.5†									
Puerto Rican	1,489	64.68	.81	7.12	21.29	30.69	15.85	14.44	9.80
Black	626	33.33	.16	5.43	15.97	27.00	15.02	17.73	18.69
White and other	606	13.70		1.82	5.45	12.37	9.24	16.33	54.79
Total	2,721	30.74	.48	5.57	16.60	25.86	14.23	15.68	21.58
Grade 8.5†									
Puerto Rican	235	64.68	2.98	7.66	1.28	4.68	2.55	2.98	13.19
Black	138	33.33	5.80	11.59	3.62	7.97	3.63	5.07	28.99
White and other	489	13.70	3.88	7.57	5.52	6.54	4.50	5.52	52.77
Total	862	30.74	3.94	8.24	4.06	6.26	3.83	4.76	38.17

* Because the academic year is 10 months, scoring intervals consist of 5 months each.

† Tested midway through each of these grades.

Source: Institute of Public Administration, *The Administration of Services to Children and Youth in New York City* (New York: Research Center, Columbia University School of Social Work, 1964). Data compiled by Robert Cloward, Director of Educational Research, Mobilization For Youth, Inc.

ratio, however, is not evenly distributed across the three ethnic categories. The proportion of nonwhite dropouts far exceeds white dropouts. In the elementary school of this district, whites are in the minority, with Puerto Ricans outnumbering them more than 2 to 1. Five years later, however, the trend reversed. Population shifts and school reassignments are a partial explanation, but the chief reason for the shift is that the most disadvantaged children have failed in school and have dropped out by grade 8.5.

Approximately 54 percent of all eighth-graders in this system are one or more years below grade level in reading. Almost 33 percent are severely retarded (three or more years below placement). More shocking are the ethnic breakdowns of retardation: 47 percent of the white and other children are below grade level; 86 percent of the Puerto Rican and 71 percent of the black children are below grade level in reading. Table 3 scores are two years older than those reported in Table 2. If the school-reported scores are, in fact, spuriously high, then the difference could represent a marked further decline in reading achievement over the two-year interim. Another possible explanation for the difference in results is the fact that each set of scores was compiled by using different tests.

A second agency, not connected with the schools, reported results similar to those shown in Table 3. Regardless of which report is accepted as more reliable, both sets of numbers indicate serious problems of reading retardation in schools attended by socially disadvantaged children and youth. In this same school district a structured sample of junior high school pupils revealed that over 30 percent of children in grades 7 to 9 did not know the alphabet. A similar survey of retarded readers in Pittsburgh turned up a figure closer to 50 percent. These findings are typical of the reading retardation problem of disadvantaged children and youth throughout the country. Although this reading retardation pattern reflects a cumulative deficit phenomenon in the area of verbal learning, it testifies more to the school's inability to teach reading effectively. For if the school can only succeed with advantaged children who need, at best, mediocre formal instruction to learn to read, then it has little indeed to boast of.

Summary

Racial and class prejudice is already a debilitating factor for any cultural minority, but, when this social problem is compounded by conditions of poverty, a predicament that we call "disadvantaged" develops. The complexity of the predicament has been described—economic deprivation breeds poor physical health, which in turn perpetuates economic deprivation by rendering its victims less employable. The resulting pattern becomes more complicated to break and more frustrating for its victims to endure, because of language, cognitive and perceptual development deficits, cultural conflict, political impotence, and their psychological concomitants—all of which interact as both causes and effects to perpetuate the cycle.

From the school's point of view, these factors culminate in a "cumulative deficit phenomenon" that manifests itself, among other aspects, in severely retarded reading achievement scores for disadvantaged children. From the point of view here, the solution to this problem lies in materials and methods; that is, a better pedagogy will teach disadvantaged children to read, write, and do arithmetic adequately in spite of their predicament. The next chapter treats this problem by describing the models upon which this pedagogy must be built.

References

1. Michael Harrington, *The Other America* (New York: Macmillan, 1963).
2. S. Bernstein, *Youth on the Streets* (New York: Association Press, 1964), p. 18.
3. L. H. Keyserling, *Progress or Poverty* (Washington, D.C.: Conference on Economic Progress, 1964), p. 660.
4. U.S. Bureau of the Census, *Report* (Washington, D.C., 1961).
5. Frank Riessman, *The Culturally Deprived Child* (New York: Harper & Row, 1962), pp. 25–35.
6. B. Bernstein, "Language and Social Class," *British Journal of Sociology*, 11 (1960), 271–76.

7. ———, "Social Class and Linguistic Development. A Theory of Social Learning," in Halsy, Floud, and Anderson (eds.), *Economy, Education, and Society* (New York: Free Press, 1961), pp. 288–314.

8. ———, "Social Class, Linguistic Codes and Grammatical Elements," *Language and Speech,* 5 (October–December 1962), 221–40.

9. Robert Havighurst, unpublished address presented at Fairleigh Dickinson Reading Conference, Teaneck, N.J., 1964.

10. R. D. Hess, "Maternal Teaching Styles and Educational Retardation," in Torrance and Strom (eds.), *Mental Health and Achievement* (New York: Wiley, 1965).

11. B. Bloom, *Stability and Change in Human Characteristics* (New York: Wiley, 1964).

12. A. Davis, "The Education of Children from the Lower Socio-Economic Groups," in R. D. Hess (ed.), *The Urban Lower Class* (New York: Holt, Rinehart and Winston, 1963).

13. Selective Service System, *Special Groups,* Monograph No. 10 (Washington, D.C.: 1953), p. 147.

14. O. Klineberg, *Negro Intelligence and Selective Migration* (New York: Columbia University Press, 1935), p. 59.

15. M. Deutsch, "The Role of Social Class in Language Development and Cognition," *American Journal of Orthopsychiatry,* 35 (January 1965), 78–88.

16. D. D. Durrell, *Durrell Analysis of Reading Difficulty* (New York: Harcourt, Brace & World, 1955).

Chapter Three

Intelligence and Learning

Introduction

Are socially disadvantaged children less intelligent than middle class advantaged children? IQ tests indicate they are; these tests are accurate and dependable. But the meaning of IQ and "intelligence," while clear enough to trained psychometricians, has been seriously misunderstood by practicing educators, and this misunderstanding has been equally injurious to advantaged and disadvantaged children. Before we consider some models on which to build effective methods for teaching reading, we must correct this misunderstanding. In doing so, we will discover some important insights about intellect, cognition, perception, achievement, and aptitude that will help us understand the disadvantaged condition. From these insights we will derive four models to guide us in teaching *all* children.

Intelligence

"Intelligence" means general scholastic aptitude, intellectual potential or ability, problem-solving, information-processing, or primary mental abilities. The term itself refers to what we *can* do in contrast to what we do; that is, aptitude rather than achievement. Intelligence usually refers to verbal and perceptual behaviors often described as knowledge amassed from past learning.

Intelligence Tests

The "progenitor" of all intelligence tests in use today in the United States is the *Stanford-Binet,* an individually administered test developed by the French psychologist Alfred Binet. In 1905, Binet and Simon published a test to predict success of pupils in the French schools. A number of translations and adaptations later appeared in the United States, the most famous of which was L. M. Terman's *Stanford-Binet,* published in 1916. Practically speaking, every intelligence test is now validated on the *Stanford-Binet* or on other "established" intelligence tests that were originally validated on the Binet.

Measurements of potential in both the physical and behavioral sciences purport to measure what an entity *can* do, the amount of "work" it *could* produce. Ironically, although the literature makes a distinction between aptitude tests and achievement tests, we can only measure aptitude by observing achievement. That is, we can predict what Tommy *could do* tomorrow by what he *did* today and yesterday. We can measure the potential of an electric circuit by making it perform work (pushing a spring-set needle on a calibrated meter). When we see how much work it has done, we can predict how much work it will probably do in the future. This predicted workload is called "potential."

By presenting a child with a series of word and picture problems, we can observe how well he works (achieves) in various verbal and perceptual areas. If we use this information to measure what he has learned in the past, the observation is called an *achievement* test. If we use this information to predict how well he will perform similar tasks in the future, it is called an *aptitude* test. If we sample a wide spectrum of verbal and perceptual behaviors, we have a "wide-range" achievement test or a general aptitude test: an *intelligence* test.

The Use of IQ Tests with Socially Disadvantaged Pupils

Past learning, as measured by intelligence tests, largely determines what we can presently achieve. Thus, intelligence tests really tap achievement. But unlike most achievement tests, intelligence tests try to tap basic general *learning* that is common to achievement in all areas of school functioning. In contrast, formal achievement tests try to tap specific areas of learning. By attempting to tap general areas basic to all academic behaviors, the IQ test becomes a useful tool to predict how well groups of children will do in the school as it presently functions. These groups can be advantaged or disadvantaged, and the test can perform this prediction well enough to guide the educational program—which is precisely the major use of these tests. If the IQ test not only predicts general school achievement, but also pinpoints strengths and weaknesses in specific areas of basic learning, then the test can be an indication of the behaviors that should be taught to children in order to help them succeed in school. If we can design educational programs to modify the verbal and perceptual behaviors tapped in IQ tests, we can make a breakthrough in educating socially disadvantaged children. Thus, present intelligence tests will continue to be adequate pretest and posttest measurements for assessing our ability to do this job. This opinion was strongly supported in a recent survey of test specialists working with socially disadvantaged children and youth. [1]

There is no question, then, that the verbal and perceptual behaviors we tap on IQ tests are *relatively* useful in predicting academic success in the American school no matter what the socioeconomic class of the test taker. In addition, IQ tests are good diagnoses of specific basic verbal and perceptual behaviors that are learned and that may be taught by the school. But IQ tests have other uses as well. They are relatively good, although less reliable, in predicting reading success in the early grades. Predictive correlations between measures of intelligence and reading success in these grades, for example, range from .35 to .50 in various studies. The tendency is toward the lower correlations. Intelligence tests are also useful guides for predicting reading grade levels in older socially disadvantaged children. One study of school records of 450 socially disadvantaged seventh- and eighth-graders showed correlations of .69 and .70 with reading grade levels. [2] These results indicate a relationship between reading and what we measure on intelligence tests in this type of population. At the lower end of both the IQ and reading achievement score scales, the relationships between these two variables tend to be higher than relationships over the full curve. These higher relationships between reading and IQ are understandable—much of the IQ test is a reading test.

Intelligence tests are therefore useful indicators of expectancy level in *reading,* but they may not be good indicators of inherent ability, creativity, or practical and mechanical abilities. *Reading grade expectancy level* is a rough criterion against which to measure reading achievement scores. If Tommy is in fifth grade and he reads at fifth-grade level, he is reading at grade expectancy level *only if intelligence tests and clinical judgment indicate average intelligence.* If Tommy's classmate Jane has an IQ of 130 with a fifth-grade reading achievement level, *she is a retarded reader.* Although she is reading on grade level, her IQ suggests that she should read well above her grade placement. Some schools see retardation in terms of "below grade level." They fail to recognize the largest group of retarded readers—those with above average intelligence but on-grade-level reading achievement scores.

Socially disadvantaged children tend to have below average intelligence test scores, and, ostensibly, these scores indicate lower grade expectancy levels in reading. However, important qualifications to this statement will be discussed subsequently in a further analysis of intelligence. Essentially, these qualifications revolve around two principles:

1. Environment and experience modify intelligence.
2. Intelligence, as it is presently measured and, hence, defined, involves delimited behaviors. Other behaviors are equally important in life, even though schools do not presently measure them. Research in creativity and cognitive styles may soon lead to radical changes in our use, interpretation, and construction of intelligence tests.

Meanwhile, intelligence tests are useful tools for predicting school success, for establishing rough estimates of reading grade expectancy levels, and for diagnosing specific types of intellectual deficits that may be amenable to modifications. [2] If one of our goals for disadvantaged children on Chicago's South Side is to increase their school achievement to the level of their more advantaged neighbors from the other side of town, then the intelligence test is a useful tool to gauge our progress.

Can We Modify Intelligence?

Intelligence can be modified because it is largely the result of an organism's varied responses to environmental stimuli. The more intensive and varied those stimuli, the higher the resulting level of effective stimulation upon the organism.

Hunt includes the most thorough discussion of this conclusion in *Intelligence and Experience,* in which he defines intelligence as "problem-solving capacity based on a hierarchical organization" of symbols and of "information-processing strategies." [3] The symbols, organizational patterns, and strategies for processing information are learned. Hunt reviews the research on cognitive and perceptual development based on theories of Hebb, [4] Harlow, [5] Piaget, [6] and Wiener. [7] None of these theories denies the genetic limitations inherited by an organism. All of them postulate, however, that learned patterns are cumulative and that for all practical purposes, the quantity and quality of what an organism learns now depends upon the quantity and quality of patterns learned in the past. These theories are well demonstrated by research, as will be shown in Chapter Four.

New Questions About Intelligence and the Disadvantaged. Once we grant that intelligence is determined by a variety of functions early in development—functions that are primarily experiential, motivational, and learned—and that these functions regulate what is genetically given, then it is superfluous to ask whether or not intelligence can be influenced by experience. The questions now become:

1. How much can we modify intelligence?
2. What are the optimum conditions for modification?
3. Exactly when should these conditions be introduced in the developmental flow?

4. What are the best methods for introducing these conditions?
5. How late in the development of cultural deprivation can these methods make a difference?

Research has not yet given us adequate answers to these questions, and without adequate answers, the effectiveness of programs for the socially disadvantaged is severely limited. An educational technology for the socially disadvantaged child is not yet developed, and at this point money could be better used toward this goal than toward action programs. When research is successful in determining the best way to utilize available know-how, then more successful programs can be developed.

Answers We Already Have. The answers that we have involve knowledge of intellectual development and attainment of reading ability in socially disadvantaged children. We know, for example, that certain types of cultural deprivation and subsequent reading retardation is partly irreversible. Existing deficits in reading tend to increase with age. In Table 3, Chapter Two, for example, the reading retardation rate for eighth-graders is more extreme than for third-graders. Limitations of tests for third-graders account for part of this gain in retardation, but they do not explain all the increase, especially when we consider that some of the worst readers had already left school before these children were tested in grade 8.5.

An analogous conclusion was made by Meyer, Borgatta, and Jones in their attempt to intervene in the process of delinquency in adolescent socially disadvantaged girls [8] Here the experimenters were acting upon psychosocial, rather than cognitive, development. Intensive social work services this late in life were not enough to reverse such tendencies as school dropout, failure in school subjects, truancy, and suspension. These were conclusions drawn from group data. Anyone who has worked with socially disadvantaged adolescents can describe the individual whose retardation has been dramatically reversed late in development. But for most socially disadvantaged youngsters, compensatory education, whether it goes by the name of remedial reading or "social work intervention," will be, at best, only better than nothing.

Thus we can make the following generalization: *The earlier we apply compensatory, high-intensity education, the better the results are likely to be.* In an elementary school, early intervention in kindergarten or first grade, and preferably in prekindergarten, is the best attack on retardation in the culturally deprived child. The intermediate grades are dangerously late, and junior high school compensatory education yields meager results. Some adult illiterates may be taught minimal functional literacy, but at the present level of educational know-how very few stand much chance of becoming true readers. Most will not be able to master reading effectively enough to read technical manuals or teaching machine programs designed to make them more employable. Job Corps may be able to take the highly motivated school dropout reading at sixth-grade level and move him to eighth-grade level, but it will be only an occasional corpsman who is able to read the technical journals necessary for retraining into more highly skilled areas. The corpsman who enters the camp truly illiterate (third-grade level or below) will be lucky, indeed, if he can read *The New York Times* two years later.

The few answers we have, then, concern the timing of intervention. These answers indicate that if we are trying to teach basic skills on which later learning depends, we must try to teach them as early in development as possible. From intelligence test results we have been able to pinpoint some of the basic skills that underlie success in later learning. The unanswered questions deal with methodology; to help answer these questions, we can use the models described in the following sections.

Model Building

In the physical and behavioral sciences we collect observations as ideas; from these ideas we construct theories. A theory is man's attempt to give rational coherence to a body of observations. [9] When we restate a theory as a practical explanation, we call it a model. For example, observations lead us to theorize that man's brain with its ancillary apparatus (receptors and effectors) is an electrochemical computer; man's central nervous system operates as a computer. The description of this operation is really an explanation of the theory. Such an explanation is called a *model*.

To explain a theory (to build a model) requires statements that are, in effect, testable hypotheses. If a theory is correct, every statement used to explain that theory can be tested. Thus, a scientific process involves observation, a coherent rationale for what appears to be related observations (theory), and an explanation of that theory (model) that states testable hypotheses. Hypotheses can be tested in an antiseptic laboratory or in practical everyday application; as long as a model works (that is, the hypotheses are borne out), the model is accepted as true. To accept a model, the following two requirements must be met:

1. It must work when applied.
2. It must take us beyond the original observations from which the model was drawn and must lead to further testable hypotheses.

Novices must be cautioned that *reality,* in the sense of what really exists, is not an issue in model building. As long as a model works when applied, it is true. When it does not work, or when a different model works better, it is no longer true.

The Use of Theories

Some teachers tend to be hostile to "theory," a term they use to mean anything "not practical." Early in every teacher's career, he meets a veteran colleague who advises him to "Forget all that theory—it never works in practice." The irony is, of course, that most graduates of teacher-training programs have few theories of their own in the true sense of the term. They usually have bits of information, hunches, biases, and disorganized ideas. No wonder, then, that their theories are not practical. Often, teachers operate from implied or unstated models that they refuse to recognize, because to do so would force them to admit to invalid models. By refusing to face their implied models, they can avoid fallacies in their classroom methodology. This is an old technique of escaping responsibility by resorting to ignorance, sometimes called the "ostrich syndrome."

For example, consider the myth discussed in Chapter One in which reading readiness is believed to be a natural result of development or growth. It is not uncommon for teachers to recommend no promotion for a nonreading first-grader under the assumption that he needs to mature and that more time to grow or develop will breed certain habits or behaviors conducive to learning to read. Without recognizing it, such teachers are applying an unsound theory that explains child development as an unfolding process in the tradition of Arnold Gesell or the 1940 progressivists who believed that "children will get there if you don't push; just give them time." An alternative model of child development does not simply derive from a different philosophy; it is the result of careful observation and experimentation in development by such researchers as Piaget, [6] Harlow, [5] and many others. A teacher cannot begin to evaluate his malpractices until he recognizes them, and *that* often requires the recognition of the implied models that underlie his practices.

Without models, teaching is inconsistent and usually ineffective. Unless the teacher has a step-by-step set of procedures that represent someone else's model, he does not even have a method. Unless the teacher is an automaton carrying out someone else's model, he must have his own models to guide his teaching. With a model, the teacher has a method without necessarily resorting to a "cookbook." The models he selects should be scientifically valid, clear, and concise. He should be able to explain to himself exactly what process is occurring in his classroom in terms of them. In other words, the activities of the teacher and the pupils should be the primary test of the models that he selects. Some practical models and examples of them in application are discussed in the remainder of this chapter.

Four Models

The four models that we have found to be useful in controlling the learning processes of socially disadvantaged children and youth are:

1. The *information-processing model,* which describes the central nervous system as a modified electrochemical computer.
2. The *hierarchy of needs model* to explain psychodynamic factors in behavior change.
3. The *syndrome model,* which establishes a scientific basis for considering a "whole child."
4. The *reading model,* which defines the reading act.

The information-processing model is a convenient explanation of human behavior that is currently being used in psychiatry, neurophysiology, neuropsychology, perception, and learning. In one sense, it is a "macromodel"; that is, the other three models describe processes that are subsumed under the information-processing model. This macromodel is an all-inclusive theory that includes smaller models or "micromodels," and by which all theories of psychology can be explained.

The hierarchy of needs model explains one part of the macromodel—the affective domain. Although the information-processing model includes the "whole child," it particularly emphasizes the intellectual or cognitive aspects. The hierarchy of needs model elaborates the nonintellectual, or emotional, component of the macromodel. It is less complex, for example, than a Freudian theory, and more directly applicable than most psychodynamic theories. Teaching children to read requires cognitive processes interacting with emotional or affective processes. An effective pedagogy must consider both aspects of behavior.

The syndrome model is a further elaboration of the macromodel and demonstrates the practical implications of the progressivists' concept of the whole child. One of the weaknesses of the whole-child theory was its inability to communicate the practical implications of the fact that man is a psychophysical organism, which means that all his "subsystems" interact. The syndrome model demonstrates this for us. Therefore, the whole organism must be considered in the learning process. This is a good example of how one model is better than another. The whole-child model (if it can be called a model at all) did not work well—not because it was incorrect, but because it was not precise enough to be applied. The syndrome model does not refute the whole-child theory; it is, in fact, a restatement of the theory in a way that demonstrates its practicality—the syndrome model works better.

Finally, the reading model is a simple definition of one part of the information-processing system. Because this book is about reading, it is necessary to develop a working model of the reading process that is neither so broad that it is impractical, nor so narrow that it is useless. The remainder of this book will apply these models in the further analysis of learning problems and in the suggestions for effective prevention and remediation of reading retardation in disadvantaged children.

The Information-Processing Model

In 1948, Norbert Wiener published the culmination of two decades of intellectual ferment, *Cybernetics*. [7] Wiener, the father of modern computer theory, had been working with neurophysiologists in applying this new science to man's central nervous system. Today, the analogy between man's brain and a digital or analog computer has exceeded the comparison state. We have fully accepted the cybernetics or information-processing model to explain human behavior because it has worked better than any competing model and because it has opened up endless paths of knowledge about human behavior. In every phase of medicine, psychology, and education, the cybernetics model can be applied. It is our most useful macrotheory because it encompasses such key theories as homeostasis, [10] stress, [11] and even psychoanalytic theory.

Man is an electrochemical information-processing system with enormous potential and complexity. His brain processes 3 million impulses per millisecond supplied by sense organs and proprioceptive, kinesthetic, and chemical inputs. Nature's crowning achievement is the evolution of this brain, an amazingly efficient processing system. Awake or asleep, the rest of the organism helps it store, process, and transmit staggering amounts of data.

At birth, the human computer is not a *tabula rasa* ready to record impressions. It has been processing data *in utero*. Programs may even be inherent in its structure. How the human computer processes information tomorrow depends upon how it is programed today. In fact, the quantity and quality of information processed in the first three or four years of life will determine how it will process information for its subsequent lifetime. K. S. Lashley describes the complexity of data processing in the brain:

> Input is never into a quiescent or static system but always into a system which is already actively excited and organized. In the intact organism, behavior is the result of interaction of this background of excitation with input from any designated stimulus. Only when we can state the general characteristics of this back-

ground excitation, can we understand the effects of a given input. [12]

Thus, behavior is determined less by the stimulus and more by the ongoing process already in the system. The child who has been programed to accept abuse from adults may perceive an input that his teacher meant to be friendly as an abusive or negative signal. The "background of excitation" molds the input signal to fit the computer's program.

The background of excitation includes three processes:

1. *Scanning*. The alpha wave observed on the electroencephalograph appears to be a scanning wave. [13] This scanning device selects memories pertinent to the given stimulus situation. Incoming information to the brain is carried by the scanning wave through a memory bank. The carrier wave tries to match previous information stored in the bank with the new input.

2. *Feedback*. All input (stimuli) is regulated by feedback from neural output. [7] Thus, how a child responds to a stimulus is not only determined by the nature of the stimulus and the program already in the computer (brain, personality, and so on), but also by a feedback system that connects responding behavior (output) to input. The child perceives a stimulus partially as a result of his responding behavior. For example, consider a situation in which the letter *e* is presented to a child. Suppose he tends to twist his body to one side and tip his head down, so that he orients himself obliquely to this visual stimulus. Such behavior is typical of first-graders and may be a response pattern to all letter stimuli. But this response pattern (output) immediately distorts the input so that the letter is perceived from an angle, which, to a novice, gives it a very different shape. In fact, many young children do not recognize a letter viewed from a side angle as the same letter viewed head on. Thus, feedback from output directly influences input of the stimulus.

3. *Affective tone*. Information from the total organism can be stored and can influence ongoing background activity, as well as input, output, and feedback. Affective tone has been called attitude, motivation, and set. Its influence on scanning and feedback controls the entire perceptual process. For example, as in the description of feedback above, a child twists his body as a response to letter stimuli. Letter stimuli may account for 50 to 60 percent of school activities in the early grades. The con-

tinuous twist of the body is a postural distortion that increases muscle tonus and, in fact, causes a subliminal discomfort of the body. Over a period of time, children subjected to these stimuli may, on a subconscious level, begin to associate letter stimuli and postural discomfort, this leading to a negative feeling associated with letter stimuli. This negative feeling or attitude becomes part of the affective tone that influences the information processing of letters.

Figure 1 shows a simplified diagram of the information-processing model.

Figure 1　Diagram of the Information-Processing Model

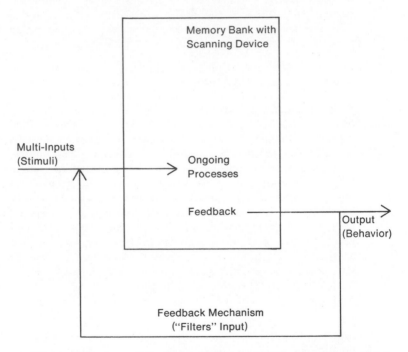

Through the use of the information-processing model, teaching attempts to program or reprogram the system. The teacher must first observe the total system to discover how it was programed. He does this by analyzing input (stimuli) and output (resulting or responding behavior). This analysis then leads him to some hunches about the ongoing process or background of excitation that he can never see directly. In other words, he observes how the child operates and then decides how the child *should* operate. How much of this decision is influenced by the child's desires and how much is controlled by human engineers (teachers, parents, clergymen, and so on) discriminates between self-directed behavior change and brainwashing. Most adults prefer brainwashing, the most common form of child training in or out of the school.

Ideally, the teacher should be an aide to the pupil, the instrument through which the pupil learns to analyze his own information-processing system. With the teacher indicating the wide range of possibilities, the pupil decides which modifications he desires. The teacher then devices the correct series of stimuli to reprogram the computer.

Just adding more information to the memory bank rarely effects significant behavior change. Conditions must be arranged that present inputs to both memory bank and affective tone. Only then will the background of excitation or ongoing process change. The teacher observes the change indirectly through new outputs; new outputs to old stimuli signify changes in memory bank, affective tone, and feedback system. For example, Sylvia Ashton Warner, working with Maori children, developed an organic vocabulary system consisting of inputs that affected both memory bank and affective tone. [14] By teaching emotionally loaded words peculiar to each individual child, she was able to influence affective tone. Such words as *ghost, monster,* and *skeleton* had been particularly emotionally tinged for these children. With this system, the background of excitation was influenced. Her reports show that the feedback system no longer filtered out reading; behavior changed, and her children began to read. The output was evidence of these changes.

The teacher's major job, therefore, is to devise sets of stimuli that will program the computer to handle appropriate information. A sixteen-year-old school dropout with perceptual problems was unable to learn simple subtraction by the usual methods. So we changed the stimuli. First, we presented seven sticks; we removed three, and he was able to count four remaining. When we asked him to do this "in his head," he was unable to see sticks in any quantity. We tried a different input. We told him to keep his eyes closed and use his nose as a finger to draw five imaginary sticks. Then we told him to remove two of these sticks. He was able to count three remaining. We had changed the quality of the input (kinesthetic stimuli) and increased the input quantity.

Models are often rejected by schoolmen as being too "mechanistic," a loaded term in education. However, a model is, in effect, a systematic diagram of a process, thus being mechanistic almost by definition. To apply models to a human being is not to dehumanize him, but to engineer his behavior. Here is the crux of why some educators refuse to define their models. Whether they admit it or not, all teachers—and all adults—control human behavior. As adults, we have no choice but to teach our children, and even when we try not to, our behaviors influence them. When we teach them without analyzing what we are doing, we are manipulating them blindly. This is antihumanistic because it allows us to engineer their behavior without subjecting our own to evaluation. But when we admit to human engineering, we are forced to appraise our strategies and subject ourselves to ethics and morals. Because we must manipulate their behaviors, we should do so carefully from models that allow us to observe and evaluate. The method of applying the model, the conditions under which it is applied, the personalities using the model, and knowledge of the effects of the model—all offer balances between mechanistic and humanistic modes.

Applying the Information-Processing Model. Using an information-processing model, it is obvious how the memory bank becomes the target of the school. The easiest path for the teacher is to stuff information into the computer. Some teachers believe that the more they stuff, the more is liable to be retained, or at least, regurgitated. Facts are fed in, and something resembling the facts appears at the output. Some signal loss is expected along the way.

Unfortunately, children, like computers, refuse to operate in such a simple manner. In the slum school, teachers often deluge the child with stimuli, but output is meager. How, for example, can eighth-graders sit year after year in the classroom and still be illiterate? Such children exist in larger numbers than most junior high school administrators admit. Like computers, these children cannot accept information (input) unless they are programed to do so. The ongoing process must be able to handle the input. If, for example, the memory bank and affective tone include experiences (information) about *lawns,* including seeing, touching, cutting, smelling, rolling on, and the infinite specific "lawn experiences," then a teacher can try to stuff in the spoken symbol /lawn/. If, however, the child has not been programed with these experiences, then the scanning device finds nothing in the memory bank or affective tone to integrate the new input. Or it selects substitute data in the memory bank that is unacceptable to the teacher; that is, the child gives a "wrong" response to the spoken word /lawn/. Or the feedback filtering system blots out the input because it does not fit the ongoing process; that is, there is no program to handle the information. Teachers usually describe this filtering process as "tuning out." During the filtering process the child appears to turn off the input channel.

The information-processing model demonstrates dramatically why quantity will not solve the educational problems of disadvantaged children. More of the same—more experiences and more training—is analogous to stuffing more data into a computer that has no program to process it. What we need is reprograming, not more data—qualitative change, not quantitative. This is the challenge of compensatory education. According to the model, the ongoing process involves five subprocesses: input, output, memory bank, affective tone, and feedback. The school environment presents input in the form of a curriculum. Output is the child's behavior that results from the total process—"what he has learned." Feedback is the filtering system that results from memory and affect. It manifests itself in attention or perceptual set. The memory bank holds cold data. The key to changing ongoing process is the affective tone, but it is the most difficult to engineer. Here is what we call motivation, attitude, feeling, affect. Affective tone controls feedback together with memory bank. If we are to program the disadvantaged child, we must not only decide what cold data to feed the computer, we must also decide how to influence the affective tone. The hierarchy of needs model is a guide to reaching this goal.

The Hierarchy of Needs Model

The ability of a system to change is determined by its flexibility. Affective tone can prevent change in the ongoing process by rendering the system inflexible, but, on the other hand, affective tone also can render a system more flexible. The problem is how to keep the system open, or how to ensure an affective tone that will keep the system flexible.

Maslow's theory of prepotency of needs [15] offers a practical model for influencing affective tone. Research evidence indicates that when psychological and physiological needs are satiated, lower animals still manifest a need and a natural curiosity to seek new experiences. We can see the same phenomenon in infants whose needs appear to be gratified. They display a basic need to seek new experiences and integrate them into the system. The infant appears to seek information, data, or experiences to fulfill his potential. This process is the one by which the child builds a unique self—a person different from all other persons. It has been called the process of "becoming." [16, 17]

When major psychophysical needs are not satiated, the organism appears to be sidetracked from "becoming." Out of necessity, affective tone seems to limit data processing by focusing the system on inputs to gratify these needs. It directs the feedback system to filter out extraneous information—in this case, anything that does not gratify these major psychophysical needs is extraneous. Thus, the system becomes less flexible; it sharply delimits itself. On the other hand, when psychophysical needs are gratified, the system is open, seeking any kind of data the environment can offer—the system is "becoming," or in Maslow's terms, the system is meeting its need to "self-actualize." Self-actualizing opens the system; meeting lower needs closes the system. For example, the hungry child organizes his energy to seek food. He delimits areas of interest; input and output fixate on that one need. The more intense the hunger or the fixation, the more constricted the system becomes. Because his behavior is fixated on one need, this child's behavior is highly predictable; he is inflexible. In contrast, the satiated child is unpredictable. His roving eyes and body may take him anywhere: from input to output he is open.

Maslow lists five basic needs in order of prepotency. [15] A system's energy centers on needs according to the order of prepotency. For example, the amount of energy a child can devote to self-actualizing depends upon the energy he needs to expend on gaining self-esteem. However, the amount of energy available to gaining self-esteem depends in turn upon the amount of energy spent in quest of love or learning how to love. The "lower needs" must be satisfied in order to make energy available to higher needs. Energy is applied according to the following hierarchy:

Self-actualization
Self-esteem
Love
Safety
Physiological (hunger, sex, warmth, and so on)

To effect change in the system's ongoing process, we must increase its flexibility. We must make it more open to different inputs. To accomplish this with any child, disadvantaged or not, we must build methodologies, provide materials, and staff schools with teachers who can gratify basic needs. These needs are the domain of affective tone. By using a third model, the syndrome theory of behavior, we can increase the possible methods of influencing affective tone.

The Syndrome Model

A syndrome is an organized, structured group of behaviors that are integrated and interdependent. Within a syndrome are feelings and behaviors that, although they appear to be different from each other, overlap and intertwine. [15] To analyze how a system processes information, we group behaviors into syndromes. For example, in one child we may decide to note such syndromes as reading disability, school retardation, seeking self-esteem, or lack of love. There is no end to the number of syndromes we can isolate in any child by grouping related outputs (behaviors).

In doing so, we find that almost all specific behaviors can be members of more than one syndrome. For example, Juan's inability to maintain visual fixation was part of a vision deficiency syndrome involving problems of binocularity. It was also part of his reading disability syndrome, his acting out syndrome, his perceptual-dysfunction syndrome, and so on. Different professions often disagree about the nature of the child's problem because they specialize in different syndrome clusters. The pediatrician includes Juan's behavior as part of a vision deficiency syndrome. The reading specialist describes the same behavior as part of a reading retardation syndrome. The psychiatrist is sure that the poor fixation is a perceptual style consistent with a particular neurosis syndrome. Actually, each specialist may be correct, and Juan's problem might be solved by any one of them. The best approach can be determined by a team diagnosis, which is usually unavailable because it is so costly. The syndrome model increases the number of alternative actions for solving the child's problems.

Applying the Syndrome Model. Syndromes have two important characteristics that enable us to influence affective tone or any part of the ongoing process:

1. We can cause change within a single syndrome by affecting one or two specific behaviors. Why? Because a total, single syndrome tends to change when any part of it changes.
2. We can cause change in the total ongoing process (often called "total personality") because the total personality is a combination of syndromes. In this case what is true of a single syndrome is also true of the total personality; that is, a change in a single syndrome tends to influence all the syndromes.

The hierarchy of needs model can be used for illustration. If Peter feels insecure because of the lack of a father in the home, he may fixate most of his ongoing process on seeking safety. His safety need syndrome dominates his input-output. Suddenly a male third-grade teacher spots Peter's problem and allows Peter to "latch on." A change in Peter's safety need syndrome occurs. According to the hierarchy of needs theory, energy is now available for gratifying self-esteem and love needs. As more energy is available for these higher needs, Peter finds more ways of gratifying these needs, especially if the teacher helps him gain self-esteem and love. Now more energy is available for self-actualizing. The system loosens up, affective tone changes, and flexibility allows more and different inputs. Peter begins to achieve in reading. This self-actualizing achievement feeds back to safety, self-esteem, and love, and more energy is released for self-actualizing. A change in only one part of Peter's safety need syndrome was enough to shift the whole syndrome. This shift resulted in a total personality change as one syndrome influenced another.

The trick is to select behaviors most accessible to teacher manipulation and most likely to cause a shift in the syndrome. The selection depends upon the available talents, assets, time, and resources. If a male identification figure were not available to Peter, an intensive remedial reading program may have been able to bring about the same type of chain reaction. The number of syndromes in which a teacher may utilize his skills is quite large because the behaviors and syndromes are interdependent. We teach the *whole child*. Thus, the ongoing process, and the affective tone, in particular, is accessible to reprograming. One more model will give us the four guides we have found most successful in manipulating learning processes in disadvantaged and advantaged children. This model is simply a working definition of reading.

The Reading Model

Reading is the processing of a symbol of a symbol of experience. Thus, it is two steps removed from reality. The written symbol c-a-t represents the oral-aural symbol /cat/, which represents the experiencing of a cat. When a child reads the letters c-a-t, it is not enough that he decode into the spoken word /cat/. That is merely replacing one symbol with another. He must take it a third step by picking out of his memory bank those experiences involving cats, including associated affective tone.

Thus, when we introduce "code busting" or formal reading instruction at the level of printed symbols, that is, when we present the letters c-a-t to children, we assume:

1. The children have the word in their oral-aural vocabularies.
2. The children have sufficient experiences with the concept or thing that the spoken symbol represents, allowing them to associate the spoken symbol with various contexts, to evaluate the concepts, and to participate in some reasonable form of dialogue.

The reading process is diagramed as follows:

$$\text{Experience} \longleftrightarrow S_1 \longleftrightarrow S_2$$

in which S_1 (symbol one) is the oral-aural symbol, and S_2 (symbol two) is the written symbol. To move from S_2 to S_1 is to "bust" the written code. Reading requires the child to perform two code-busting processes; first, the written code and, second, the spoken code. Unless S_2 takes him back to experience, he has not read. In order to read, the child must have the experience or concept, the related oral-aural symbol (he must be able to say the word or to recognize it when said to him), and the ability to translate S_2 to S_1.

Middle class children entering first grade have oral-aural vocabularies estimated at from 8,000 to 10,000 words. Teaching them to read is primarily a problem of teaching them to code bust S_2 to S_1. Certainly, experiences and concepts they associate with S_1 must be sharpened and enriched, but they come to the school well equipped with S_1 and experience. In contrast, culturally deprived children lack S_1. The job of teaching them to read is not simply teaching them to bust the written code; teachers must also preteach S_1.

Most teachers of the culturally deprived also claim that these children lack experiences, but our own observations suggest that this problem is less intensive than most classroom teachers think. Teachers tend to confuse deficiencies in S_1 with deficiencies in experience. For example, almost all disadvantaged children in East Harlem have experienced the *curb*. They have sat on it, tripped over it, banged their heads on it, and thrown a ball at it. The *curb* is part of their experience, but they may not have the oral-aural symbol /curb/. True, disadvantaged children lack many experiences, but even more serious is their lack of oral-aural symbols (S_1) for the experiences they have had.

Summary

Intelligence tests are useful instruments to measure learned behaviors, most of which are verbal and perceptual. These tests are relatively useful in predicting school success, but their primary value is in diagnosing basic perceptual and verbal deficiencies on which to base compensatory educational programs for disadvantaged children. Similarly, these tests can be used to gauge the effectiveness of such compensatory programs. The problem is to determine which behaviors can be taught at what point in development to influence children's general ability to learn.

Thus, intelligence is essentially the basic program within the "human computer" that determines the quality and quantity of intellectual functioning, problem solving, or information processing. Using this computer model, we can think of basic education as a means of programing children to function effectively in life. One key to this programing is the emotional or affective component of man. This component determines the flexibility of the information-processing system that was used in this chapter as the behavioral model for man. A flexible system is open to new experiences. In more familiar terms, the child who feels happy, satiated, safe, loved, and feels good about himself is one who is open to change, and change is the crux of learning.

A version of Maslow's prepotency of needs theory lends itself neatly to manipulating affect for optimal learning. The human organism seeks new experiences if basic physiological, safety, love, and self-esteem needs are relatively satiated. Under these conditions, man will self-actualize; optimal learning will occur. But when one or more lower needs are unfulfilled, most of a person's energy will center on that need. This tends to rigidify the organism and delimit the information-processing system. To break this rigidity we apply a syndrome model. By categorizing specific responses (behaviors, outputs) into syndromes, one or more of a number of areas can be treated because related behaviors within a syndrome affect each other. Moreover, because different syndromes affect each other, the possible methods of changing children's behaviors are extended.

Although these models apply to any area of human behavior, they are used in this book to help solve the problem of teaching reading. Reading is defined as the processing of a visual symbol into an oral-aural symbol that elicits intellectual and emotional responses drawn from experience. In order to read, a child must have memory traces, associated affective tone, and a socially acceptable oral-aural symbol for these processes *before* he tries to decode the letters that represent the spoken word.

The extent and intensity of the disadvantaged condition and

models to use to change some of this condition—at least that portion within the grasp of the school—have been presented. The next chapter will introduce the first step in this change: diagnosis of the specific reading needs of disadvantaged children.

References

1. I. Sigel *et al., Practitioners' Perspective on Psycho-Educational Tests* (Chicago: Merrill Palmer Institute, 1965).
2. S. Alan Cohen, "A Study of Relationships Among Measurements of Reading, Intelligence and Vision Development, Using a Dynamic Theory of Vision in Socially Disadvantaged Junior High School Children" (Unpublished doctoral dissertation, Boston University, 1965).
3. J. McV. Hunt, *Intelligence and Experience* (New York: Ronald Press, 1961), p. 109.
4. D. Hebb, *The Organization of Behavior* (New York: Wiley, 1949).
5. H. Harlow, "The Formation of Learning Sets," *Psychological Review*, 56 (1949), 51–65.
6. J. Piaget, *The Psychology of Intelligence* (London: Routledge and Kegan Paul, 1947).
7. Norbert Wiener, *Cybernetics* (New York: Wiley, 1948), p. 97.
8. H. Meyer, E. F. Borgatta, and W. C. Jones, *Girls at Vocational High School* (New York: Russell Sage Foundation, 1965), pp. 205–17.
9. F. H. Allport, *Theories of Perception and the Concept of Structure* (New York: Wiley, 1955), p. 4.
10. W. B. Cannon, *The Wisdom of the Body* (New York: Norton, 1939), pp. 23–25.
11. H. Selye, *The Stress of Life* (New York: McGraw-Hill, 1956).
12. K. S. Lashley, "Problem of Serial Order," in L. A. Jeffries (ed.), *Cerebral Mechanisms in Behavior* (New York: Wiley, 1951), p. 112.
13. W. S. McCullough, "Why the Mind Is in the Head," in Jeffries, *op. cit.,* p. 100.
14. Sylvia Ashton Warner, *The Teacher* (New York: Simon and Schuster, 1963), pp. 28–66.

15. A. H. Maslow, *Motivation and Personality* (New York: Harper & Row, 1954), pp. 32, 80–106, 146–54.

16. ———, *Toward a Psychology of Being* (Princeton, N.J.: Van Nostrand, 1962).

17. G. Allport, *Becoming* (New Haven, Conn.: Yale University Press, 1955).

Chapter Four

Diagnosing Reading Disabilities

Learning involves behavior change, and the first step in changing behavior is to determine what needs to be changed. Educators call this *diagnosis,* which requires formal and informal testing. The tests that we have found to be most useful in understanding the specific needs of disadvantaged children who have trouble learning to read are presented in this chapter. Descriptions of the reading disability patterns of this population revealed by these tests are also included. First, however, we must consider the purpose of tests, the meaning of diagnosis, and the misassumptions about testing all children. Tests should serve three major purposes. For the classroom teacher, these purposes fall into an ordered list of priorities, as described in the section on Three Uses of Tests.

The Controversy over Standardized Tests

A standardized test is merely a tool, not an end in itself. If standardized tests are designed to help meet the three priorities described below and these priorities are not being met, it does not seem wise to blame the tool. For example, some school systems have eliminated standardized intelligence tests for various reasons.

One of these reasons is that teachers and administrators tend to label (predict) children as "below average" in intelligence, which leads to an educational self-fulfillment of the prediction. The problem is not a test deficiency but a deficiency in the use of the tests; the solution is teacher training, not elimination of the IQ test. Another reason sometimes cited for eliminating the test is that they are standardized on middle class children and therefore put lower class children at a disadvantage, because these children perform poorly. But IQ tests are general scholastic aptitude tests and are relatively good indicators of academic success for large groups; disadvantaged children as a group are poor achievers in schools that have middle class expectancies. Therefore, the IQ tests are accurate descriptions of the academic performance of large groups of disadvantaged children in American middle class schools. In other words, the test does exactly what it is designed to do.

To replace these tests with achievement tests does not eliminate the problem of misuse. To replace global intelligence tests with newly constructed tests that divide results into categories of behavior is an equal waste of time and money. Multifactor IQ tests and multiple achievement and aptitude tests already exist. To build new norms using lower class populations is unrealistic. Black parents in Watts do not want their children to achieve as well as black children in Chicago slums. They want them to achieve as well as the middle class children from white suburbia with whom they must compete in American society. Thus, the sentiment against standardized tests and/or the elimination of them is a poor solution to the problem of professional incompetence.

Three Uses of Tests

To Teach

The school's responsibility is to promote learning. Therefore, unless tests contribute to this goal, they should not be included in the curriculum. The first priority of a test, then, is to teach. A test should sample behaviors or information that is important for the child to remember. If a history test asks a child to regurgitate the date of Hawaii's annexation to the United States, we are assuming that of all the information a child could glean from a study of late nineteenth-century America, the date of Hawaii's annexation is one of the more important facts. Consider instead the following question:

> The year 1898 marks an important period
> of American imperialism. Discuss.

> Or

> What new lands did America obtain in
> that year?

This question reemphasizes an important point previously taught by the teacher and reinforces the concept of classical imperialism. It also leads to the possibility of the following test question later in the year:

> The date 1898 was the high-water mark of America's period of "classical imperialism." The mid-twentieth century ushered in what some people consider a new form of American "imperialism." Compare the two forms of imperialism. What kinds of new possessions were involved in each type of imperialism?

These test questions reinforce important ideas, and thus become effective teaching tools. In order to answer them, the student must think about what he has been taught, and then apply as much appropriate information as he can. The primary emphasis is on learning, with evaluation as a secondary outcome. Therefore, the test serves as a review or as a point of departure for further discussion or debate.

In the same way, consider a test question in which the child is asked to select the single statement that best emphasizes the main idea of a reading selection. This question can lead to a discussion of what constitutes a statement of main idea, and become a lesson. The teacher and pupils focus on the discussion, rather than on an evaluation of performance. If a child selects the wrong main ideas in a test following a teaching unit on main ideas, the test does not become a record of his achievement. It becomes, instead, one more teaching tool—a step toward further work in this skill. When a child finally masters main ideas as manifested in a later test, his test performance should not become a permanent record of achievement. It should be, instead, a signal to both teacher and pupil that it is time to move to a new skill. The new test result also becomes an intrinsic reward as well as a motivating device to move on to new achievements.

To Diagnose

Most classroom teachers have succumbed to "Friday's disease," an established behavior pattern characterized by a tendency to administer quizzes or tests on the day that ends a teaching unit, usually a Friday. One of the most effective antidotes for Friday's disease is to infect teachers with "Monday's disease," a behavior pattern characterized by a tendency to administer quizzes or tests at the beginning of a teaching unit. The purpose of infecting the profession with Monday's disease is not to eliminate Friday's disease, but to balance it by changing the teachers' and the pupils' perceptions of testing.

When a teacher teaches and then evaluates pupil behaviors (related, we hope, to the behaviors or information taught), the teacher has no way of knowing whether or not learning has occurred. That a child can spell ten out of ten words correctly on Friday's test is no indication that he has learned anything, because he might have been able to spell these words before the teacher ever taught them. For such a child, the week's work in spelling may have been a waste of time. The argument that he could use the review is absurd in the light of many other needs a child has at any level of achievement. Thus, the second purpose of a test in order of priority is to diagnose needs. The child should be pre-tested before instruction and post-tested after instruction to allow him to observe the quantity and quality of his own learning. For the child, pretesting should establish what behaviors or information he needs to learn; for the teacher, it should establish not only what the child needs to learn, but the level and rate at which he should learn it. In other words, pretesting is the major determinant of each child's curriculum.

This proper use of testing is avoided by most schools, not because it is time-consuming, but because it would require that the school then meet the individual needs thus diagnosed. That requires skilled teachers, hard work, an abundance and variety of material, and careful planning to make full use of the data gathered in pre- and post-testing.

To Evaluate

The third priority of a test is to evaluate teacher and pupil performance and to measure the effectiveness of materials and methods. Evaluation, which uses group, rather than individual, scores is the basis for general curriculum planning. The amount of time and effort devoted to this priority should be commensurate with its position in the hierarchy of uses; in fact, meeting the first two priorities will also fulfill the third objective, because they will provide the needed group data.

Seven Ways Not to Use Tests

These three uses and their order of priority apply to both teacher-made and standardized tests. Unfortunately, a number of malpractices have developed in the use of tests with both disadvantaged and advantaged children. These are spelled out in the following passage.

1. Tests are not designed to be negative reinforcers. They are not meant to quantify a child and thereby qualify him for life.
2. Standardized tests are not designed to be filed away in guidance office records. Unless the test information is given to teachers, pupils, parents, and curriculum directors for intelligent use according to the three priorities, the administration and storage of tests are absurd.
3. Not to make this information available to teachers because of their inability to use it wisely is no reason to withhold the information. Intensive in-service training for teachers who do not know how to use test information is required.
4. The elimination of standardized tests from a school program because of their misuse is not an answer to, but an avoidance of, the problem. In-service training is again required.
5. The confusion of achievement and aptitude by many educators is also unnecessary. Standardized tests of aptitude, including tests of general aptitude currently in use, are essentially forms of

achievement tests constructed and statistically standardized to tap general areas of achievement. It is dangerous and unwise to interpret aptitude test results as measurements of genetic or intrinsic aptitude. These test results are usually the accumulation of past learning over long periods of time. To label a child as permanently lacking a math or reading aptitude is erroneous. If he is taught skills, he will tend to develop an aptitude.

6. To predict future success in a given content area on the basis of aptitude tests for any individual is dangerous. The predictive correlations for standardized tests are high enough to generalize predictions about future success of *groups* of students, but they are not high enough to predict for *individual* students. Certainly, reliable test results at the extreme ends of the curve are significant, but 66 percent of the population falls between plus or minus 1 standard deviation of the mean. The predictive correlations of most tests are not high enough to predict for these individuals with much better than a fifty-fifty chance of accuracy. Furthermore, many other factors, such as motivation, personality, environmental opportunity, and luck, wield greater influence than test performance.

7. Grouping for instruction on the basis of gross measurements of achievement or aptitude is a useless practice. This will be discussed in a later chapter. Standardized or teacher-made tests contribute to effective grouping for instruction only when they diagnose specific subskills weaknesses in reading or other curriculum areas, telling us specifically what each child needs to learn.

Tests to Meet the Three Priorities for Disadvantaged Children

An efficient testing program will use a variety of techniques to meet all three priorities simultaneously. In projects with disadvantaged children, researchers have used combinations of standardized group tests, standardized clinical tests, and unstandardized clinical tests. Examples of intelligence tests that have been used to diagnose needs, to pinpoint specific cognitive areas that might be affected by remedial instruction, and to evaluate long-range effects are described below.

Intelligence Tests. The Wechsler Intelligence Scale for Children (WISC) [1] is a multifactor test that pinpoints specific areas of

Figure 1   **Example of WISC Report Form**

Wechsler Report _____

Name _____

Age _____ Grade _____ Date _____

How To Interpret the Scores Below: These scores are recorded in percentiles. A percentile of 55 means that your child performed as well as or better than 55 percent of the cases on which the test was standardized. The performances used as the standard are a sample of performances of children in your child's age group.

Verbal Tasks

A. General range of information about the world and life around him.   _____
B. Ability to use his information in practical situations.   _____
C. Arithmetic reasoning and ability.   _____
D. Ability to note essential similarities, verbal abstractions.   _____
E. Memory for digits, auditory attention, concentration.   _____
F. Word knowledge, general cultural and educational level.   _____

Performance Tasks

G. Ability to note details, discriminate between essential and nonessential details.   _____
H. Social intelligence or ability to comprehend a social situation, to comprehend subtleties in interpersonal relations, story sense.   _____
I. Ability to deal with part-whole situations when the goal is known, to handle space abstractly.   _____
J. Ability to deal with part-whole situations when the goal is not known.   _____
K. Ability to learn a new task involving speeded eye-hand coordination and visual memory.   _____
L. Capacity for planning and foresight, involving visual and motor control.   _____

Summary

Verbal Intelligence _____   Significant Highs _____
Performance Intelligence _____   Significant Lows _____
Total Intelligence Score _____   Expected Grade Level _____

Source: S. Alan Cohen, Ferkauf Graduate School, Yeshiva University; adapted from a report form developed at the Boston University Secondary Reading Clinic.

strengths and weaknesses. Many clinicians prefer it to the Stanford-Binet [2] because the latter is too verbal and does not tap certain cognitive and perceptual behaviors at various levels of mental maturity. The WISC, of course, is an individually administered psychological test and must be given by qualified psychometricians. Figure 1 is an example of a WISC test analysis form used in one educational center. (This particular form was originally developed at Boston University Secondary Reading Clinic by Dr. Mabel Noall and was revised for use in the Yeshiva University Ferkauf Graduate School Reading Center.) The value of a multifactor analysis of intelligence is shown. A scatter of scores across the WISC subtests indicates to the clinician the specific areas of weakness that should be given attention when planning instruction. It allows him to pinpoint specific cognitive or perceptual needs. The form clearly describes the types of behaviors that make up intelligence.

When groups are too large or when psychometricians are unavailable, group multifactor intelligence tests, such as the *California Test of Mental Maturity, Short Form* (CTMM), [3] or the *Primary Mental Abilities* test (PMA), [4] are good substitutes. Figure 2 is an example of the CTMM test analysis form, again pinpointing specific areas of need, most of which lend themselves to remediation. Depending upon the level, the PMA yields separate scores for cognitive and perceptual skills that underlie IQ: picture vocabulary, sight or reading vocabulary, number sequence, arithmetic problem solving, verbal and number reasoning, and speed of visual perception. Other multifactor group tests of intelligence exist and may be equally useful. Even tests yielding global scores of IQ can be used diagnostically if teachers take the time to study each child's pattern of errors by doing an item analysis. Tests like the CTMM and PMA make this job easier for the teacher.

Group Reading Tests. As a group test, the Reading Center at Yeshiva University finds the *California Reading Test* (CRT) [5] at all levels to be particularly useful because it provides both subskill and item analyses. Probable areas of strengths and weaknesses for each individual are pinpointed, thus enabling us to tailor instruction to individual needs. The norms on the CRT tend to be easier than on other standardized tests, but we find that this fact is

Figure 2   **Example of CTMM Report Form**

**California Test of
Mental Maturity Report**

Level _____

Form _____

Name _____   Sex____ Grade____ Age____

Address _____

Factor	Test	Raw Score	% Correct
Spatial relation-ships	1. Sensing right and left 2. Manipulation of areas		
Logical reasoning	3. Similarities 4. Inference		
Numerical reasoning	5. Number series 6. Numerical quantity		
Verbal	7. Verbal concepts		

Language IQ
Nonlanguage IQ   Highs
Full-scale IQ   Lows

Source: Reading Center, Ferkauf Graduate School, Yeshiva University.

irrelevant to diagnosis. For all types of surveying, research, and group evaluation, the CRT norms are adequate. At many levels, the CRT seems to yield slightly higher scores than such tests as the *Metropolitan Achievement Tests,* [6] *Stanford Achievement Test,* [7] *Gates Reading Tests,* [8] *Iowa Tests of Basic Skills,* [9] and so on. This shortcoming of the test, however, is no problem as long as educators realize that standard scores do not reflect "real" reading grade levels. Reading grade levels are number systems used by test publishers to designate a point on the curve of score distribution for the sample used to standardize their tests. Because different populations are used to standardize each test, the reading grade levels on one publisher's test would not be expected to conform exactly to the same level on another publisher's test. In fact, a fifth-grade reading level on one level of a test will not usually correspond to the fifth-grade reading level on a different level of the *same* test.

Many projects have used Metropolitans, Stanfords, Gates, and Iowas for research and pre- and post-surveying in a number of projects with disadvantaged children, and these tests demonstrated their usefulness. Again, item analyses for errors have yielded specific skills weaknesses. Figure 3 is an example of a test analysis form used to report diagnostic patterns on the CRT, grades 7, 8, 9, and other tests. Results of the CRT, shown in the shaded portion, illustrate the contrast between tests that merely report global scores and the CRT, which reports results for specific skills weaknesses. This is the difference between survey and diagnostic tests. The question of the reliability and validity of these subskills measurements is irrelevant for classroom teachers; for all practical purposes, this type of test gives the practitioner a useful indication of the probable subskill weaknesses of children.

Individual Reading Tests. Teachers should not use informal reading tests in the classroom when standardized (formal) tests are available. It requires as much teacher training to use informal instruments as it does to use standardized instruments, such as the *Durrell Analysis of Reading Difficulty.* [10] The Durrell kit is a series of short diagnostic tests that can be used as a complete battery or as spot tests of various subskills of reading. The Reading Center's use of the Durrell kit is merely the result of the staff's training, for the *Gates-McKillop Reading Diagnostic Tests* [11] or the newer *Diagnostic Reading Scales* tests by Spache [12] will do equally as well. These are excellent test kits through grade 6 for most children and for retarded readers at all levels.

All elementary school teachers in the first four grades should be thoroughly trained in the teaching of reading and in the use of these diagnostic tests. Because reading is the most important skill taught in the early grades, teachers who have not mastered the pedagogy of teaching reading, which includes diagnosis, should be taught, even if this involves a radical change in teacher-training programs.

Figure 3   **Example of CRT Report Form**

Name ....

Address...

Age...... Date of Birth............ Grade .... School ....

Date of Testing ....

Tests	Gr. Lev.	% ile	% Cor.	Tests	Gr. Lev.	% ile	% Cor.
Speed of Reading				Interpretive Comprehension			
Mich. _____							
BTRC _____				Inferences			
				Details			
California Reading				Central idea			
				Organizing and seq.			
Level _____							
Form _____				Phonetic Spelling			
Total Vocabulary				Vis. Mem. for Word			
Math voc.							
Science voc.				Spelling			
Social science voc.				Auditory Dis.			
General voc.				Word Analysis			
Follow Directions				Oral Recall			
Simple choice							
Definitions				Written Recall			
Math directions				Outlining			
Map directions							
Reference Skills				Keystone Vision			
Parts of book				Benton Vis. Ret.			
Dictionary							
Index							
Contents							
Graphs							
Library infor.							
Select ref.							
Maps							

Source: Reading Center, Ferkauf Graduate School, Yeshiva University.

Clinical Tests of Reading. A number of clinical tests of reading have been developed by the author and other staff members on various projects. One is a *Diagnostic Test of Word Attack Skills* (DTWAS), which appears in two forms. [13] The first form, the *Word Analysis Test,* [14] was developed in collaboration with Dr. Mabel S. Noall at Boston University. It consists of an individually administered word reading test that pinpoints most of the specific word-attack skills in five minutes or less. A group-administered version concentrating on important phonic skills was developed in collaboration with Dr. Robert Cloward, Director of Educational Research at Mobilization For Youth. This test consists of ten short tests, each taking four minutes or less, that can be given as a complete battery or as single tests to individuals or groups. Both forms are based on the analysis of word-attack skills outlined in Gray's *On Their Own in Reading.* [15]

A third test developed with Dr. Cloward is the *Basic Test of Reading Comprehension* (BTRC). [16] Figure 4 is an example of one page of this speed of comprehension test based on a technique used in the *Michigan Speed of Reading Test,* now out of print. The BTRC consists of 65 passages (1 to 3 short sentences), each passage 22 syllables long. One word near the end of each passage spoils the meaning. Vocabulary is limited to grade 3.5 level or below. The subject reads against time and crosses out the word that spoils the meaning in each passage. This test is used from grade 3 through adult level as a quick survey to classify groups into one of four teaching categories: illiterate, poor reader, adequate reader, good reader. Instead of taking from forty minutes to an hour to find the general reading level of a group, the BTRC supplies this information in seven minutes, leaving plenty of time for the teacher to use other diagnostic tests to determine individual needs. Reliability of the BTRC is high, and correlation coefficients with standardized tests of reading run from .72 to .80+.

Both the DTWAS and BTRC were initially developed to test disadvantaged urban children. These children tend to be test shy, but the BTRC has met with unusual success because the children enjoy it as a game.

A third test, the *Oral Reading Test of Functional Literacy,* was developed in collaboration with Carol Grossberg at Mobilization

Figure **4   Basic Test of Reading Comprehension Sample**

Directions: *Cross out the word near the end of each numbered passage that spoils the meaning.*

(1) Heat the water in the pot on the stove. When the water is hot we will make a box of tea. (2) We made a swing by tying a rope to the limb of a tree. It is fun to slide on the swing. (3) Jan lost her pocketbook on the way to school. It was very careful of her to lose it. (4) The water in the pool was too cold for us, so we swam in the lake where it was much colder.

(5) Mary likes to make her breakfast cereal very sweet. That is why she puts so much salt on it. (6) If you eat green apples they will make you sick. They give you a pain in your ear if you eat them. (7) We made a bed in a box for our dog. That way the dog will not have to sing on the cold floor. (8) Mother made cookies today. When we get home she will give us a fire full of cookies to eat.

(9) I help my mother by washing dishes in the sink. I have to scrub them to get them dirty. (10) Save your money by putting it in a bank. That way your money will be gone when you need it. (11) In the wintertime we have wars with snowballs. We build forts out of snow and throw rocks at each other. (12) Whenever you need a cup of sugar, you can go next door and borrow some flower from friends.

STOP! DO NOT GO ON TO THE NEXT PAGE UNTIL YOU ARE TOLD TO DO SO.

For Youth. Figure 5 is an example of a portion of this test. Many oral reading paragraphs are inappropriate for semiliterate young adults, because such paragraphs provide childish content that embarrasses examinees. As a result, they refuse to read the paragraph orally and appear to be illiterate. The problem was to develop a high-interest, low-vocabulary test paragraph. The result was an oral reading paragraph, written at the functional literacy level (grades 4 to 5), but containing language suitable for urban adults. This useful tool can be developed for any environment. Using a list of graded vocabulary, a paragraph can be constructed and then tested on groups who have known reading levels.

Figure **5** **Example of the Oral Reading Test of Functional Literacy**

Robert drives the car in the city. There are many people and cars so he does not drive fast. He sees a red light. A red light means stop. Robert steps on the brakes. The light turns green. A green light means go. Robert looks both ways. No cars are coming. Robert takes his foot off the brakes and steps on the gas. Then Robert hears a siren. A fire engine turns the corner and it does not slow down for the light. Robert knows he has the right of way but the engine is in a hurry and Robert waits for it to go by. The engine speeds by . . . .

Sources: Developed by Carol Grossberg and S. Alan Cohen at Mobilization For Youth, New York City, 1965.

All three tests are currently in use in experimental form throughout the country. They point up the need for more diagnostic and functional tests that meet the unique needs of specific groups in specific environments. Tests to meet these needs can be developed and statistically standardized locally.

Visual Perceptual Tests. At the lower levels, the Reading Center has used Frostig's *Developmental Test of Visual Perception* [17] and has found it more useful than reading readiness tests to predict success in the first grade. The Frostig test is diagnostic and is keyed to specific materials and methods of teaching the skills measured in that test.

Keystone Visual Survey Tests, [18] and the *Ortho-Rater,* [19] have been the most useful screening devices. The usual criticism of them involves overreferral, but a good reading clinician who focuses on the process of responses, as well as on the nature of the responses, will not overrefer. By asking himself how the subject performs the survey tasks, the clinician collects much more valuable information than merely recording normal or subnormal responses. More often than vision clinicians admit, overreferrals are a problem of underdiagnosis on the part of optometrists or ophthalmologists who are unaware of the types of visual-perception behaviors important to reading teachers. A solution to this problem is to find one or two optometrists or ophthalmologists who "speak" the language of the teacher, because all vision specialists are not equally attuned to children's school needs. In addition to clinical observations, the Reading Center uses Benton's *The Revised Visual Retention Test* [20] administered to small groups to detect perceptual-motor dysfunctions. In individual cases (especially in the early grades) the center has administered *The Bender Gestalt Test for Young Children,* [21] using Koppitz' method of scoring.

Reading Disability Patterns in Disadvantaged Urban Children

Test response patterns on the instruments described above have been analyzed at the Yeshiva University Reading Center. The following description of reading disability patterns was based on at least 50 and at most 284 urban disadvantaged children and youth in the New York City area. Most of these children were black and Puerto Rican Americans entering the center's clinic for diagnosis. Referral sources were parents, school personnel, medical specialists and school agencies. The children ranged in age from four to nineteen.

On the WISC, these children tend to score low on block design (I) but do adequately on the coding (K) subtest, with the exception of very young children who tend to do poorly on both subtests. (Letters in parentheses refer to WISC subtests listed in Figure 1.) The more sophisticated block design appears to be sufficiently sensitive to detect visual perceptual weaknesses that are not detected on the coding subtest. The latter taps visual perceptual and motor skills that underlie these more sophisticated skills. Thus they are more apparent at a younger age but get covered up as children grow older. On Frostig's *Developmental Test of Visual Perception,* lowest scores appear on the shape constancy subtest. In fact, in one study this subtest was a better predictor of low reading achievement than any other Frostig subtest, Stanford-Binet scores, Bender Gestalt protocols, or Metropolitan reading readiness scores. It is unclear whether some factor in the test administration or the content of the test was the crucial variable in this correlation. Total WISC IQs tend to be lower than average in disadvantaged children and youth, but they rarely dip below 90. Nonverbal IQs tend to be a few points higher than verbal IQs. The trend rather than the degree of difference appears to be more significant. A number of children, however, show very high verbal and lower nonverbal scores in spite of all other symptoms of poor verbal development.

The WISC information (A) and vocabulary (F) subtests tend to be lower than comprehension (B) subtest scores. This appears to be a persistent pattern that differentiates socially disadvantaged children, as a group, from advantaged children. In fact, the scores of most middle class children with reading problems tested at the center tended to be the reverse. Children from the wrong side of the tracks appear to lack information about the world as perceived by middle class children, but they are more capable in making their way in the practical aspects of everyday life. This is the only WISC pattern that differentiated the retarded readers from different socioeconomic levels.

The digit span (E) subtest may be high or low, depending upon anxiety level and concentration ability. Puerto Rican girls were usually lowest in this subtest. Arithmetic (C) subtest scores are low and appear to be more a result of poor school achievement than anything else. What has surprised the Reading Center staff is the similarities (D) subtest, which appears to tap verbal abstraction ability and concept formation. Some disadvantaged children scored very low—which fits the stereotype of cultural deprivation. But a large number of cases with depressed total IQs scored above average on this subtest. The similarities subtest is not one of the strongest subtests in the battery, but we are still unable to explain this relatively consistent finding. The WISC performance scatter showed block design (I) low but nothing else that might discriminate disadvantaged children from more advantaged children with reading problems. The subtest scatter appears to be more pronounced on the verbal than on nonverbal tests.

Analysis of the center's protocols and research with larger groups of schoolchildren using the *Diagnostic Test of Word Attack Skills* described above have supplied abundant data for firm conclusions about word-attack skills patterns in this particular population. Most black and Puerto Rican urban children tested in various projects over the past three years are sight readers. They have never learned the relationship between grapheme and phoneme. Over 50 percent of junior high school pupils in one slum school district did not know the alphabet when asked to write it, and many elementary school disadvantaged children cannot blend sounds.

Visual discrimination of letters is weak, but it is better than scores on auditory discrimination of sounds in words tested on various levels of difficulty (matching, identification, reproduction). Beginning consonants are usually heard well enough, but ending consonants, beginning blends, ending blends, and medial vowel sounds are almost always missed by these children. Ability to hear beats in words, however, is excellent once the children understand what is asked of them. The relationship between pronunciation (output) and auditory discrimination of sounds in words (input), even in blacks and Puerto Ricans with heavy regional or ethnic dialects, is not a simple 1-to-1 relationship. One study at the Reading Center showed, for example, that seven sounds most commonly misarticulated by a group of blacks were also the same ones most often missed in a test of auditory discrimination. However, this did not hold for other sounds, nor did it apply to all individuals. Visual memory of unknown words is lower than visual discrimination of known words, but this, too, is far below expectancy. From these patterns, we cannot help concluding that the specific behavior deficits mentioned are usually found in most retarded readers, economically disadvantaged or not.

Oral reading scores are low, of course, but comprehension scores are high. Listening comprehension scores are significantly higher than oral reading scores. Usually, listening comprehension scores are at grade placement or above, indicating skills problems rather than problems of intellectual potential. Thus, disadvantaged children can evidently comprehend, but are unable to "bust" the written code. Again, this is the usual pattern in retarded readers regardless of ethnicity or economic status.

Much has been said about oral language patterns of black and Puerto Rican children, most of which has no basis in fact. The Reading Center data indicated that there were no differences in the incidence of speech impediments between middle class and lower class retarded readers. The test protocols report differences in articulation and dialect patterns between blacks and Puerto Ricans, but most studies show no differences in the verbal productivity of middle and lower class children except when the latter are requested to speak to adult authority figures. No evidence indicates that dialect differences or mild articulation problems interfere with learning to read in disadvantaged children, nor is there evidence that oral language training in prekindergarten or kindergarten causally affects reading achievement. The evidence shows that urban black and Puerto Rican children with heavy dialects and relatively poor articulation learn to read when they are taught without special oral language development training.

No differences were observed in emotional problems of retarded readers from middle class homes compared to lower class homes. Nothing observed or measured at the Reading Center indicates that urban black and Puerto Rican retarded readers are more or less emotionally disturbed than white middle class retarded readers. Both groups appear upset over their lack of school achievement. Furthermore, no observations or measurements at the Reading Center indicated that psychosocial problems of urban black and Puerto Rican retarded readers are particularly difficult to overcome in the remedial reading process. The very basis of clinical treatment and the classroom curriculum is a therapeutic atmosphere, one in which the child feels safe enough to test new behaviors. Under these conditions, rare in most schools but necessary in all, most of these children learn to read and write adequately. The Reading Center records show no differences in percentage of success scores resulting from the center's clinical treatment between disadvantaged and advantaged retarded readers.

Conclusions About Reading Disability
Patterns in Disadvantaged Children

It appears that disadvantaged children have a higher incidence of perceptual dysfunctions than test norms predict. Intelligence, a term describing a collection of test results tapping various learned cognitive behaviors, is lower in these populations but still within the normal range. As a measurement of scholastic aptitude, intelligence scores accurately predict the lack of school success experienced by so many of these children. WISC subtest patterns show disadvantaged youngsters operating exceedingly well with a minimum of information and with marked verbal deficits. The WISC also shows deficits caused by perceptual dysfunctions; this is also revealed in other tests of "pure" perception.

According to our studies, poor visual discrimination of letters, the usual p-b-d-q reversals, poor visual memory for unknown words, and poor visual recognition of known words are common among these children. Add to these factors a myriad of socioeconomic and cultural conditions that contribute to general deprivation, and we have a difficult case of reading disability. On the other hand, the specific behaviors that form the disability syndrome are not peculiar to disadvantaged children. Qualitatively, the patterns described here are found in many middle class children seen by the Reading Center with the possible exception of the one WISC pattern noted above. The difference between the two socioeconomic groups appears to be a quantitative one; that is, more of the socially disadvantaged have more of these disabilities than do middle class children.

Finally, work in the Reading Center, as well as numerous curriculum projects conducted during the past three years, demonstrates that most of these children learn to read and write in spite of their language deficits. Most of the disabilities are remediable without resorting to magic mirrors, talking typewriters, or any other mechanical device. Most of these children will learn to read and write if the schools teach them thoroughly.

Summary

Tests are tools for diagnosis. Difficulties encountered in the use of tests, from the evidence now available, seem to point to the retraining of those who administer and analyze tests rather than to the abandonment of the tests. That retraining must focus on using tests as diagnostic tools that aid teaching, not as evaluative instruments. Diagnosis pinpoints a specific behavioral need of a child, whereas evaluation assigns a value to a child's behavior. The latter is relatively useless and dangerous because it usually leads to the self-fulfillment of this value. Children who are labeled stupid tend to behave stupidly.

A good criterion for selecting tests is how well they pinpoint these needs. Such tests used at the Yeshiva University Reading Center have drawn a behavioral profile of disadvantaged, retarded readers from urban areas that is not very different from retarded readers from middle class suburbia. This fact suggests that the methods of combating reading retardation in disadvantaged children may not be radically different from existing methods already employed with all kinds of children.

One problem often observed in the diagnostic patterns of young retarded readers is perceptual dysfunction, a term used to describe poor information processing on a motor and visual-motor level. Research in child development suggests that these behaviors are crucial for "primary learning," or building the basic program of the human computer. We have previously called that basic program "intelligence." The next chapter includes descriptions of studies of this problem in disadvantaged children and suggestions for preventing these dysfunctions from interfering with learning to read.

References

1. D. Wechsler, *Wechsler Intelligence Scale for Children* (New York: The Psychological Corp., 1949).
2. L. M. Terman and M. A. Merrill, *Stanford-Binet Intelligence Scale,* 3rd edition (Boston: Houghton Mifflin, 1960).
3. E. T. Sullivan, W. W. Clark, and E. W. Tiegs, *California Test of Mental Maturity* (New Cumberland, Pa.: California Test Bureau, 1957).
4. T. G. Thurstone, *Primary Mental Abilities* (Chicago: Science Research Associates, 1963).
5. E. W. Tiegs and W. W. Clark, *California Reading Test* (New Cumberland, Pa.: California Test Bureau, 1958).
6. *Metropolitan Achievement Tests* (New York: Harcourt, Brace & World, 1958).
7. T. L. Kelley *et al., Stanford Achievement Test* (New York: Harcourt, Brace & World, 1952).
8. A. Gates, *Gates Reading Tests,* all levels (New York: Bureau of Publications, Teachers College, Columbia University, 1958).
9. *Iowa Tests of Basic Skills* (Boston: Houghton Mifflin, 1964).
10. D. D. Durrell, *Durrell Analysis of Reading Difficulty* (New York: Harcourt, Brace & World, 1955).
11. A. Gates and A. S. McKillop, *Gates-McKillop Reading Diagnostic*

Tests (New York: Bureau of Publications, Teachers College, Columbia University, 1962).

12. G. D. Spache, *Diagnostic Reading Scales* (New Cumberland, Pa.: California Test Bureau, 1963).

13. S. Alan Cohen and R. Cloward, *Diagnostic Test of Word Attack Skills,* experimental edition (New York: Reading Center, Yeshiva University, 1962).

14. Mabel Noall and S. Alan Cohen, *Word Analysis Test,* experimental edition (New York: Reading Center, Yeshiva University, 1962).

15. W. S. Gray, *On Their Own in Reading* (Chicago: Scott, Foresman, 1962).

16. S. Alan Cohen and R. Cloward, *Basic Test of Reading Comprehension,* experimental edition (New York: Reading Center, Yeshiva University, 1965).

17. Marianne Frostig *et al., Developmental Test of Visual Perception* (Palo Alto, Calif.: Consulting Psychologists Press, 1961).

18. *Keystone Visual Survey Tests* (Meadville, Pa.: Keystone View Co., 1956).

19. Ortho-Rater (Rochester, N.Y.: Bausch and Lomb Optical Co.).

20. A. Benton, *The Revised Visual Retention Test* (New York: The Psychological Corp., 1955).

21. E. M. Koppitz, *The Bender Gestalt Test for Young Children* (New York: Grune and Stratton, 1964).

Chapter Five

Problem of Visual Perception

Introduction

Man is a visually dominant animal. [1, 2] Of the 3 million impulses processed by the brain per millisecond, two-thirds come through the visual channels. All man's perceptual processes are directly or indirectly linked through visual perception, [9] and it is through visual perception that we can best understand his cognitive development. When we use an information-processing model to explain behavior, we must recognize that input to the electro-chemical computer, the brain, is a visually dominant process.

Evidence exists that visual perceptual development in socially disadvantaged children is poorer than in middle class children. This chapter presents the evidence and reports on a new study of visual perceptual development in disadvantaged first-graders. Discussions include the implications of visual perceptual development as it relates to cognition and reading and the visual perceptual dysfunctions that are found in disadvantaged children.

Because visual perceptual development is so basic to cognitive processes, we could expect poor development in this area to result in poor learning potential. Add this to the negative psychosocial factors that influence school achievement, and we begin to appreciate the extent of the effort needed to ensure a positive reading achievement prognosis for socially disadvantaged children. At the present time, we have little know-how in promoting social change. Because *this* facet of the problem cannot be influenced significantly, other factors must be considered—visual perceptual development (in this chapter) and methods and materials for influencing perceptual development (Chapter Six).

What Is Perceptual Development?

"Perceptual development," a term synonymous with "learning to learn," means the process by which the organism builds basic information-processing strategies needed to learn other skills and information. Some experimental psychologists call this process "primary learning." Others use the term "learning set." Harlow, for example, demonstrated learning sets or strategies for learning to learn in rhesus monkeys. [3, 5] Essentially he demonstrated that learning discrimination tasks at an earlier point in development facilitated learning more complex discrimination tasks at a later time.

The most thorough statement of this theory and its supporting evidence is provided by Hebb. [4] Long before Hebb, psychologists had concluded that learning was more than the process of a new response to a stimulus; something called "mediational processes" was also present. Hebb called these mediational processes *autonomous central processes* (ACP). He showed that in man attention, perception, thought, and learning are controlled less by the immediate stimulus and more by ACP than in lower animals. [6] In reviewing research, Hebb showed how simple relationships are learned as promptly by lower animals as by higher. Furthermore, he restated what psychologists have long known—that the earliest learning (primary learning) actually takes longer in man than in lower animals. Autonomous central processes (ACP) result from this early primary learning. Man takes longer to develop ACP because he has more to develop. Compared to all other known animals, a larger proportion of man's brain is devoted to ACP than to stimulus receptor mechanisms. Harlow's experiments in learning to learn demonstrate Hebb's theory of ACP—

that the quantity and quality of later learning depend upon ACP resulting from early primary learning. Hebb's theories underlie empirical evidence in learning psychology and neurophysiology. Thus, for example, attention or set, as observed by the psychologist or as measured by physiological changes in the eye and the retina, is evidence of ACP. Hunt concludes that "invention" and "insight" in adults are dependent upon ACP. [7]

Hebb conceived of primary learning as perceptual experience. Being a visually dominant animal, man depends more upon visual and visual-motor processing for adequate development of ACP than any of the other higher animals. Early perceptual deprivation would, therefore, result in retarded development of ACP. (It must be remembered that the earliest visual perceptual development involves motor, tactual-motor, and kinesthetic learning.) The literature is full of experimental evidence indicating that deprivation of visual, motor, and kinesthetic processes early in development retards ability to learn in species of all levels from rats [8, 9, 10] and chimps [11, 12] to humans. [7]

Perhaps the best descriptions of the development of these processes in human infants has been provided by Piaget in his research reports on "sensorimotor intelligence" and by Gesell in his reports on vision development in infants and children. [13, 14] Although Gesell and Piaget differed in their basic philosophies of development, the reports of what they observed in children are strikingly similar. Using Gesell's model, every child organizes his visual space world in three fields—skeletal, visceral, and cortical. On a skeletal level, the child seeks and holds a visual image, and at this stage, tactual, proprioceptive, and kinesthetic perception dominate visual perception. On the visceral level he "discriminates and defines the image." Visual perception leads but is dependent upon motor (skeletal) reinforcement. On the cortical level, he interprets, integrates, and processes the image. At this level, Gesell includes association and higher mental processes comparable to Piaget's cognitive stages in the development of intelligence. All three levels develop jointly, but not uniformly. The lower functions (skeletal and visceral) are operative more often than higher functions (cortical) at any early stage. This explains a child's need to touch and to taste whatever catches his eye. The adult fulfills many lower functions by covertly including them in higher functions, which Hebb implies in his statement that every visual act includes a motor correlate. [1]

Further evidence that visual development moves from a motor, to a perceptual, to a cognitive level comes from Bender, [15, 16] Frostig, [17] Jersild, [18] and Siegel. [19] Three classic texts, by Coghill, [20] Hooker, [21] and Sherrington, [22] establish the same principle of development; that is, the basis of higher processes is perceptual-motor behavior. When Titchener explained his core-context theory in 1910, he too stated that all cognition is originally a "kinesthetic" process. [23] The evidence is compelling: The ability and readiness of a stimulus to affect present behavior is determined largely by the organism's previous perceptual experience. Genetic limitations undoubtedly exist, but we learn to learn. The earliest experiences are visual perceptual, visual motor, tactual, and kinesthetic. Children from deprived environments appear to lack certain quantities and qualities of these experiences. This deprivation becomes most apparent at the reading readiness and early elementary levels when the trained observer detects the dysfunctions described below.

A Definition of Visual Perceptual Dysfunction

When the central (contrasted to the peripheral) information-processing system is faulty because of

Organic impairment
Developmental lag
Lack of learning
Genetic inheritance

or any combination of these, a child suffers a "perceptual dysfunction."

Various professionals viewing the dysfunctioning child from their particular disciplines have pet nomenclatures for visual perceptual dysfunctions or for phases of this dysfunction: neurological disorder, dyslexia, minimal brain damage, visual motor problems, specific language disability, strephosymbolia, specific reading disability, and so on. These terms symbolize diagnostic patterns related to perceptual and perceptual-motor behaviors. When many of these behaviors are grouped into a syndrome, we call that the *perceptual dysfunction* syndrome. The cause of this syndrome is relatively unimportant, since no profession has been able to perfect a specific diagnosis based on "true" etiology. There are many types of perceptual behaviors that could be dysfunctioning, and all children have, at various times, many of these symptoms. The important thing is to observe the specific perceptual behaviors and to either correct dysfunctions or teach children to compensate for them. When a retarded reader has a large number of these perceptual symptoms, we may conveniently think of his perceptual problems as dominant, just as we might think of a severely emotionally disturbed retarded reader as having dominant psychological problems. Often, we may decide to remediate these dominant problems before we teach the child to read. But there is no such thing as a "pure" case of perceptual dysfunction: to categorize children into such a stereotype is dangerous as well as futile.

Behaviors Found in Perceptually Dysfunctioning Retarded Readers

The following list describes behaviors observed by teachers in elementary schools with retarded readers. The list consists of two groups of behaviors: Syndrome One, which describes behaviors commonly found in retarded readers, and Syndrome Two, which describes behaviors directly related to visual perceptual development in both retarded and nonretarded readers. When both groups of behaviors are found together in a child, there is a current vogue to assign to this child's difficulties the label "perceptual dysfunction" or one of the variations described above. Such labels are, at best, convenient shorthand symbols for these behaviors and, at worst, an excuse for not teaching children to read.

Syndrome One

Perceptually dysfunctioning children often have difficulty learning to read and write. Behaviors listed in this category are found in most reading disability cases, but are more often found when other symptoms of perceptual problems are present.

Reversals. Almost all children in the early grades confuse *d* and *b,* *was* and *saw,* and so on. When this becomes a persistent problem beyond grade 4, it may be part of the dysfunction syndrome.

Distorted Handwriting. Perceptually dysfunctioning children usually have handwritings distorted to the point of illegibility. This may be the result of eye-hand-motor and spatial problems discussed in Syndrome Two.

Spelling. Dysfunctioning children may misspell as many as 90 percent of their words.

Oral Reading. These children have great difficulty holding their place on the page. In grade 4, they may still retain line-skipping and word-reversing behaviors that we see in normal first-grade beginning readers. Adverbs and *w* and *th* words seem to give these children particular trouble. Often, they begin to read smoothly and then suddenly "short-circuit" when they reach the first adverb.

Blending. If these children are taught phonograms in isolation, they will be unable to blend word parts into wholes. Blending sounds is particularly difficult for these children.

Visual Discrimination. Although these children can often discriminate the isolated *e* from *a,* they confuse these letters in words. They may see *pet* as *pat,* or *pat* as *pal.*

Other Reading Symptoms. The symptoms listed above are most often present in perceptually dysfunctioning children. The symptoms listed below are usually found in these children, but seem directly related more to reading disability than to perceptual dysfunction:

1. Cannot discriminate sounds in words
2. Cannot remember the alphabet
3. Has weak visual memory of words
4. Has tendency to use sight vocabulary as the only word-attack skill in repertoire

Diagnosis and Correction. For many perceptually dysfunctioning youngsters, the symptoms listed above can be corrected without perceptual training. That is, an intensive remedial reading program can reduce these symptoms to a point where a child is reading at grade level. However, teachers must expect a much tougher time when they row against the tide than when they row with it; they must expect that in a large group of children, most of whom have visual perceptual dysfunctions and most of whom have little else working for them to compensate for their dysfunctions, the probability of success in teaching reading is greatly reduced.

Syndrome Two

Children with visual perceptual problems manifest symptoms not directly related to reading. These symptoms are, in fact, the core behaviors of the visual perceptual dysfunction syndrome. Those directly observable in the classroom are listed below. Other symptoms can be detected only on neurological and psychological tests administered by trained clinicians.

Poor Kinesthetic Awareness of One's Own Body. Kinesthetic cues are insufficient for the dysfunctioning child. He must look and touch to make sure where his body parts are in space. He has not learned to judge where his total body begins and ends in relation to the world around him. He cannot feel where his arms, legs, or head are, so he bumps into things or knocks books off his desk. His body image is inaccurate. A kinesthetic, visceral, autonomic sense of body direction is called "laterality."

Poor Laterality. A child with poor laterality has never learned a sense of two-sidedness. Although he may be able to verbalize left and right, he does so by using outside cues, such as his ring hand, his writing hand, or a side of the room. He has not developed a *sense* of right and left, even though he may have a *knowledge* of them. He has not learned to use his own body as a point of reference for up-down, right-left, in-out, forward-back.

Poor Directionality. The projecting of a sense of laterality to the outside world is called "directionality." This sense enables a child to manipulate space beyond his body. He can handle spatial problems, such as discrimination of *p, b, d;* he can manipulate spatial figures "in his head" and can do arithmetic "without writing it down." This spatial manipulation is extended to time, so that he can handle time sequences and chronological order. The child with perceptual dysfunctions, therefore, often has both weak laterality and poor directionality.

Inefficient Hand-Eye Dominance. All normal children develop a dominant side. Being a two-sided, bilobed animal, the human being develops one lead side and one supporting side. To have two leading sides would be most confusing; they would compete with each other and render the organism helpless. Most people tend to be right-eyed and right-handed; that is, they learn to use the left side as a support for the right. A small number of people develop left-sided dominance, with the right hand and eye used to support the functions of the left. Perhaps a small number more, for one reason or another, develop mixed or cross dominance. Such people may be left hand-dominant and right eye-dominant, or the reverse.

Left or right hand-eye dominance is not directly related to cerebral dominance. For example, normal left hand-eye-dominant people have the same brain-center control areas as right hand-eye-dominant people. Furthermore, the language center for almost all people is in the left hemisphere of the brain regardless of hand-eye dominance. [24] Dominance tendency appears to be genetically determined, [14] but like most inherited propensities, it is also subject to environmental influence. Thus, the behaviors we observe as indicating hand-eye dominance are largely learned. Mixed or cross dominance is *not* a symptom of perceptual dysfunction or of reading disability. [25] A right-handed, left-eyed child may be, for example, very efficient in his hand-eye coordination.

The key to understanding the symptom is *efficiency.* Regardless of which side is dominant or of the presence of cross-dominance, any inefficient hand-hand, eye-eye, or hand-eye operation is part of the perceptual dysfunction syndrome. Such inefficiencies can be suspected when we see the written page with sloping lines exceeding a 10-degree angle from the 90-degree axis. This same child is one who usually holds his writing tool in an awkward, pinched, or infantile grasp. Inefficient dominance joins poor laterality, weak directionality, and inaccurate body image as symptoms of poor motor coordination.

Lack of Imagery. Many children with visual perceptual problems have difficulty visualizing numbers, letters, shapes, and scenes. Without this visual imagery, they are unable to have the visual memory necessary for recalling sight vocabulary. The reader is cautioned not to reverse this statement: Many children with poor visual memory for words have good general visual imagery.

Hyperactivity. The visual-perception problem child may appear overactive. He lacks ability to concentrate and to fixate visually on a target for any significant length of time. That which appears to be hyperactivity may be the result of a number of factors in the syndrome, both psychological and physiological. There is evidence, for example, that perceptual dysfunctionates are neurologically hypoactive, and that overt hyperactivity may represent peak responses of overcompensation. This speculation is based on observations of hyperactive children who have been given stimulants rather than depressants and as a result show decreases in hyperactivity. Regardless of the cause, perceptually dysfunctioning children appear to be overactive and have great difficulty in concentrating and fixating visually.

Inefficient Saccadic Eye Movements. The normal eye moves in short, staccato movements rather than smooth sweeps across a page. These movements are called "saccadic eye movements." Because of many factors, some listed as symptoms above, the dysfunctionate's saccadic eye movements are inefficient. As a result, he loses his place on the page, regresses in his eye movements, and skips lines. His ocular pursuits are usually choppy and uncontrollable.

Poor Binocularity. The human being has two eyes and two visual areas of the brain, one in each cerebral hemisphere. The functional relationships between these pairs are learned. Binocularity is more a learned result of function than it is a product of physiology or structure. Usually children with poor visual perceptual development have not learned to use both occipital areas of the brain and both ocular mechanisms together. More fortunate children learn to suppress one image cortically (in the brain) or motorically (covering one eye with a hand). They are one-eyed readers (monocularity) and may be more successful at reading than those children with unsteady, intermittent binocularity, or than those children whose fragile use of both images together is achieved only with peak energy output. Such children tire quickly. If they are bright enough, they may protect the organism from the agony of over-work by avoiding reading. Children with perceptual dysfunctions tend to have either fragile binocularity or—more likely—unsteady, intermittent binocularity.

Inconsistent Ocular Findings. When a thorough vision survey is used, such as a telebinocular exam, or when a standard ocular exam is performed, the dysfunctionate's performances tend to be inconsistent. This behavior often fools examiners, because they record the patient's best response to each ocular test. Thus, for example, a child may have binocularity at one moment and double vision the next. Or, he may have 100-20 acuity in his early re-sponses, but then work himself up to 20-20 acuity in two or three minutes. Such findings indicate an inconsistent organism struggling to perform efficiently, but an organism that is unable to maintain itself consistently.

Tactual-Motor Reinforcements. Because of all these symptoms, the child with visual perceptual dysfunctions cannot trust his higher processes (vision, audition, and cognition). He resorts, therefore, to his basic information-processing level—tactual-motor. He must reinforce vision, for example, by touching.

Poor Multisensory Coordination. In addition, the dysfunctionate has trouble coordinating simultaneous auditory, visual, and tactual stimulations. To mix these multi-inputs with ongoing cortical processes is too difficult for the child with visual perceptual problems.

Poor Reproduction of Shapes. These children have great difficulty reproducing figures from tests that require them to draw figures or geometric shapes. Although they may eventually recall the shapes, they will either distort geometric drawings or severely constrict them.

Disheveled Clothes. The dysfunctionate's shoelaces are often untied, or if they are tied, they hang precariously in an awkward attempt at a bow. His buttons may be out of line with the buttonholes, and one button is often undone. His shirttail may be out, and his belt buckle may be off-center.

Splinter Skills. In spite of poor hand-eye coordination, the perceptually dysfunctioning child may be an outstanding athlete, or he may achieve in an area even though the particular skill required is listed above as one which the dysfunctionate performs poorly. He may be, for example, an outstanding reader. But when we look at the total picture, we will see that the perceptually dysfunctioning child will only have one or two outstanding splinter skills against a background of deficiencies in most areas.

Diagnosis and Correction. Unless the behaviors under Syndrome Two accompany the Syndrome One symptoms, a retarded reader cannot be considered a visual perceptual problem. This is an important point. Some overeager visual perception specialists tend to include most disabled readers in this category. *If we look closely enough at all children, disabled readers or not, we can find some lags in visual perception development.* This fact does not justify, however, our treating all disabled readers as visual perceptual problems, although they may be treated for specific visual perceptual weaknesses, such as visual discrimination or visual memory for words. We do not know what percentage of all retarded readers are visual perceptual problems, but some indication of this figure for socially disadvantaged children will be presented below.

Perceptual Dysfunctions in Socially
Disadvantaged School Populations

Pasamanick and Knobloch, after investigating the incidence of perceptual dysfunctions in socially disadvantaged children, reported a significantly higher than average incidence of "organic factors" related to school retardation. [26, 27] Deutsch's work with preschool children also refers to the high incidence of perceptual problems in disadvantaged children. [28] On New York's

Lower East Side, visual perceptual problems at all age levels were apparent to the MFY staff in various educational programs. Clinics and programs servicing underachievers deal with select populations, however, and clinicians working in such programs can be easily seduced into a distorted view of a more general population. Realizing this, the MFY staff maintained as conservative a view as possible concerning the quantity and quality of perceptual dysfunctions in Lower East Side schoolchildren. As a test of their general approach, the MFY staff decided to experiment with a visual perceptual training program for 15 mildly retarded second-graders who the staff thought would be relatively high in visual development. Severely retarded readers and organically damaged children had been screened out by the school system, leaving what school officials considered a second-grade population typical of Lower East Side classrooms—mildly retarded-reading, hyperactive children of lower socioeconomic status from Puerto Rican and black homes.

The MFY staff was astounded at the severity of the dysfunctions when close examination of 10 children was made. For example, in one examination each child was seated before an examiner who first took time to set the child at ease. The examiner then placed a beam of light about 1 foot from the child's nose and asked the subject to fixate, reminding the child again and again to keep looking at the light. The longest fixation was 9 seconds, and median fixation time for the 10 subjects was slightly more than 4½ seconds. The first 4 subjects examined for kinesthetic awareness of body parts were unable to move their left legs in a standing position without resorting to postural distortions similar to spasticity. As a result of these observations, a survey of the incidence of perceptual dysfunction was taken in 1965 in eight schools offering a representative sample of socially disadvantaged first-grade children on New York's Lower East Side. Eight specialists were trained to administer Frostig's *Developmental Test of Visual Perception* [29] to 120 first-graders in eight schools. The eight schools geographically represented the sixteen elementary schools in the area. An alphabetical list of first-graders in each school was divided by the appropriate number, resulting in the selection of 15 children from each school for inclusion in the survey. Children were tested in groups of 4 or 5.

A check of the sampling technique is the ethnic distribution shown in Table 1. The percentage of each ethnic group is similar to estimates of total school ethnic distribution provided by Mobilization For Youth demographic studies in 1963 and 1964.

Table 1 **Ethnic Distribution of Sample in First-Grade Visual Perceptual Survey***

Ethnicity	Number	Approximate %
Puerto Rican	65	55
Black	39	32
White	9	8
Chinese	6	5

*n = 119.

Frostig's *Developmental Test of Visual Perception* taps five areas of functioning:

I. *Eye-motor coordination,* involving the drawing of continuous straight, curved, or angular lines between guide lines of various widths, or from target to target without guides.

II. *Figure-ground,* involving perception of figures against increasingly complex grounds.

III. *Constancy of shape,* involving the recognition of geometric figures of various sizes, shadings, textures, and positions in space, and their discrimination from similar geometric figures.

IV. *Position in space,* involving discrimination of reversals and rotations of figures presented in series.

V. *Spatial relationships,* involving analyses of simple forms and patterns. These consist of lines of various lengths and angles which the child is required to copy using dots as guides.

Perceptual skills tapped by this test screen for handicaps that result from any one of the following four etiologies: organic impairment, developmental lag, lack of learning, or genetic inheritance. These skills are relevant to performance in nursery school, kindergarten, and early school years. As Frostig states:

> The fairly well-directed eye movements necessary for accurate response in Subtest I are a precondition for reading. Eye-hand coordination is prerequisite for writing. A sufficient ability to shift

in figure-ground perception is necessary for the analysis and synthesis of words, phrases, sentences, and paragraphs involved in reading. Form constancy must reach a certain point in development before a child can recognize a word in varying contexts. On the accurate perception of position in space and spatial relationships depends the ability to differentiate similar letters like *b* and *d*, and to recognize the sequence of letters in a word and words in a sentence. [30]

The normative data for the Frostig test was based on 2,116 "unselected" schoolchildren from preschool to third-grade levels. Experience with the test in the Northeast indicates that the norms are conservative. (This factor must be taken into consideration when interpreting the data below.) Thus the 50th percentile or the "perceptual quotient (PQ)" of 100, by definition the mean or average score, is at best a minimal expectancy for normal children. We would expect a PQ of 104 or the 60th percentile as an adequate score on this test.

Tests were administered in April of the school year. Thus, the average chronological age of the population was approximately 6.6 years. In the following tables, subtest means are reported in age equivalents; 6.6 should be used as average age criterion against which to evaluate age level scores. In other words, an age equivalent score of 6.5 or 6.6 on a subtest is the norm; it yields a PQ of 100. An age equivalent score of 6.9 is above the norm, while 6.3 is below. The total battery of subtests yields a PQ with an average of 100 and a standard deviation of 15.

Table 2 reports means, standard deviations, and maximum and

Table **2   Mean, Standard Deviation, and Minimum and Maximum Perceptual Age-Level Scores of Sample First-Graders***

Subtest	$\bar{X}$	S.D.	Min.	Max.
I	5.97	2.51	1.00	9.60
II	6.12	1.43	3.00	8.30
III	5.44	1.56	2.60	9.00
IV	6.02	1.23	3.30	8.90
V	6.29	1.23	0.00	8.30

* *n* = 119.

minimum age equivalent scores for the total sample population on each subtest. Table 3 reports the average total PQ, standard

Table **3** **Perceptual Quotients of Sample First-Graders***

$\overline{X}$	S.D.	Min. PQ	Max. PQ
95.87	13.22	67.00	126.00

* $n = 119$.

deviation, and range for the entire population. Both tables reveal wide ranges in age equivalent scores from ages 0 to 9.6. The PQs range from 67 to 126. The average PQ and average age equivalents for all the subtests are consistently and significantly below average for the entire first-grade population. If we analyze these figures in terms of a curve of distribution, we find over 40 percent of the population scoring at age levels under four, a score that indicates severe visual perception problems.

Analyzing the population by sex in Tables 4 and 5, we can see differences among males and females, none of which are statistically significant. Minimum scores for females are not quite as low as for males. Maximum scores represent test ceilings inherent in the test. Generally speaking, lowest scores tend to be earned by males, but boys may have slightly higher PQs than girls. Although differences are not statistically significant, this trend of males scoring slightly higher PQs than females is consistent in all tables.

Comparing age level scores for each perceptual subskill and PQs according to ethnicity, we see striking differences across ethnic groups. (New York City public schools do not record ethnicity on pupil records nor do they condone research in their schools that records ethnicity. In this study, MFY examiners recorded ethnicity on the basis of their observations of the children in the testing session, first and last names and, in cases of black children who had some evidence of Spanish culture, by asking the child if Spanish was spoken in the home. Blacks and whites with one or more Spanish parents were classified as Puerto Rican.) Tables 6 and 7 compare scores for four ethnic groups. The sample white and Chinese populations, although accurate ratios of the total population from which the sample was drawn, are too small

Table 4   **Mean, Standard Deviation, and Minimum and Maximum Age-Level Scores of Sample First-Graders Compared by Sex***

Subtest		$\bar{X}$	S.D.	Min.	Max.
I	M	6.21	2.56	1.00	9.60
	F	5.66	2.44	1.00	9.60
II	M	6.14	1.45	3.00	8.30
	F	6.08	1.41	3.90	8.30
III	M	5.32	1.61	2.60	9.00
	F	5.59	1.49	2.60	9.00
IV	M	6.04	1.28	3.30	8.90
	F	5.99	1.03	4.00	8.90
V	M	6.38	1.07	4.00	8.30
	F	6.17	1.42	0.00	8.30

* Male: $n = 67$; female: $n = 52$.

Table 5   **Perceptual Quotients of Sample First-Graders Compared by Sex***

Sex	$\bar{X}$	S.D.	Min. PQ	Max. PQ
Male	96.87	13.69	67.00	126.00
Female	94.58	12.62	73.00	121.00

* Males: $n = 67$; females: $n = 52$.

to be statistically significant. However, they are probably accurate in demonstrating the superiority of these subgroups in visual perceptual development, for this is consistent with other cognitive measurements and with clinical observations of the populations.

Table 6 reveals a shockingly lower PQ among Puerto Rican and black children compared to white and Chinese. The curve for Puerto Rican and black compared to white and Chinese shows a much higher incidence of severe perceptual dysfunctions. Table 7 gives a finer analysis, showing, for example, that all groups are

Table **6** **Perceptual Quotients of Sample First-Graders**
Compared by Ethnicity

Ethnic Group	N	$\bar{X}$	S.D.	Min. PQ	Max. PQ
Puerto Rican	65	95.26	12.59	70	119
Black	39	92.56	12.35	67	118
White	9	103.44	11.88	82	121
Chinese	6	112.50	13.63	93	126

retarded in eye-motor coordination (Subtest I) 80 percent of the way through grade 1. Black children score almost to grade level, but Puerto Rican, white, and Chinese are approximately a year retarded in eye-motor coordination. This is the only case of members of the two lowest socioeconomic subcultures (Puerto Rican and black) surpassing white and Chinese in this survey.

In interpreting the data in Tables 6 and 7, two points must be reemphasized:

1. The test norms are conservative.
2. The inherent test ceiling prevents discriminating among groups at the high end of the curve.

Both points increase the significance of the low scores.

Table 7 indicates that Puerto Ricans are higher in figure-ground perception (Subtest II) than are white pupils. This difference, however, did not reach statistical significance. In every other subtest the trend is reversed, with white and Chinese scores exceeding Puerto Rican and black scores to a significant degree. Lowest scores for Puerto Rican and black are in shape-constancy (Subtest III). In other subtests where minimum scores vary among ethnic groups, Puerto Rican scores are lowest with black scores second lowest. In shape-constancy, not a single Puerto Rican was able to score at maximum in spite of a sample population three-fifths larger than black, seven times larger than white, and almost eleven times larger than Chinese. In other words, in a test that has low ceilings, of 65 Puerto Rican children, not a single one was able to "max" the test, although *at least* 1 out of 6 Chinese, 1 out of 9 white, and 1 out of 39 black children did earn a top score.

Table 7   **Mean, Standard Deviation, and Minimum and Maximum Perceptual Age-Level Scores of Sample First-Graders Compared by Ethnicity***

Subtest	Ethnic Group	$\overline{X}$	S.D.	Min.	Max.
I. Eye-Motor	PR	5.96	2.56	1.00	9.60
	B	6.20	2.15	1.00	9.60
	W	5.32	2.91	1.00	9.60
	Ch	5.58	3.75	1.00	9.60
II. Figure-Ground	PR	6.18	1.41	3.00	8.30
	B	5.78	1.29	3.90	8.30
	W	6.08	1.51	4.00	8.30
	Ch	7.63	1.63	4.30	8.30
III. Shape-Constancy	PR	5.19	1.41	2.60	8.30
	B	5.27	1.47	3.00	9.00
	W	6.71	1.59	4.00	9.00
	Ch	7.25	1.84	4.00	9.00
IV. Space Position	PR	6.00	1.21	3.30	8.90
	B	5.71	.92	4.00	7.00
	W	7.04	1.23	5.00	8.90
	Ch	6.62	1.38	4.90	8.90
V. Spatial Relations	PR	6.34	1.30	0.00	8.30
	B	5.83	1.00	4.00	8.30
	W	6.89	.94	6.00	8.30
	Ch	7.83	.36	7.60	8.30

* Puerto Rican (PR): $n = 65$; black (B): $n = 39$; Chinese (Ch): $n = 6$; white (W): $n = 9$.

Other data, not included here, report perceptual differences related to sex among ethnic groups. With the exception of one case, there are no significant differences in PQs between sexes within each ethnic group. The one exception was between male and female whites, where a PQ difference of 98.20 and 110.00 was reported in favor of males. These figures are highly unreliable because of the small number tested. However, within every ethnic group, male scores tended to exceed female scores, although not to a statistically significant degree.

Summary. Socially disadvantaged first-graders on New York's Lower East Side were significantly retarded in visual perceptual development. How much of the perceptual dysfunctions were due to organicity, and how much to emotional instability, developmental lag, or lack of learning is impossible to determine at this time. Black children appear to suffer the worst dysfunctions, although Puerto Rican children's scores were so close that differences between these Black and Puerto Rican children were not statistically significant.

The visual dysfunctions uncovered were so serious that beginning reading taught by traditional methods would fail with a large percentage of these children regardless of the teacher's skill and the size of the class. When visual perceptual dysfunctions are combined with auditory perceptual dysfunctions, substandard verbal environments, and psychosocial deficits associated with disadvantaged children, present attempts to teach reading in grade 1 will result in even a larger percentage of failure.

Causes of Perceptual Dysfunctions in Disadvantaged Children

Pasamanick claims that most of the dysfunctions found in the Deutsch studies reflect organic impairment. [27] He postulates that these conditions stem indirectly from short- and long-range effects of the deficient diet, poor general living conditions, and poor prenatal care experienced by members of disadvantaged minority subcultures. Deutsch suggests that developmental lag and lack of learning play an important role. [28] Deutsch's theory tends to be more probable because most of the behaviors that are observed as dysfunctioning are learned. However, the efficacy of Pasamanick's claim, that is, that organicity may be present, cannot be denied, especially when we consider the likelihood of brain damage during birth being undetected or untreated because of the inadequate care socially disadvantaged women receive. However, minimal organicity should be compensated for by the incidental perceptual learning during early years of development. This may be the key factor. Both the advantaged and disadvantaged child may suffer the same minimal brain lesions at birth. The environment of the former, however, may offer the opportunity to learn compensatory skills, an opportunity not given the latter. Thus, not just more organicity, but also less opportunity for perceptual learning, is the probable cause of the shockingly high incidence of visual perceptual dysfunctioning in the disadvantaged children tested by MFY. I suspect, however, that similar findings would result if the same perceptual survey were taken of poor rural whites and other culturally deprived minority children.

Perceptually Dysfunctioning Children
Can Learn to Read

In spite of the claims of some advocates of perceptual training, many perceptually dysfunctioning children will learn to read if they have other things going for them. It is folly to underestimate the human organism's ability to compensate for dysfunctions. One factor may play a major role in determining whether or not a child reads, but that major factor gains its status only in relation to others.

If a child with perceptual dysfunctions lacks the psycholinguistic background conducive to success in reading, then the perceptual dysfunction appears to be a very important factor. If he lacks, in addition, motivation to read, perceptual dysfunction looks even more important. Add a family history of low school achievement and low achievement expectancy by his teachers and community, and the presence of perceptual dysfunction looms as an insurmountable impediment to success in reading. On the other hand, give a perceptually dysfunctioning child any one or combination of these factors and he usually parlays them into success in reading. Why? Because the human organism is always imperfect and always using its assets to compensate for its liabilities whether those liabilities are psychodynamic, physiological, or perceptual.

For example, an emotionally disturbed, withdrawn Puerto Rican girl (factor 1), who rarely spoke (factor 2), whose oral-aural language experiences were minimal (factor 3), whose family was illiterate in both Spanish and English (factor 4), but who was perceptually sound (factor 5), had resorted to fantasy through reading (factor 6). In spite of factors 1 through 4, which usually contribute to reading disability, Maria had a tremendous need to read (factor 6). Reading was a convenient escape mechanism for her. She also had some advantages, such as factor 5, and others not included in diagnosis. As a result, she read on grade level in grade 4. Clinton had severe perceptual dysfunctions. He was disoriented in space, hand-eye coordination was poor, and visual imagery was weak. But he had a literate mother who insisted that he read and who spent the first three years of Clinton's schooling drilling him nightly on phonics. When he was fourteen years old, Clinton was a "phonic plugger," able to hold to his grade level by sounding out each word. He was a crippled reader, but was not disabled. He paid a high price for his school success and obviously needed some type of perceptual training, but even with his handicap, he had learned to read because he had other advantages.

Although Clinton and Maria learned to read, however, we cannot expect such success for most socially disadvantaged children. They often do not overcome this handicap of visual perceptual dysfunction because they do not have very much else going for them.

Summary

Although some children with visual perceptual dysfunctions can learn to read, we cannot expect a large number of such children to do so when they are so culturally deprived. Not just the visual perceptual problem, but this problem in combination with the others that constitute cultural deprivation, stack the cards against disadvantaged children. This is an important point to remember, because there is a current vogue to write off bright underachievers as "perceptually dysfunctioning" children. Perceptual difficulties may not alone *cause* reading retardation. In many —perhaps most—cases, a perceptually dysfunctioning child, not so extremely impaired as to be noticeably dysfunctioning to the layman's eyes, does not need visual perceptual training in order to learn to read. The Yeshiva University Reading Center and project classrooms are full of dysfunctioning children who read well because they were taught well. But when we analyze the mass of retarded readers who are also disadvantaged on many dimensions, visual perceptual development stands out as *one* of the more important deficiencies that must be considered in preventing retardation, particularly in schools where the quality of teaching reading is not good enough to offset this and other deficits.

Visual perceptual functioning is basic to verbal skills, cognitive development, and intelligence. [7] Because perceptual dysfunction is a widespread problem among socially disadvantaged children of all subcultures, this training must be part of the regular curriculum, rather than part of separate remedial services. It should be one core of a preschool or kindergarten program for socially disadvantaged children. The next chapter includes an outline of such a program and the published materials that are available.

References

1. D. O. Hebb, *The Organization of Behavior* (New York: Wiley, 1949), chap. 5.
2. G. Walter, *The Living Brain* (New York: Norton, 1953), p. 78.
3. H. F. Harlow, "The Formation of Learning Sets," *Psychological Review,* 56 (1949), 51–65.
4. D. O. Hebb, "Primate Learning," in H. Helson (ed.), *Comparative Psychology* (Englewood Cliffs, N.J.: Prentice-Hall, 1951), pp. 81–83.
5. ———— and J. M. Warren, "Formation and Transfer of Discrimination Learning Sets," *Journal of Comparative Physiology and Psychology,* 45 (1952), 482–89.
6. ————, "Man's Frontal Lobes: A Critical Review," *Archives of Neurological Psychiatry,* 54 (1945), 1–24.
7. J. McV. Hunt, *Intelligence and Experience* (New York: Ronald Press, 1961), p. 87.
8. D. O. Hebb, "The Innate Organization of Visual Activity: I," *Journal of Genetic Psychology,* 51 (1937), 101–26.
9. ————, "The Innate Organization of Visual Activity: II," *Journal of Comparative Psychology,* 24 (1937), 227–99.
10. K. S. Lashley, "The Mechanism of Vision: XV," *Journal of Genetic Psychology,* 18 (1938), 123–93.

11. A. H. Reisen, "The Development of Visual Perception in Man and Chimpanzee," *Science*, 106 (1947), 107–8.

12. ———, "Plasticity of Behavior: Psychological Aspects," in H. Harlow and C. N. Woolsey (eds.), *Biological and Biochemical Bases of Behavior* (Madison, Wis.: University of Wisconsin Press, 1958), pp. 425–50.

13. J. Piaget, *The Origins of Intelligence in Children* (New York: International Universities Press, 1952).

14. A. Gesell *et al.*, *Vision, Its Development in Infant and Child* (New York: Hafner, 1967), pp. 48–50.

15. L. B. Bender, *A Dynamic Psychopathology of Childhood* (Springfield, Ill.: Charles C Thomas, 1954), pp. 14–15.

16. ———, *Child Psychiatric Techniques* (Springfield, Ill.: Charles C Thomas, 1952), p. 61.

17. Marianne Frostig *et al.*, "A Developmental Test of Visual Perception for Evaluating Normal and Neurologically Handicapped Children," *Perceptual and Motor Skills*, 12 (1961), 383–94.

18. A. T. Jersild, *Child Psychology* (Englewood Cliffs, N.J.: Prentice-Hall, 1960), pp. 94–111.

19. A. I. Siegel, "A Motor Hypothesis of Perceptual Development," *American Journal of Psychology*, 66 (1953), 301–4.

20. G. E. Coghill, *Anatomy and the Problem of Behavior* (Cambridge, Eng.: Cambridge University Press, 1929).

21. D. Hooker, *The Prenatal Origin of Behavior* (Lawrence, Kan.: University of Kansas Press, 1952).

22. C. Sherrington, *The Integrative Action of the Nervous System* (New Haven, Conn.: Yale University Press, 1948).

23. P. Schilder, *Contributions to Developmental Neuropsychiatry* (New York: International Universities Press, 1964).

24. W. Penfield and L. Roberts, *Speech and Brain Mechanisms* (Princeton, N.J.: Princeton University Press, 1959), p. 137.

25. R. I. Coleman and C. Deutsch, "Lateral Dominance and Right-Left Discrimination: A Comparison of Normal and Retarded Readers," *Perceptual and Motor Skills*, 19 (August 1964), 43–50.

26. B. Pasamanick, "The Intelligence of American Children of Mexican Parentage: A Discussion of Uncontrolled Variables," *Journal of Abnormal and Social Psychology*, 46 (1951), 598–602.

27. ——— and H. Knobloch, "The Contribution of Some Organic Factors to School Retardation in Negro Children," *Journal of Negro Education*, 27 (1958), 4–9.

28. M. Deutsch, "The Disadvantaged Child and the Learning Process," in A. H. Passow (ed.), *Education in Depressed Areas* (New

York: Bureau of Publications, Teachers College, Columbia University, 1963), pp. 163–74.

29. Marianne Frostig, *Developmental Test of Visual Perception* (Palo Alto, Calif.: Consulting Psychologists Press, 1963).

30. ————, *Administration and Scoring Manual, Developmental Test of Visual Perception* (Palo Alto, Calif.: Consulting Psychologists Press, 1964), p. 1.

Chapter Six

Solutions for Visual Perception

Introduction

The survey reported in Chapter Five supports other research findings and clinical observations of staffs working in poverty projects which indicate that the incidence of severe visual perceptual dysfunctions in socially disadvantaged children is unusually high. The causes of such dysfunctions are open to speculation—how much is minimal damage and how much is poor general development is unknown. Whatever the cause, we can expect a tendency toward lower school achievement among these children when we consider this dysfunction in the light of other widespread deficits. As discussed in the previous chapter, *one* strategy that can be used to offset the visual perception deficit is visual perceptual development training as part of the disadvantaged child's school program. But, considering the magnitude of the problem, perception specialists working in a separate remedial program is not a sufficient solution—the problem must be solved in every class-room. Teachers of the early grades should be trained in such strategies. This teacher training should include a thorough grounding in child development, a grounding that provides more than Freudian psychology. Every teacher should be acquainted with enough developmental neurophysiology to understand the theory underlying perceptual training.

An experimental program in visual perceptual training for the carliest developmental stage conducted by the author and Dr. Barbara Berger, formerly of Mobilization For Youth, is described in this chapter. In addition, other published programs and descriptions of programs available to schools are presented. However, the reader is cautioned on three points:

First, most commercially published programs stress visual perceptual training at a much higher level of development than is necessary, perhaps because such training lends itself to the paper-pencil-workbook materials that schools and publishers are used to. The methods presented here are geared to programs at a much lower level of development; the other programs are reserved for use at later stages or when appropriate for the particular situation.

Second, a number of administrative technicalities and professional taboos must be ignored if a perceptual training program is to be implemented. For example, children lying and rolling on the floor, much movement and noise in the classroom, and careful structure and control in kindergarten and prekindergarten are practices not currently in vogue in the large city school systems and are, in many instances, contrary to school policy.

Finally, a word of caution must be offered to those who will recognize many of the specific exercises as those used in their own methodology. Some critics will argue on this basis that these programs are already being carried out in early childhood and kindergarten classrooms. There is some truth to this argument, but a pedagogical universe exists between "some activities" and a tight, thorough, sequential, repetitive, structured developmental program based on a defined rationale. Educators must understand that *programs* not *activities* bring the results we seek. An activity may be exciting and effective, but unless it is part of a complete, thorough, and sequential series, lasting behavior change usually will not occur. In evaluating perceptual training activities for incorporation into the preschool curriculum, educators must seek complete programs that have sound rationales, thorough sequences of activities, day-to-day reinforcements, and adequate measurements of progress. In addition, such programs must be presented in detailed, step-by-step outline form so that the majority of teachers can follow them with a minimum of pretraining.

Visual Perceptual Training

Perceptual training attempts to provide structured, formal experiences to substitute for the informal primary learning that some children have missed. Because the effects of deprivation are cumulative and because the optimal time for learning these experiences has passed, we can no longer rely on the child's ability to learn informally or incidentally. Perceptual training tries to offset this disability by a high-powered, "all-out push" to help the child reach the point at which he is no longer working at a disadvantage. To do this requires a thorough, structured attack. The attack consists of visual perception training built on a sequence of steps analogous to perceptual development in normal children.

The earliest form of primary learning or the basis of autonomous central processes (ACP) is visual perceptual learning at the skeletal, motoric, and kinesthetic level. The training program described below starts at this level and moves up the developmental scale. It does not, however, encompass the total perceptual development process, but is concentrated instead on the basic level observed as dysfunctioning in the population reported in the previous chapter. Specifically, this program was aimed at affecting the behaviors that underlie visual perceptual development tapped by the Frostig test. [1] These behaviors coincide with clinical observations of the following specific behaviors in early elementary school children from New York City's Lower East Side reported in the preceding chapter.

1. Lack of flexibility in posturing—rigid, stiff postures
2. Limited body awareness and kinesthetic differentiation
3. Poorly developed sense of laterality (minimal kinesthetic awareness of right and left sides of body and inability to differentiate cognitively)
4. Inadequate spatial orientation with reference to their own bodies, as well as positioning of objects in space (tendency to rotate designs in copying block designs and in constructing geometric figures on pegboards)
5. Poor sense of directionality

6. Poor visual-motor coordination
7. Faulty figure-ground perception
8. Constant motor overflow—minimal voluntary control of motoric impulses
9. Inability to attend, listen, and assimilate directions

Materials

1. Individual chalkboards that can be tilted at various angles to help children make transition from vertical to horizontal.
2. Floor mats for exercises, because a dirty floor inhibits children and curtails their enjoyment and concentration in body work on the floor.
3. Individual series of stationary block models for spatial positioning practice with concrete objects.
4. Individual series of stationary pegboard models representing a progression in complexity of figure-ground perception.
5. Sets of bongo drums for rhythm training.
6. For form-perception training with concrete objects, it is especially important to have materials suited to the gross muscle coordination of the group. For example, pegboard exercises for kindergarten demand large, easily manipulated pegs and pegboards with holes spaced far enough apart for children to handle easily. Those currently on the market present problems even for seven- and eight-year-olds, because the pegs are too small; their manuipulation is too difficult and the activity therefore not enjoyable. The pegs, moreover, should be brightly colored and the boards a neutral shade to emphasize the figure-ground distinction, since picture-ground perception is the purpose of these exercises.

All these materials can be easily and inexpensively constructed in a do-it-yourself workshop.

Focus

Training activities at the early stage of perceptual development, which are focused directly on the body, are designed to promote the following kinds of learning:

1. Increased flexibility of posture and large muscle coordination.
2. Body awareness and body schema, specifically in relation to

laterality. The major effort is directed toward developing ability to differentiate between right and left sides of the body and between up and down.

3. Spatial orientation and positioning exercises involving the entire body, and similar exercises with arms and legs.
4. Increased motor control to combat tendency toward motor overflow.
5. Balance training using square balance boards and walking rails, varied motor exercises, and games.

Some training is also given in form discrimination, moving from motor action stage (skeletal) to manipulation of concrete forms representing various shapes (visceral), to visual paper and pencil exercises from Frostig's *Kit for Development of Visual Perception* (cortical). [2] This training includes:

1. Motoric conditioning to different abstract shapes (children walk floor patterns of circles, squares, triangles, and so forth).
2. Visual motor training with abstract shapes (children trace around templates and finally move to freehand).
3. Spatial positioning drills with wooden triangles.
4. Copying simple block patterns constructed by the teacher. Attention is focused on positioning blocks correctly in relation to their bodies.
5. Paper and pencil exercises on spatial positioning, numbers 1 through 15 in the Frostig kit. [2]
6. Pegboard exercises emphasizing figure-ground relationships.
7. Exercises in figure-ground perception in the Frostig kit. [2]

Three principles of development underlie these training activities. First, the training activities are sequentially presented from a sensory-motor level (activities focused on the body), to manipulation of concrete objects, to abstract discrimination by visual exercises. Second, the sequence progresses from large-muscle activities to fine motor coordination and control. Third, the sequence progresses from the simple to the more complex.

A Program in Visual Perceptual Training

The exercises outlined were tested in a pilot program with 15 retarded-reading second-graders. [3] They are offered as the beginning of a motor training program for basic perceptual development. In addition, the books, kits, and items listed in the References at the end of this chapter contain basic perceptual exercises that can be used to develop an individual program.

I. Articulation of Body Schema

This series of exercises covers kinesthetic awareness of body, identification of body parts, and isolation of body parts on a motoric level.

A. Kinesthetic Awareness of Body
   (To be done by children with their eyes closed.)
   1. Curl up on your *right* side.
      a. Knees to chest.
      b. What do you feel like now? (Ask different children.)
      c. Let's listen to our hearts beat. Sh-sh-sh quiet! (Try to induce a semihypnotic state.)
      d. Let's listen to ourselves breathe.
   2. Roll onto your back (repeat *a–c* above).
   3. Straighten out your legs.
      a. Back flat on the floor.
      b. Press your belly back.
      c. Spine flat.
   4. Repeat (1) on *left* side.
   5. Repeat 2.
   6. Repeat 3.
   7. Jump to a standing position.

B. Identification of Body Parts
   1. Children first learn the names of parts of the body. Teacher stands in front of the class, touches different parts of her body, and children imitate. As they touch a given part, the children call out the name in chorus:

head	leg	eyes
shoulders	arm	chest
stomach	neck	back
hand	mouth	fingers
foot	ears	

2. Differentiation of body parts
    a. Teacher calls out commands to class, à la "Simon Says": Touch your elbow, touch your foot.
    b. Practice in different positions—"Hokey Pokey" (At this stage do not require children to make right-left discrimination of arm or leg.)
    Children in a circle—all facing the same direction: Put your little arm in. Take your little arm out. Put your little arm in and shake it all about. (Repeat with foot and head.) Put your whole self in. (Children jump into circle.) Take your whole self out. (Children jump back to original place.) Put your whole self in and turn yourself about. (Children complete jump turn.)
3. Laterality discrimination in motion: Repeat game—having children all fall in opposite directions. They will be using different arms and legs.
4. Right and left discrimination: Play this game using jingle wristlets and anklets on *right* side only. Now they sing: Put your *right* hand in; take your *right* hand out.
5. Play the game using jingle wristlets and anklets on *left* side only.
6. Motoric isolation of body parts I: To isolate these parts of the body and control movement.
    a. Children on backs on floor—eyes closed.
    b. Slowly raise just head off the floor.
    c. Slowly raise just shoulders off the floor.
    d. Slowly raise just chest off the floor until they are sitting up.
    e. Now reverse—start sitting up—and return to prone position.

II. Working Toward a More Flexible Posture

This series of exercises covers changing body postures, spatial reorientation of the body, and moving through space.

A. Changing Body Postures (Floor Exercises), Horizontal to Vertical
    1. Children lie on floor—on backs—eyes closed.
    2. Everybody sit up.
    3. Bring your knees to your chest—feet flat on floor.

   4. Jump up.
   5. Repeat, performing each action to a single drumbeat.
   6. Children are standing up.
   7. Everybody sit down—knees hunched up—feet on floor.
   8. Straighten legs—sitting position.
   9. Backs to floor.
  10. Try sequence 6–9 with drumbeat.

B. Spatial Reorientation for Body
   1. Teacher stands with back to class—assumes different poses involving entire body (standing, prone, sitting), changing relationship of her body to the floor; children imitate.
   2. Teacher repeats exercises but at increasingly rapid tempo. Teacher begins by changing positions slowly, progressively speeds up tempo. Children take turns playing leads. Each one assumes a different pose, and the others imitate.
   3. "Statues"
     Teacher plays music, children move around. When the music stops, they freeze in position.

C. Moving Through Space—Assuming Different Body Positions
   1. Duck walk: crouched position, waddle across the room, hands behind back.
   2. Kangaroo hop: Jump across the room with feet together.
   3. Spider walk: Crawl across the room, hands at side.
   4. Crab walk: Everybody down on all fours, bodies off the floor. Hands walk alone—forward 3 steps. Now feet walk forward to join hands.

III. Localization of Body Parts in Space

This series of exercises covers spatial positioning, arms only; spatial positioning, legs only; and spatial positioning, arms and legs.

A. Spatial Positioning, Arms Only
   1. Teacher stands with back to class, performs sequence of arm movements; children imitate, using the same arm.
    a. Unilateral (right arm only).
    b. Bilateral.
    c. Cross lateral. [4]
   2. Repeat the exercise, but substitute a stick figure on the board for the teacher. Have children close their eyes each time. Change position of the stick figure; have children

open their eyes and arrange themselves in imitation of the figure.

B. Spatial Positioning, Legs Only
Repeat (A).

C. Spatial Positioning, Arms and Legs
Teacher stands in front of the class, assumes different poses —shifting leg position, shifting arm position. Repeat sitting on a chair; repeat kneeling on the floor.

IV. Laterality Training: Kinesthetic Differentiation

This series of exercises covers standing—"Bumps-a-Daisy," "Angels in the Snow" variations, and balance-board training.

A. Standing—"Bumps-a-Daisy" (One-sided)
   1. Teacher demonstrates: Shifts weight to the right, pushing out right hip.
   2. Children line up side by side with bodies touching.
   3. Teacher calls children's names, starting with the child at the extreme left.
   4. As each name is called, the child does "Bumps-a-Daisy" to right and holds position.
   5. Practice by repeating at faster tempo and with varied cues. Make sure children respond on cue.
   6. Repeat entire sequence to the left.

B. "Angels in the Snow" Variations (Two-sided)
   1. Children lie on their backs with eyes closed.
   2. Hold piece of chalk in hand and in right foot (between toes).
   3. Raise and lower on cue:
      a. Arm.
      b. Leg.
      c. Both.
   4. Repeat with left side.
   5. Repeat in different positions:
      a. On stomach.
      b. On all fours.
   6. Partners variation.
      a. One child lies down.
      b. Other child kneels to right.
      c. Kneeling child touches arm, leg, hand, foot sequentially.

    d. Child lying down moves each part as it is touched.
    e. Repeat with left side.
    f. Partners switch roles.

C. Balance-Board Training (Use 22- to 24-inch Balance Boards)
  1. Children stand upright on board without tilting, eyes open.
  2. Repeat with eyes closed.
  3. Use various cues (visual and/or auditory) to indicate direction and have children tilt boards to rhythm.

V. Laterality Training

More practice with variations emphasizing discrimination of right and left sides of the body.

A. "Hokey Pokey"
  1. Play games as directed in I-B.
  2. Now repeat sequence outlined, but have children remove wristlets and anklets, and require independent discrimination of right and left.
  3. Now alternate right and left directions: Put your right hand in, take your right hand out; put your left hand in, take your left hand out.

B. Laterality: Right-Left Discrimination in Walking
  1. Floor pattern for right and left feet (see Kephart [4]).
  2. Use red and green tape Xs to discriminate between right and left feet.
  3. Mark children's feet with appropriate color tape.
  4. Have children practice walking pattern, master R-L discrimination and problem of adjusting size of their steps to pattern.
  5. When they can do this, have them walk to rhythm (metronome, drumbeat).
  6. Have them go as fast as they can, *leaping.*
  7. Final stage: Have children follow R-L patterns without any marking on their feet.
  8. Repeat the process, *crawling.*

C. "Hopscotch"
  1. Mark pattern on floor with chalk.
  2. Have children jump the number sequence, starting L-R.
  3. Alternate rows R-L.

4. Have children follow this pattern hopping on right leg.
5. Next have them do it hopping on left leg.

D. "Hopscotch" Variation
 1. Have children hop on right foot—A to B.
 2. Jump from B to C (both feet).
 3. Hop on right foot from C to D to E.
 4. Jump from E to F (both feet).
 5. Repeat with left foot.

E. Body Parts Identification
 1. Pin picture of right hand, outside view (as in Frostig pictures) on chalkboard.
 2. Have children hold up the same hand. If they do not know which hand it is, have them come up and experiment by matching each hand to the picture.
 3. Repeat with a picture of right hand, inside view.
 4. Repeat with picture of left hand.
 5. Next day, pin up several at once. Have children identify their matching hands.

VI. Development of Motoric Control

This series of exercises covers controlling motor overflow, oculamotor pursuits training, and eye-hand coordination.

A. Controlling Motor Overflow
 1. Control and coordination of movement—I.
    a. Have children march around the room to different tempos of drumbeat. Sequence: slow-faster-slow.
    b. Repeat exercise, skipping.
    c. Have children practice moving and stopping on a given signal.
    d. Repeat for walking, skipping, and jumping.
    e. Have children practice interruption of flow of movement with large arm movement to a given signal.
    f. Have children swing one arm in a circle to the right—continuous movement, then stop the flow of movement at a given signal.
    g. Repeat in opposite direction.
    h. Repeat with arm at lateral extension.
    i. Do similar exercises with legs.
 2. Control and coordination of movement—II: "Mirror" game. (Teacher should demonstrate first with another child, and be sure to stay at child's level.)

   a. Have children take partners.

   b. Partners stand facing each other, looking into partner's eyes at all times. The leader slowly initiates movement with different parts of the body, which the other child performs simultaneously—as in a mirror image.

   c. Encourage children to experiment: Up and down movements, lateral movements, balancing on one foot, asymmetrical positions, moving in different directions, turning around, moving together as one person. The leader then must move very slowly so the other child can keep up.

   d. Have different pairs of children perform the game before the class.

  3. Motoric control and coordination.

   a. Teacher tells the children a caterpillar is crawling over her hand, wrist, lower arm, elbow, shoulder. She wiggles each part independently as the caterpillar crawls over it. Children imitate.

   b. Teacher repeats the procedure, starting with the same foot, ankle, leg, knee.

   c. Teacher then repeats the entire procedure on the other side of the body.

   d. Next, the teacher asks one child to be the leader—he is to wiggle only that part of his body on which the caterpillar is crawling. The other children imitate.

   e. The children take turns. Each must use a different part of the body.

B. Oculamotor Training—L-R, R-L

  1. Have children do the following exercises (first standing, then sitting):

   a. Move their eyes left to right across the ceiling of the room.

   b. Follow with their eyes, left to right, a pointer with a handkerchief tied to the end.

   c. Follow a flashlight beam left to right across the room.

   d. Follow a pencil with a white tack stuck in the eraser from left to right in front of them (see suggestions for training in Radler's *Success Through Play*). [5]

C. Eye-Hand Coordination and Control

  1. Bean bag toss game (children keep score).

   a. Chalk targets on the floor, using different geometric shapes to foster awareness of form differences.

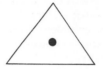

  b. Bull's eye (middle of target) is 10 points; outside area
   is 5 points.
 2. See the Frostig kit for more eye-hand coordination exercises. [2]

VII. Directionality Training

 This series of exercises covers in-out training; up-down training; in-out, up-down moving in space; and projecting bodies in space.

 A. Concepts of In-Out in Relation to Own Body ("belly button" is reference point)
  1. Floor exercises:
   a. Children lie flat on their backs, arms outstretched, legs together.
   b. Bring legs to belly button, *in*.
   c. Stretch legs away from belly button, *out*.
   d. Repeat with arms.
   e. Repeat with arms and legs simultaneously.
    (1) Bring arms and legs *in* (arms hug knees)
    (2) Stretch arms and legs *out*.
   f. "Angels in the Snow" (see Kephart [4]).
  2. Standing exercises:
   Repeat with arms *in* and arms *out*.

 B. Up-Down in Relation to Own Body
  1. Each child imitates a flower growing "up-up-up."
  2. Have them crouch on the floor and gradually grow taller and taller, until they have stretched as tall as they can on tiptoe.
  3. Then have them slowly come down to a crawling position.

 C. Directionality—Up-Down, In-Out—While Moving Through Space
  1. Have children do *in-out* with arms while moving across the room to rhythmic drumbeats.

2. Have children do *up-down* movement patterns across the room to rhythmic accompaniment:
   a. 3 walking steps—flat foot—(soft drumbeats).
   b. 1 up on tiptoe (1 loud drumbeat).
   c. 3 steps on tiptoe.
   d. 1 flat foot.
3. Let children improvise movement patterns to music, utilizing *in-out* extensions and *up-down* changes with arms, legs, and bodies.

D. Projecting Bodies into Space in Different Directions
   1. Have children play any games requiring moving through space in different directions—forward, back, sideways.
   2. "Giant-Step": Children march in formation (groups of 3 or 4). Call out commands: Two giant steps forward. Three giant steps backward. One giant step to right side. One giant step to left side. Orient each directional command to some concrete part of the room (window, cupboard, walls, blackboard).
   3. Have children perform a series of quarter-turn jumps involving directional reorientation of bodies.
      a. Children line up in rows of 4.
      b. Teacher-demonstrator stands in front of the group.
      c. Children make a series of quarter turns until they are back in their original positions. Teacher calls out the reference point each time they jump a quarter turn: To the window. To the desk. To the closet. To the chalkboard. (Back to original position.)
      d. Similar drill doing a half-turn jump.
      e. Final drill—whole-turn jump.

VIII. Form Perception

This exercise covers motoric awareness of forms and shapes, manipulation of concrete forms and motoric differentiation of forms and shapes, and figure-ground differentiations.

A. Motoric Awareness of Form and Shape
   1. Chalk circles, triangles, squares, diamonds on the floor.
   2. Children march around them, hop around, jump around outlines.
   3. Children draw imaginary triangles, squares, and so on in the air with their noses or with upper torso bent forward, using their heads as pencils.

B. Manipulation with Concrete Forms and Motoric Differentiation of Forms, Shapes

1. Children trace around wooden templates of different abstract forms. (They should use large, colored chalk, and work on rectangular chalkboards laid out on floor.)
2. Children try copying their forms freehand with chalk.
3. Children construct the various forms with matchsticks or straws—on a felt board.

C. Figure-Ground Differentiation—Working with Concrete Objects

1. Pegboard exercises constructing simple geometric forms. (See Kephart on form perception [4]).
2. Practice in rotating positions of these constructions to match a demonstration model.
3. Pegboard exercises, constructing more complex designs. (See Frostig pegboard designs [2]). As a variation, use marble boards. Assign only a single color of marble or peg to a child. Cautions: Use large pegs (easily manipulated). Use bright contrasting color of pegboard (not a neutral shade like tan). If using marbles, follow the same principle.
4. See Getman's template exercises in P.A.S.S. manual. [6]
5. Also see Frostig's *Kit for Development of Visual Perception.* [2]

This outline is suggested as a basic visual-motor training program for early childhood classrooms. It should be supplemented by the Getman and Frostig programs, which are the best visual perception programs currently available on the commercial market. In early childhood classes for socially disadvantaged children, auditory perception, oral-aural language development, and school orientation should constitute three more parts of the four-pronged attack on educational retardation in disadvantaged children (see the discussions in Chapters 7, 8, 9).

Results of This Program

Although the pilot program was not continued long enough to warrant systematic measurement of growth, observations of the children's progress indicated that they were learning and improving, particularly in the training areas stressed most repetitively. At the end of the sessions, they were visibly more aware of their own bodies; more adept in laterality, directionality, and balance; and more flexible and confident in using their bodies. One tangible indication of their progress was the contrast in their draw-a-person productions prior to and following training. Examination of pre- and post-drawings revealed visible improvement in spatial positioning and balance. For example, some of the post-drawings had spatial boundaries for the figures, whereas the pre-drawings had none. The figures in post-drawings were more vertical, upright, and better balanced than in pre-drawings, in which they were tilted off-balance in one direction or the other. There was also a consistent trend in the post-drawing series indicative of a more solid and affirmative sense of self. The post-drawings were larger, showed a firmer stance, and were noticeably less rigid, more relaxed, and more movement oriented. They displayed more projection of self into space (arms extended) than pre-drawings. This technique of measurement, improvised to provide some index of growth in body schema, seems to show promise as an assessment device for future programs of this kind.

An effective developmental curriculum for early childhood requires a graduated sequence of training activities in each skill area that aims at developing learner mastery at increasing levels of complexity. Moreover, to make learning stick, particularly at younger age levels, curriculum construction requires building in a fair amount of repetition and reinforcement through a variety of training exposures and practices in each skill area. In this pilot program, 30- to 40-minute sessions enabled the staff to do three different kinds of activities per session, and frequently to combine in one session exercises on different levels of abstraction (bodies, objects, paperwork). The implementation of a training program within the preschool or kindergarten routine would probably allow no more than 30 minutes of formalized work each day. This time should be spent as follows:

1. An initial period concentrating exclusively on body work. (This initial period should be at least six weeks, and certainly it could be up to two months.)
2. A second phase introducing manipulation with objects (geometric forms, blocks, pegboards) for training for spatial posi-

tioning, spatial relationships, figure-ground perception, and perceptual constancy—but still continuing sensory-motor training (three months).

3. Final phase, introducing Frostig-type materials for the remainder of the school year.

The plan outlined prolongs the sensory-motor training aspect. This rationale is based on the developmental fact that success on this level of learning is crucial to adequacy in succeeding stages of perceptual development; that is, unless perceptual discrimination is truly operant in the sensory, kinesthetic, and motor realms, children's responses to pencil and paper type training will be mere surface learning.

A few observations on the Frostig materials came out of this pilot experience. The scope of her program does include activities on various developmental levels (body, objects, and abstract pencil and paper work). The major limitation, however, is the suggested training curriculum on the sensory-motor level. Although the activities suggested are good per se, they are not organized to the extent necessary to provide developmental and organic progression. For this purpose, Getman and Kephart are superior, as is much of the creative dance training approach currently being utilized with four- and five-year-olds.

Problems of Methodology in Using This Type of Program

The major difficulty in treating poor perceptual development is how to do a corrective job with individual children in a large group situation, when so much body awareness work demands close teacher supervision. The most feasible solution to this problem is to introduce teacher aides to reduce teacher-pupil ratio to 1 to 5 in prekindergarten and kindergarten and, if possible, through grade 2. These are critical years in the educational development of children.

The problem of teacher-pupil ratio becomes crucial in the following types of training activities. Laterality exercises that require children to make unilateral responses of arms and legs ("Angels in the Snow") are difficult in large groups. A solution is to pair children. With this method, one child can provide tactual cues to the child doing the exercises by touching the appropriate arm or leg and then checking and notifying the teacher when the subject is uncertain or in error. At least in initial exposure to this type of practice exercise, the teacher should work with only half the group at a time, structuring a helper-observer role for the rest of the children. Chalkboard exercises as in Kephart [4] or in the P.A.S.S. [6] manual are difficult to supervise in large groups. Because it is important to correct the child while he is doing the exercise, the teacher must stand over him and provide immediate assistance. Even working with three children at a time is difficult. Group practice on balance boards and walking planks presents a problem. Here, however, the issue is less one of effective supervision and more a problem of kinesthetic concentration by a child in a group situation. In order for children to really profit from these activities, they must be able to concentrate and feel their bodies. One can work effectively with three children on balance boards, or two on walking planks, *if* the other children are occupied.

Effective techniques for getting children's attention quickly are a problem, although perhaps less so for the experienced classroom teacher. The use of some auditory signal is helpful—drum, bell, or piano. In the same manner, much work must be done in developing techniques for giving simple, clear directions. How to do this with a minimum of words is likely to be a major challenge for the teacher. Children become easily confused by wordy instructions; they cannot assimilate verbal directions easily.

Two other aspects of training discussed below present specific technical difficulties:

Exercises in Body Positioning. In this exercise the children imitate the teacher, who is the demonstration model. The teacher must position himself with his back to the group so that children can observe and copy the positioning. Yet the teacher must still manage to observe individuals. When children have mastered these exercises, they must be taught to do them with the teacher-demonstrator facing them. This is a more complex skill requiring cross-lateral orientation of the child's body in relation to the teacher. On this level, there is difficulty among those who cannot make the required switch; they continue to mirror-image the teacher. In these exercises, success among four- and five-year-olds will demand better methodology than is presented in this program. This is especially important if the teacher expects to prepare children for the beginning Frostig exercises in body positioning (see the Frostig manual). [2] Young children's abilities to master Frostig's learning tasks depend upon their developing a strong kinesthetic sense of laterality, as well as upon an effective teaching technique.

Spatial Positioning Exercises with Blocks. One purely technical problem in this exercise involves setting up block design models for groups of children. The problem here is how to position the demonstration block model for the children to copy with their own set of blocks in such a way that the model is positionally equivalent for all the children. When working with several children at once, it is not possible to position the model similarly for all children. If children are seated at an angle to the model, as opposed to having it squarely in front of them, their products will be rotated to some extent depending upon the seating angle. This situation may confuse the teacher in checking individual products; it may confuse the children in comparing their constructions with each other. The same problem exists in working with pegboard designs on a group basis. One solution is to seat the children in a straight row with the demonstration model in front of them. Under these conditions, the group size limit is four or five children. The best solution, of course, would be a complete demonstration model series for each child. In this way he can work individually following a progression from simple to more complex block designs or figure-ground pegboards.

Summary

The ability to observe and quantify visual perceptual development in children outstrips our abilities to influence this process. That is why the program described above is labeled "pilot." At best, it is a first try in an area relatively new to the educator. For this reason, it may be wise for schools to seek out a developmental vision optometrist under the Optometric Extension Program (see Chapter Eight), the only professional group that has so far systematically developed a repertoire of perceptual training techniques. Educators must become aware, however, of the difference between this type of training and traditional vision or orthoptic training practiced by many conventional vision specialists. Visual or orthoptic training is an effective approach to a very different category of problems, an approach that is not generated from a developmental model. Educators should also be aware of the intensive professional rivalry between ophthalmology and optometry and between developmental vision optometry and conventional optometry. These rivalries often break into open hostilities with children and educators caught in the crossfire.

Finally, the whole role of visual perception in the development of cognition and reading is still being researched. Certainly more must be discovered about the relationship between perceptual development, cognition, and reading, and much more needs to be discovered about methods of influencing this development. While the literature includes many studies implicating visual perceptual dysfunctions as *one* correlate to learning disability, especially when these disabilities are found in lower socioeconomic class children, other correlates, described in the following chapter, must be given equal weight in any consideration of the total problem of educating disadvantaged children.

References

1. Marianne Frostig, *Developmental Test of Visual Perception* (Palo Alto, Calif.: Consulting Psychologists Press, 1963).
2. ———, *Kit for Development of Visual Perception* (Cleveland: Follett, 1963).
3. S. Alan Cohen and B. Berger, "Perceptual-Motor Training Program for Early Primary Grade Children," in S. Gordon and R. Golub (eds.), *Recreation and Socialization for the Brain Injured Child* (East Orange, N.J.: New Jersey Association for Brain Injured Children, 1966), pp. 61–75.
4. Newell C. Kephart, *The Slow Learner in the Classroom* (Columbus, O.: Merrill, 1960).
5. D. H. Radler, *Success Through Play* (New York: Harper & Row, 1960).

6. G. N. Getman and Elmer R. Kane, *The Physiology of Readiness: An Action Program for the Development of Perception for Children* (Minneapolis: P.A.S.S., Inc., 1964). Includes a template kit.

Chapter Seven

The Role of Preschool

Introduction

Whatever else may result from the War on Poverty, a rediscovery of the potential of early childhood education has certainly emerged. Faced with millions of children who begin school at a distinct disadvantage, the federal government has sparked a reemphasis on reaching children early—on giving disadvantaged children a "headstart." Unfortunately, the state of the art and science of early childhood teaching has not kept pace with this new demand. Headstart programs and early childhood education in general are still geared to the three goals stated twenty years ago by the National Association for Nursery Education. [1] According to the association, early childhood preschools were designed to meet the needs and interests of children; to stimulate independent, fearless, creative thinkers; and to lay the groundwork for social attitudes of cooperation needed in a democratic society. All these goals are admirable, indeed, but they are not peculiar to disadvantaged children. Because all children should be subjected to programs that foster these qualities, the goals do not offer the curriculum director of Headstart programs very much to build upon. More important, perhaps, is the lack of specificity in these goals and in the five outcomes that the association assumed would derive from them: *physical well-being, mental well-being, increased social maturity, richer emotional life,* and a *happy reunion with parents* as a result of the preschool experience. [2] This lack of specificity seems to be an occupational hazard at all levels of professional education, but early childhood educators, especially, would be able to serve their children and themselves much better if operant or behavioral descriptions were available, rather than these generalities. It is not a question of being for or against these goals and outcomes; it is, instead, a problem of replacing them with realistic behavioral descriptions that would give the preschool teacher practical guidelines for developing her own classroom methods.

The material in this and the following chapters is concentrated on the problem of developing practical models from which to teach. This chapter will lay the theoretical groundwork by establishing what preschools should do for disadvantaged children, the guidelines for doing it, and two rules of thumb for implementing effective preschool programs. Also included is a review of the difference between a genotypic theory of child development that, although no longer valid, still underlies most educational practice, and a phenotypic theory that contemporary psychologists have demonstrated as valid. Finally, the crucial difference between learning readiness and reading readiness, and the pedagogical necessity for recognizing this difference in practice, will be established. The following two chapters will describe methods of teaching children learning readiness and reading readiness.

Effectiveness of Kindergarten Programs

The professional literature assumes that children who attend kindergarten achieve better in school than those who do not attend a preschool of some type. [3, 4] But almost all the studies underlying this assumption were done on middle class children. One study of disadvantaged children shows that reading achievement scores through grade 5 are higher in those who have attended kindergarten than in those who have not. [5] Researchers, on the basis of these studies, tend to explain this better achievement in terms of general experience, but none of the studies statistically pinpoints the behavioral factors that make the difference. The consensus of opinion seems to be that children who attend kindergarten are more manageable in later grades, although the terms used by the researchers are "mature," "better able to concentrate," and "more ready to learn." However, over 50 percent of the twenty relevant studies that I surveyed did not establish statistically significant differences in school achievement between those who attended kindergarten and those who did not. Yet, they concluded in favor of the former.

At the time of the Marlowe study, [5] there were no published studies of the effects of kindergarten on school achievement of disadvantaged children. At Mobilization For Youth, we collected data on 721 culturally deprived Puerto Rican, black, and white children, 464 of whom had attended kindergarten. The remaining 257 had begun school in grade 1. We compared the kindergarten group (experimentals) with the nonkindergarten group (controls) on the *Metropolitan Reading Achievement Test,* Form A, administered at the middle of grade 3. The overall reading scores of this population were approximately similar to the scores reported in Table 3, Chapter Two.

The difference between a mixed population of black and white children who attended kindergarten as opposed to those who had not was *not* statistically significant, whereas the difference between Puerto Rican children who attended kindergarten compared to those who had not was highly significant. It appears that kindergarten experience was more potent for socially disadvantaged Puerto Rican children than for black and white children. This factor accounted for an overall finding in which the entire group of white, black, and Puerto Rican experimentals were better readers than those who had not attended kindergarten. This same study showed that kindergarten attendance made more of a difference for boys than for girls, regardless of ethnicity, but that Puerto Rican boys benefited most from kindergarten experience when we used third-grade reading scores as our criterion. The important implication of this study is that regardless of what preschool training *really* does, we cannot assume it has the same effect on all children. It is necessary to tailor the preschool program for the particular group that we are dealing with.

A Misassumption about Child Development

In our attempts to introduce sound readiness practices into preschool and kindergarten classrooms for disadvantaged children, we are often met with the universal cry of many preschool specialists: "They're not ready for that." Underlying this statement is the same theory that determines a given chronological age as optimal for school entrance. This is the *genotypic* theory of development, now twenty years behind the research.

The genotypic concept views development as an unfolding of relatively predetermined processes. The best-known advocates of this theory were G. Stanley Hall and his student, Arnold Gesell. Gesell exploited the normative study of child behavior. By describing the children's characteristic behaviors at each age, Gesell implied that development is genotypically predetermined. [6] A genotypic theory tells us to wait and observe; when certain behaviors begin to emerge from the child, we know he is ready for a particular set of stimuli. *Whether they admit it or not,* genotypic theorists imply that the potentials for behavior are locked inside at birth ready to unfold according to predetermined time and sequence scales. Hall, Gesell, and other researchers of this school gave us excellent normative studies of child development; they isolated crucial variables that we continue to observe as basic processes of development. But their underlying genotypic theory is no longer accepted by researchers in child development in the light of more recent research. Gesell, himself, seemed to modify his stand in the last of his most important researches. His study of vision development in children, [7] which was a radical departure from the traditional optic theory of vision, was, by its very nature, *phenotypic,* rather than genotypic. [8]

A phenotypic theory describes development as a continuous interaction between the innate growth mechanism and environmental conditions. [9] Piaget [10] and Bruner [11] are good examples of researchers who embrace phenotypic development as a process resulting from the succession, quality, and quantity of environmental encounters experienced by the genotype. According to a phenotypic theory, we cannot explain behavior simply by means of a developmental chart. We must, instead, study the organism's interaction with its environment now and in the past. This means that learning affects development. The opportunity to be affected by certain quantities of stimuli will shape behavior at any age.

A Realistic Goal for Preschool Education

The developing child will be influenced by his environment whether or not preschool specialists wait. The wisest course for the educator is to control the quality and quantity of stimuli to ensure types of behaviors that will aid the child. The choice of these stimuli should not be left to whim, but must stem from the results of controlled research and from the analysis of future behaviors demanded of the child in the real world. For children, that world is a reading world, a school world, in which disadvantaged children's egos are shattered in first grade by demands they cannot meet. It is a world difficult enough to inhabit when one's skin color or a few of one's mores or perceptions are different from the power culture's. It is a world in which the power culture's children learn to read and write in first and second grade, not in sixth grade or in Job Corps camps.

Early childhood programs must recognize the realities of the world in which disadvantaged children compete. They must recognize that *what* we teach to children at any age is within their grasp if we adapt the method of teaching to the level of the child. Adult adjustment problems are part of that reality, but in the list of priorities for preschool curriculum development, the very first job of the school is to prepare the child to be successful in elementary school, where literacy is the chief goal. A phenotypic theory makes this goal possible, for research underlying the phenotypic theory establishes beyond question that we do not need to wait for a child to *become* ready; we *make* him ready. We use methods that fit the child's style, level, and rate of learning to help him succeed in the real world. If we wait for "unready children" to become ready to do what their peers can already do, we can be sure that they will bear the scars of this disadvantage for life. If, on the other hand, we can make "unready children" ready—able to compete successfully in the real world of the elementary school—many adult problems can be avoided. The old shibboleths that reading instruction or "formal" teaching in preschool is traumatic or injurious to children must be discarded, because there is no evidence that early formal instruction in reading is injurious. The important factor is the quality of this early instruction, for ineffective and inappropriate instruction can be injurious at any age.

Guidelines for Building Preschool Curriculums

Because the language skills of many socially disadvantaged, culturally deprived preschoolers are grossly inadequate for present preschool curriculums, preschools and elementary schools should first focus on teaching language development and prereading skills, and then on reading, writing, and arithmetic. These are the primary goals of the American school. Obviously, preschools and elementary schools should not try to operate as psychotherapy centers, social change agents, human relations workshops, or vocational institutes; they may perform some of these functions *only* as a means of reaching their primary goal. This guideline does not preclude other goals: It establishes, instead, a priority that must be met before other goals are assumed. Only by analyzing educational goals into specific operations and by pinpointing these specific behaviors can we ensure the success of instructional programs. The use of a phenotypic theory of child development expands the possible behavioral goals we can choose, for we are no longer restricted to the limitations of the genotypic theory.

Educators must also make a distinction between two categories of readiness: readiness to *learn* and readiness to *read*. Learning readiness includes basic skills that do not relate directly to reading but prepare the child to learn in the school environment. Reading readiness skills relate directly to the formal teaching of reading. The payoff to reading readiness is the book. The distinction between the two types of readiness is important if we are to be specific about behavioral objectives and if we are not to delude ourselves into teaching behaviors that do not further primary goals.

The following two rules of thumb are useful in ensuring success in preschool learning programs:

1. Define learning goals operationally. Be specific. Using "ability to read" as a learning goal is too general; "ability to read preprimers" is better. Better still is "ability to read Book X." Another example: "Ability to match a triangle stimulus to a like triangle imbedded in a square and circle" is more specific than "visual discrimination training."

2. Do not depend on transfer of learning. *Transfer* describes the shifting of responses learned in one situation to responses in another. Because they do not specifically define the stimuli and responses, many educators erroneously assume transfer of learning from one set of responses to another. But the sets may be operationally different, and transfer may therefore not occur. There is no convincing evidence to assume, for example, that auditory discrimination of a tinkling bell transfers to auditory discrimination of oral language sounds. In fact, evidence indicates that mastering the former is not a prerequisite to learning the latter. Many standard preschool activities have little transfer to reading readiness or related language skills. Even "just talking" may not relate significantly to achieving the types of language skills necessary for school success. It is useful, therefore, to train children for specific operational goals rather than for transfer. This is a sort of "play-it-safe" policy, because some transfer is bound to occur. As long as we do not bet on it, however, we can ensure the learning of specific operations and be delightfully surprised when transfer occurs.

Summary

The deprivations that lead to language and perceptual deficits in some children may be so severe that they cannot be remediated. The children of *some* lower socioeconomic class families are certainly this disadvantaged, and the technology of preschool education is not sufficiently developed to compensate for such extreme deprivations. We do not know enough about which methods are most valuable for these children, nor do we know the correct sequences and intensities of stimulations necessary to offset their deprivations. We do not even know the dimensions of these deficits.

If we add to these problems strict limitations of time and facilities, we find the preschool in the potential position of trying to attempt more than is possible. The preschool program can be filled with activities that keep children busy but are a waste of the already limited time to attain the basic goal—preparation for elementary school. This misuse of resources is one major finding in the Headstart evaluation studies reported by Wolfe. [12] In the first year of the program, many Headstart staffs were honest enough to admit that they were not sure they were serving their children's needs. But they consoled themselves with the old rationalization, "At least the program will do them no harm." The fact is that this situation is detrimental to disadvantaged preschoolers because time increases the amount and intensity of their deficits. That is why we must delimit preschool goals to the specific behaviors that ensure disadvantaged children's success in the early elementary grades. A preschool program for disadvantaged children should prepare them to learn to read the books and write the words that will be expected of them in grades 1 and 2.

If reading is defined as the processing of a symbol of a symbol of experience

$$\text{Experience} \longleftarrow S_1 \longleftarrow S_2$$

then preschoolers should be given those experiences and oral-aural symbols for the words they must eventually read. They must be given auditory and visual perceptual training of sounds and letters they will meet in the preprimers, first readers, or phonic exercises. They must take trips to places that provide the specific experiences and accompanying oral language symbols they will need to read specific books. They must see pictures and hear stories that prepare them to read specific books. This is *reading* readiness. Some socially disadvantaged children are so perceptually and cognitively deprived, so unable to concentrate or fixate on an auditory or visual stimulus, so poor in perceptual development, so devoid of oral language, sequential thinking, and mastery of basic linguistic patterns, that they are even not ready for reading readiness. They need a "basic training" program geared to goals described by defining learning processes operationally: a *learning readiness program*. It is important to discriminate between the two: The first has reading a book as the operational goal; the second, reading readiness. Materials and methods geared to specific goals for each program are described in the following two chapters.

References

1. G. E. Chittenden, M. Nesbitt, and B. Williams, *Essentials of Nursery Education* (Washington, D.C.: National Association for Nursery Education, 1948), pp. 7–8.
2. J. C. Foster and M. L. Mattson, *Nursery School Education* (New York: Appleton-Century-Crofts, 1939), p. 12.
3. Y. Bergamini and W. Swanson, "Does Kindergarten Make a Difference?" *School Executive,* 74 (December 1954), 54–55.
4. National Education Association, *For Your Information* (Washington, D.C.: National Education Association, July 1952), p. 2.
5. M. A. Marlowe, "A Comparison of the Effects of Kindergarten Experience on Third-grade Reading Achievement of White, Negro and Puerto Rican Children" (Unpublished master's thesis, Yeshiva University, 1964), chap. 2.
6. A. Gesell *et al., The Embryology of Behavior: The Beginnings of the Human Mind* (New York: Harper & Row, 1945), pp. 35, 249, 258.
7. ————, *Vision, Its Development in Infant and Child* (New York, Hafner, 1967).
8. S. Alan Cohen, "A Study of the Relationships Among Measurements of Reading, Intelligence and Vision Development, Using a Dynamic Theory of Vision in Socially Disadvantaged Junior High School Children" (Unpublished doctoral dissertation, Boston University, 1965), pp. 30–34.
9. J. McV. Hunt, *Intelligence and Experience* (New York: Ronald Press, 1961), chaps. 5–9.
10. J. Piaget, *The Origins of Intelligence in Children* (New York: International Universities Press, 1952).

11. J. Bruner, *The Process of Education* (New York: Vintage, 1963).
12. M. Wolfe and A. Stein, "Long-range Effect of Preschooling on Reading Achievement" (Unpublished study, OEO Project 141–61, Study III, Ferkauf Graduate School of Education, Yeshiva University, 1966).

Chapter Eight

Teaching Learning Readiness

The learning readiness program described in this chapter consists of four major parts: teaching control; teaching routine; teaching physiological readiness, or learning to learn; and teaching language and concept development. Each section describes methods, and, where possible, materials and sources. Complete listings of these materials appear in the Appendix.

Teaching Control

The first purpose of a learning readiness program is to prepare children to operate in a schoolroom shared by other children and adults. It is erroneous to assume that all socially disadvantaged preschoolers need psychotherapy. Certain subgroups of culturally deprived children, for example, do appear to have a higher proportion of emotionally disturbed children than are usually present in the classroom. Yet, preschool programs on New York City's Lower East Side and others in the Mississippi delta region did not appear to have a higher incidence of emotionally disturbed children than middle class preschools. In fact, certain Headstart projects that I have observed appeared to serve youngsters with fewer manifestations of interpersonal problems than those in most suburban middle class preschools. Whatever other deprivations these children had, they did not seem to lack love, parental concern, and relatively good care considering their poverty-stricken environments.

Socially disadvantaged deprived children have a range of needs as great as that of middle class preschoolers. A small minority who come from overly restrictive homes need more freedom—something closer to the play therapy atmosphere. A second group needs strong structuring. The latter group, larger than the first, must be organized and directed, because they have been unable to organize themselves physiologically or emotionally. The largest group should be given more alternative activities from which to choose at the beginning of a preschool program, but fewer as the program progresses.

Whether we approve or disapprove, most schoolrooms are restrictive, and we must prepare socially disadvantaged children for the environment in which they will have to live. The goal of the preschool is to accomplish this with a minimum of stress and conflict, and to help the children retain adequate self initiative. If we educate them sufficiently, enough of them will attend the Berkeleys of tomorrow and, on equal ground, confront the system with pressures that may lead to change. Our primary job now is to get them on that equal ground.

There is so little we know about techniques for teaching control. In general, most children learn to conform more or less to the restrictive school environment. The disruptive children are so easily noticed that we tend to forget the fact that most children are not disruptive—an indication that the school environment, as it presently exists, is effective in teaching control. The problem is for most of us to get over the guilt of having to force children to "knuckle under." Their psyches are not so brittle as to suffer irreparably from this type of restriction. In fact, most children have many alternative outlets available to blow off steam and are not really "knuckling under" as much as some teachers think. The only specific suggestion that can be offered here is to alert teachers to reward children who maintain self-control *before* these children ask for reward. When a child is *spontaneously* or *unconsciously* behaving well, he should be rewarded. When he misbehaves, he should be ignored as much as possible. The emphasis should be on positive reward for spontaneous self-control.

Teaching Routine

If Johnny enters the preschool and drops his jacket anywhere, the teacher's reaction should not be punishment but redirection: she tells Johnny to pick up the jacket and hang it in an appropriate place. If necessary, she walks him through these activities in much the same way that she would teach him long division. If Sarah bounces play blocks off classmates' heads, the teacher acts to restrict her by removing the blocks and giving her something else to work with. If she prefers to play with blocks, she can be shown what to do with them and what not to do with them. The point is that the teacher *teaches;* she does not wait for the child to "discover" the correct behavior. Certain skills are best taught directly without discovery, and classroom routine is one of them.

Second, in teaching the daily routine, the teacher should not subvert. John Adams once commented that the worst type of tyranny is subtle; behind the sugary platitudes of the demagogue is deadly manipulation by the tyrant. Not only in preschool, but throughout the grades, teachers tend to hide behind rhetorical questions and false fronts labeled "discovery technique" or "nondirective" teaching. When Sarah bounces a big block off Roberto's head, the teacher should not say, "Now, Now! We don't want to do that, do we?" Sarah obviously wanted to do it. Removing Sarah or the blocks—a straightforward, direct restructuring of the situation without hostile reprisals—will teach her more efficiently than disarming facades. Children resent teachers who try to depersonalize them; they are more comfortable and healthier with an overt authoritarian than with a polite, subtle despot.

Third, early preschoolers are not cooperative animals. They tend toward parallel play, going about their activities side by side with minimal interchange. Stone and Church suggest that children gain satisfaction by other children's nearness, even in parallel play. [1] Often, other children are merely convenient objects to sit upon or to take toys from. Such interaction—or more accurately, lack of cooperation—is "natural" to early preschoolers, but it is not conducive to types of behaviors necessary for schoolroom survival. Children will eventually learn how to interact by discovering that to sit upon another child is to invite uncomfortable retaliation. However, preschool teachers ought not to overlook themselves as a potent operant in the preschooler's environment. They should not miss the chance to demonstrate and teach correct interpersonal behavior. The most important factor in demonstrating such behavior is honesty—letting the child know when his behavior is unacceptable. Such feedback is not punishment; it is knowledge, followed by a demonstration of correct behavior.

Fourth, deprived children need verbal interaction with teachers. However, verbalization must be contiguous with overt behavior. With Sarah, "No more blocks because you throw them. Let's see you make something with clay," is accompanied by removal of the blocks or relocation of Sarah. Younger children, especially severely deprived children, need to hear language for instructional purposes, although action is a better teacher at this age.

Thus, the first operations to be learned by the preschooler are those necessary for carrying out classroom routines:

1. Housekeeping
2. Interacting with peers and adults
3. Care of the self
4. Conforming to prescribed activities
5. Conforming to rules
6. Learning to handle school materials correctly

When possible, these goals are achieved by a discovery technique, but usually teacher direction will be necessary. Teaching correct behavior, not punishing incorrect behavior, is the primary method to be used. In addition, heavy emphasis on action-demonstration with accompanying verbalization, rather than verbal explanation alone, is necessary for teaching at this level.

Teaching Physiological Readiness

The literature on deprivation in socially disadvantaged children stresses two approaches. First, the Hunt school suggests the need for more early perceptual and perceptual-motor experiences in culturally deprived children. [2] The other school of thought stresses linguistic conditioning, oral language development. Both schools have the same goal: concept formation, intellectual or cognitive development. They are not mutually exclusive. In a brilliant monograph, Bereiter [3] attacks the assumption of the first school and supports the verbal or linguistic group. Although Bereiter's arguments are powerful, it is not necessary to choose one side or the other. The evidence on both sides indicates that we should provide culturally deprived children with learning to learn training both on a perceptual-motor and on a linguistic level.

Materials and Methods

In Chapters Five and Six the case for physiological readiness was presented, available programs were listed, and the experimental program for early perceptual-motor levels piloted at Mobilization For Youth was described. The following are additional selected published materials and methods for teaching physiological readiness that appear promising for culturally deprived preschoolers (see the Appendix for full data for sources of materials).

The Getman-Kane P.A.S.S. Program. G. N. Getman, coauthor of this program, is a principal investigator in Gesell's research on vision development. [4] The program consists of template forms for basic geometric shapes in two sizes, a 2-degree sloping tracing board with a series of developmental tracing patterns, a set of 35 mm tachistoscopic slides for visual memory and patterning, and a step-by-step manual that guides the teacher in conducting training in six basic areas: general coordination, balance, eye-hand coordination, eye movements, form perception, visual imagery.

Since perception of symbols is related to perceptual motor or physiological development, the sequence in Getman-Kane materials is from coordinating the body systems to balance and form discrimination to manipulating abstract space and spatial symbols. P.A.S.S. exercises first re-create the experiences of infancy and early childhood (body parts and their coordination), then the higher-level coordinations involved in visual development. The sequence then is form perception exercises, symbol perception and recall, and—finally—letters and numbers. The manual includes instructions for making and modifying other supplementary training materials. The problem with this and other similar programs is that they require a low pupil-teacher ratio. Groups with ratios above 3 to 1 are difficult to manage. The use of teacher aides is perhaps the best solution to this problem. We used school dropouts, upper-grade helpers, parents, and volunteers in one pilot project of the Getman-Kane program.

Kephart, **The Slow Learner in the Classroom.** This textbook outlines the theory and describes the activities that will teach the early levels of Getman's program. Most of Kephart's techniques are drawn from direct contact with Getman's work, and this book is a good supplement to the Getman and Frostig programs.

The Frostig Program for the Development of Visual Perception. This kit provides rexograph masters of exercises in five areas of perceptual development as measured in Frostig's *Test of Visual Perception Development.* A manual of directions with a short rationale explaining the program is included. Skills cover training from the simplest activities in discriminating body positions through complex problems of higher perception.

This program is valuable for children at slightly higher levels of development (kindergarten through grade 1) because most of the kit is made up of pencil and paper rexograph exercises. In general, we found first- and second-graders in slum schools so deficient in visual perception development that this material was too advanced for them. Although the manual covers directions for teaching earlier skills on the motor-tactual-kinesthetic levels, the presentation is too sketchy. Both Getman and Kephart do a better job on these levels. Frostig depends too much on the teacher's ability to expand on the theory and examples presented in the manual. However, coupled with the Getman package, it is an effective program in visual development on the upper levels.

The Winter Haven Lions Publications Committee Program. These sets of tests, instructional booklets, and learning materials were developed in a research project sponsored by the local Lions Club. Headed by Dr. Darrell Boyd Harmon, a committee of specialists from every major discipline set up a perceptual learning program in the local first and second grades. The result was a Getman and Kephart program (both of whom were members of the committee).

Teaching Resources. This subsidiary of *The New York Times* markets a full series of excellent perceptual materials in soft and hardware.

Consultants in Perceptual Training. Variations of the programs described have been successful in special schools and in clinicians' offices. Their incorporation into the preschool curriculum is still a problem, but the need is great enough for schools to attempt the job. A few educators and psychologists, who have had some contact with either Kephart or members of Getman-trained Optometric Extension Program study groups, can be called upon for help. Perhaps the best sources of consultants are optometrists trained under the Duncan, Oklahoma, Optometric Extension Program; the New Haven, Connecticut, Gesell Institute Vision Center; or the New York Optometric Center.

Special Equipment. Some equipment has been developed in our programs at MFY and the Ferkauf Feading Clinic. Modified balance boards and walking rails, together with sloping chalkboards and templates, can be inexpensively designed and built by school personnel.

The Montessori Method (SB 88) and *Dr. Montessori's Own Handbook* (SB 98). The Montessori preschool curriculum is the most complete learning to learn program with special emphasis on perceptual development. Essentially, Montessori programs revolve around thorough and sequential sets of manipulative materials and activities designed to teach basic perceptual and conceptual skills through discovery and self-direction. Starting with simple materials, the child moves along at his own pace to higher levels of complexity.

Included in the Montessori materials are excellent methods of teaching classroom routine and self-control. At its best, the Montessori school is probably the most promising technique for teaching culturally deprived preschoolers, but being at its best requires a flexible, nondoctrinaire Montessori teacher. Otherwise, Montessori schools can tend to be rigid; they can lack the freedom of American preschools, and they can lack adequate oral language development and verbal interaction between child and teacher.

Other Perceptual Training Programs. McLeod, *Readiness for Learning,* has a perceptual readiness kit as part of the Lippincott prereading program. A number of specific activities are clever and effective by themselves, but it is not a complete program. It would be unfair not to extend recognition to the Lippincott series for at least including an attempt to meet this important learning readiness activity, but using one of the more complete perceptual programs with the Lippincott readiness materials would make the series more effective.

Training in Sense Modality Shifts. Again in the light of Chapters Five and Six, we must recognize the probability that retarded readers, especially deprived children, will have a higher incidence of difficulty in sense modality shift, a factor to be considered under physiological readiness. Modality shift or perceptual shift involves the ability to process information through one sense modality and transfer it to another, or to coordinate information-processing through more than one modality simultaneously. Recent research indicates that there are relationships between cross-modal transfer, or poor auditory-visual integration, and reading ability. Although poor modal integration should not be considered as the cause of reading retardation, poor modality integration *may* be a contributing factor, because it fits the pattern of overall perceptual inadequacies described in Chapters Five and Six.

Birch and Belmont differentiated retarded readers from adequate readers, matched on all relevant variables, with a test of intermodal shift. [5] Retarded readers had more trouble matching a set of spatially distributed dots (visual input) with an "equivalent" set of temporally organized auditory stimuli than did adequate readers. Because one task involved processing of spatial (visual) factors and the other temporal (auditory), Blank and Bridger [6] carried the approach a step further by testing intramodal rather than intermodal shift. Instead of matching auditory stimuli (timed "beeps," second pause for short space, full second pause for long space) with printed dot patterns, two matched groups, one of retarded readers and the other of adequate readers, had to match a flashed pattern from a light source (visual stimuli but still temporally organized) with the printed dot patterns. Once again these tests were able to differentiate good from poor readers. Blank and Bridger concluded that a deficiency in applying verbal labels to physical stimuli leads to poor inter- and intramodal transfer of equivalent stimuli.

Other research related to cross-modal transfer difficulties was reported by Goins [7] and Poling [8] a decade or more ago. More recent work has been done by Katz and Deutsch [9, 10] and Lee and Loy. [11] All these studies suggest the possible value of working in inter- and intramodal shift at the learning readiness stage with children who already show retarded perceptual and language development.

No research has been done to test the effects of intra- or inter-modal training on reading achievement. In fact, no literature on methods of training exists, except what is implied in the tests of inter- and intramodal transfer. It is, then, a calculated guess that training in modality shift at the learning readiness stage might influence language and concept development. Although this hypothesis remains untested, such training should be tried in early childhood programs for deprived children. The training should be sequentially planned; it should start with simple and move to more complex stimulus-response combinations. For example, a first step would be to present auditory stimuli, such as patterns of taps on a drum or on the floor; children's responses might be tapping sequence with their feet, clapping their hands, beating on a drum, or walking according to the auditory stimulus pattern. On the simplest level, the children would produce the response motor pattern in the same way as the stimulus pattern is produced; that is, the teacher taps a pattern on a bell and the children translate this into an equivalent walking pattern. Next the auditory stimuli become patterns of short beeps or taps and long beeps or taps. Pupils match these auditory stimuli patterns to a pattern of colored sticks or paper in which red represents long and white represents short. Soon the words short and long can be used, or at least the visual symbols SH and L. The next stage would be to present the beeps and require the children to match them to equivalent dot patterns, as in the Birch and Belmont study. Finally, the stimuli can become patterns of a flashed light source matched to dot patterns, as in the Blank and Bridger research. The imaginative teacher can expand this rough scheme into many combinations of stimuli and responses that are both inter- and intramodal.

Teaching Language and Concept Development

Perhaps the most revealing research on language and concept deprivation in culturally deprived minority children has been done by Hess [12] and his students at the University of Chicago. In a number of cleverly designed projects, Hess has shown that inferior verbal interaction between mother and child in the first three years of life leads to a paucity of both expressive language and concept development in the child. This inferior verbal interaction between mother and child is reinforced by poor general verbal environment. There is some doubt that the school or any other agency can fully compensate for this early deprivation, although partial compensation may be possible. The quantity and quality of compensation can be increased if we analyze specific verbal processes and concentrate on methods of teaching the most crucial of these processes. In other words, just indiscriminately increasing the amount of verbal communication among culturally deprived preschoolers and teachers may have some minimal effect on children's language and concept development, but such minimal effects yield relatively minor educational payoff. Instead, if we define precise language goals and implement a thoroughly structured program around delimited goals, we are more likely to get closer to the quantity and quality of learning we seek.

Adjusting Methodology to Pupils: Operant Conditioning and Semi-automated Teacher Aids

Even the most culturally deprived child can be taught to associate verbal labels to specific stimuli or classes of stimuli. [13] The problem is not readiness, but methodology. That is, the fact that the child has the disadvantage of poor early verbal learning or refuses to communicate verbally is less important than the method used to teach him such skills at a later stage of development.

For example, Suzanne Salzinger [14] used a clown puppet whose nose lighted each time the child gave an appropriate oral response to a taped question. A number of research projects using operant conditioning with emotionally disturbed children or subjects who refused to communicate verbally have obtained excellent results by using automated feedback producers. The automated source (television screen, typewriter, or, in this case, clown puppet) seems to be "safer" to certain children. Whatever the reason, the use of an automated source of stimuli and feedback (reinforcers) is often an effective technique for improving oral communication. Using operant conditioning, the automated feedback operates only when the child gives the appropriate response. In her research, Salzinger found that the technique increased the children's speech rates.

Something as simple as a hand puppet and pseudoventriloquy may be more effective than "face-to-face" oral communication with those children who use minimal oral communication. The same technique as the teacher-controlled puppet can be used successfully on form boards. The child is rewarded by the "automated producer" when he makes the appropriate response; when his response is inappropriate—fitting a triangle into a space for a square—he is neither rewarded nor punished. This is an important ingredient of much of the Montessori material. On the receptive side of oral communication, certain children attend better to a tape-recorded story where the source, again, is an automated producer. I found that a group of disadvantaged Puerto Rican kindergarten children who would not respond orally to teacher-produced oral stimuli did respond to the same stimuli when the voice of the teacher was recorded on tape. By coupling a tape recorder to a filmstrip projector and isolating them by using individual headsets, the children felt safe enough to respond to the tape. A picture of a lion was presented. The tape said: "This is a lion. He is a beautiful animal. Can you say *lion?* Say the word *lion.*"

A beginning reading program using an automated visual and auditory producer called Audex is currently marketed by Educational Development Laboratories (Huntington, N. Y.) in conjunction with L. W. Singer Publishers, New York. It uses parallel reading books and requires oral, written, and push-button responses. Adaptation to early childhood programs is possible. Another more elaborate variation is the responsive environment equipment marketed by Edison Responsive Environments, Inc., New York, which has also produced the "talking typewriter." This equipment offers visual and auditory stimuli applying principles of operant conditioning. Unfortunately, programs for the machine are not yet fully developed.

The important point is that instead of waiting for the child to become ready, we invent methodology to teach the child as he comes to us. If necessary, we resort to teacher-controlled machinery that allows the child to interact with his environment to elicit positive feedback. Research indicates that a most promising methodology for teaching oral language development to preschoolers is built on this principle of operant conditioning.

Teaching Levels of Language Behavior

Vera John's analysis of language development in slum children [15] supplies us with a most useful teaching guide. John [16] and others agree that cognitive processes develop directly from the incidental learning of the structural aspects of language. In fact, according to Bereiter:

> From our earlier work in teaching concrete logical operations it became evident that culturally deprived children do not just think at an immature level; many of them do not think at all. That is they do not show any of the mediating processes which we ordinarily identify with thinking. They can not hold on to questions while searching for an answer. They can not compare perceptions in any reliable fashion. They are oblivious of even the most extreme discrepancies between their actions and statements as they follow one another in a series. They do not just give bad explanations. They can not give explanations at all, nor do they seem to have any idea of what it is to explain an event. The question and answer process which is the core of orderly thinking is completely foreign to most of them. [17]

John's analysis of language that must be taught to compensate for this severe deprivation consists of three major levels.

Labeling. Children must be taught the labels for observed phenomena. They must learn to associate simple verbal labels with foods, furniture, and colors—things they are familiar with. Most important, they must learn to understand what they hear and to say the names of the things they will read about a year or two after their preschool program. If the school system is using the Ousley and Russell *On Cherry Street* (Ginn) as a first-reader, the children must learn such labels as "birthday," "chair," "a walk," "mitten," "red," "door," "wagon," "bow-wow," "monkey," "airplane," "surprise," and "duck." In fact, counting words from the previous primer (*The Little White House,* Ginn), the preschooler destined for this bill of fare must have mastered 354 words, at least 15 percent of which involve labels largely unknown to severely culturally deprived children. Long before they are to read these books, the labels must be taught on both receptive and expressive channels of communication. Ideally, these children should learn the labels for objects in their immediate environments, and these same objects should appear in their primers. Unfortunately, most primers do not describe Harlem or an urban school; they tell stories about unreal children from Cherry Street who live in white houses. Unless training in labeling centers on things found in a white house or on Cherry Street, it may be of little help to the child in meeting the language demands made by the school.

In short, we must teach these preschoolers morphological analysis relevant to the language demands of the school. Perhaps someday the school will change its demands by changing some of the content of basal readers. Then we can teach labeling of disadvantaged children's real and immediate environments, with the assurance that these labels will be included in their first readers. Until we are assured of this, however, the preschool staff must teach the labels used in the basal readers of their respective schools if the curriculum is to pay off later, when it really counts, in terms of school success, success in life, and healthy self-concepts.

Relating. Children must be taught syntactical analysis and intra-verbal relations. After they have learned to associate the verbal label /bread/ with that thing they eat or that long brown loaf, they must put together two labels, /bread/ and /box/ to understand a second concept. They must be able to understand and to say /time/ when they mean "Time out!" or "It's time to go." They must recognize word sequences and groups taken from sentences in *On Cherry Street* that are equally appropriate for disadvantaged children's real and school environments. These are words and concepts they will encounter in grade 1.

Classifying. On this level the child must expand labels and word groups into concepts. The word received or transmitted as /bread/ must include concepts of crust, a slice, a loaf, white, soft, whole wheat, Russian pumpernickel (not in his first reader, but in his real environment), and, someday, food in general. Should bread not be associated as well with an odor or the taste of rolls, bagels, breadsticks? Is the man in the subway station selling hot pretzels, bagels, or bread? These are classifications or concepts that must be worked out by preschoolers. Some will relate to his real world, but others, unfortunately, will relate only to the middle class world of basal readers.

A Preschool Program for Language Development

How will the culturally deprived child learn these in the preschool? One of the most promising methods was developed as a direct outgrowth of John's analysis of language levels. For two years, Judy Pasamanick worked for the Institute for Developmental Studies of the New York Medical Center under Martin Deutsch and on Mobilization For Youth's Materials Development Unit staff under my supervision. During this time she observed, analyzed, and cataloged the most promising operations that occurred in a number of experimental classrooms in both Institute and MFY projects. (Some of these analyses were done for both research agencies and are on file at the Institute and at MFY). Mrs. Pasamanick edited these notes, adding some activities and materials of her own invention and deleting others. She reorganized the activities into types of language behaviors. The scheme is an elaboration of John's levels of behavior. In the Pasamanick program, labeling is called Level I: vocabulary development; Level II is called sequencing skills (relating); and Level III is called classification skills.

Within each level, Pasamanick ordered the tasks sequentially in four stages of linguistic development, progressing from simplest to most complex.

Stage I. Stage I is based upon experiences familiar to the children; that is, those experiences the children are most likely to come to school with. This stage attempts to crystallize the known and concentrates on labeling simple nouns and a few basic verbs.

Stage II. When the children have mastered Stage I, the teacher moves to Stage II, which attempts to expand the child's noun and verb repertoire.

Stage III. Stage III concentrates on expanding the use of language as an expressive and descriptive tool, so that sequencing tasks are introduced (storytelling, series of words, and so on). Descriptive words and connectors as well as nouns and verbs are developed.

Stage IV. Finally, in Stage IV the children use the language reinforced or developed in the early stages for categorizing, cataloging, and reasoning.

The sequencing of activities is carefully developed and cleverly interconnected. All the activities are built around areas of standard nursery and kindergarten materials and curriculums. They include manipulative equipment (blocks, puzzles, doll corner, and so on), discussion, stories, songs, rhythm games, dramatic play, art activities, outdoor play, trips, and snacks. Ideally, this completed program should contain three parts:

1. A manual for each stage.
2. A picture kit consisting of photos depicting multiethnic groups, concentrating upon black and Puerto Rican children in active physical and emotional states. These are used as bases for specific vocabulary tasks in the areas of verbal development and descriptive language, as well as for the teaching of sequence skills. Photographs of objects (tools, foods, animals) are used in conjunction with classification tasks.
3. A developmental series of storybooks organized cognitively to parallel the total language curriculum. The stories meet the dual function of providing children with good literature and structured learning. To achieve this latter purpose, a teacher's manual describes how to make the most of the cognitive implications within each story. A sufficient supply of inexpensive copies of each story should be available for children to borrow for home

use. Supplementary materials, records, visual aids, picture and color cards, sensory rings, and posters should be used with the books.

Pasamanick's scheme is valuable to early childhood curriculum specialists in the schools. It offers them an excellent rationale for developing ongoing Headstart and follow-up preschool programs.

A High-Intensity Language Program

One theme continues to reappear in this book: Compensatory education for culturally deprived children necessitates sharply delimited goals. Thus, in the preschool curriculum for culturally deprived children, general language enrichment as an instructional method, perhaps even as a goal, is ineffective. A high-intensity program in linguistic instruction must be superimposed on the traditional preschool curriculum. For example, 10- to 20-minute sessions of intensive instruction in language development can be interspersed among play activities. During the typical half-day session of preschool, two or three of these intensive training sessions can be spaced by periods of unstructured play and other traditional preschool activities.

During high-intensity training sessions, groups of four or five preschoolers meet with a teacher while the rest of the class is supervised by a teacher aide or assistant teacher. High-intensity sessions emphasize achievement; they are task-oriented. Children are directed to concentrate on language exercises presented by the teacher. Work, not play or competition, is emphasized—work being an exciting and rewarding stress situation. Unlike traditional "free" classrooms, high-intensity sessions require children to stay with the task. The task is selected and controlled by the teacher, who, of course, adjusts the method and the length of time to children's abilities to handle the task. No evidence exists to show adverse emotional or physical effects of such a program on children. Nor is there any evidence that children develop negative perceptions of learning. The notion that preschoolers cannot handle structured, short periods of high-intensity instruction is absurd. Not only can they handle it, but they enjoy it. Preschoolers love structure, they enjoy direction, and, before they are tainted by cultural distortions, they love to work and achieve.

A variation of this program was reported by Jean Osborn, an associate of Bereiter at the Institute for Research on Exceptional Children at the University of Illinois, in a paper presented at the American Educational Research Association convention, February 12, 1965. She reports using 20-minute periods of high-intensity teaching of grammatical structure and linguistic patterns in oral language to groups of severely deprived preschoolers. Because linguistic patterns and syntax in spoken English rely heavily on word structures (inflected endings and affixes), pronunciation or diction was included. Osborn also relied on vocabulary words that organize experience words, such as *people, food,* and *vehicles*. Finally, she applied Bernstein's model of restricted language, in contrast to elaborated language. The culturally deprived child already uses a restricted language, and he must learn a new language to succeed in school. Thus, the teacher does not start with the child's language, but instead teaches the new language as a foreign-language teacher might, using an oral-aural method of pattern drills:

Lesson goal: Teach big *and* little

T: "This block is big."
C: "This block is big." [Child *repeats* word containing concept.]
T: "Show me the big pencil."
C: Points to the big pencil. [Child *locates* concept and *demonstrates* it in action.]
T: "Tell me about that pencil."
C: "The pencil is big." [Child *uses* concept.]

The lesson expands by adding interrogative statements, negatives, and relative concepts of *big* (in which the pencil becomes small when coupled with a bigger pencil).

Lesson goal: Reinforce big *and* little, *teach negatives, teach interrogatives*

T: "This is the big apple. Give me the big apple."
C: Child gives teacher the apple.
T: "Which apple is this, the big or little apple?"
C: "This is the big apple."
T: "Which apple is that?"
C: "That apple is the little apple."

T: "Which apple is not big?"
C: "This apple is not big."
T: "That apple is not big. What is that apple?"
C: "That apple is little."

Special stress is put on the clear pronunciation of *in, on, and, or, than, big, bigger, is, isn't.* These words control meaning and are often slurred over in restricted language; the lack of precision makes meaning unclear and impedes development of the child's ability to think logically.

Prepositions and conjunctions are thoroughly presented: *in, on, above, under, beside, between, in front of, in back of, before, after.*

T: "I am on the table."
C: "I am on the table." [Child sits on table.]
T: "Where are you sitting?"
C: "On the table."
T: "Now say the whole thing."
C: "I am sitting on the table."
T: "Who is in the table?"
C: "Penny [a puppet] is in the table."

The teacher puts a big pencil on a book in a drawer and a small pencil under the book behind the paper. The child must verbalize the total series of actions: "Teacher put the big pencil. . . ." Here Osborn is training the children to manipulate words necessary for sequencing and for transferring actions to words. Children act out and speak combinations using the conjunctions. First, they learn to distinguish between *and* (two things) and *or* (choosing one of two). This is extended to three or more single things connected by *and* and *or*. In the next stage, groups of things are joined: "I picked up the white blocks and the red blocks." Using actions and words that symbolize actions, the sequencing is extended using *and* to connect words describing one object: "The red and white blocks or the red and yellow blocks." At the highest levels of complexity, words and statements are grouped in categories and these categories are labeled: "All these pictures show people. All these things are red. Those are blocks." The teacher uses pictures, books, toys, furniture from the doll corner, drawings on chalkboard, and the children themselves.

Osborn reported that this type of program showed dramatic results when the severely culturally deprived children in her experiment were post-tested on the *Illinois Test of Psycholinguistic Abilities*. The high-intensity model can accommodate any content. Osborn's language development program was geared to logical thinking, but a close look reveals how John's scheme of labeling, sequencing, and categorizing fits the program as well. The combination of high-intensity learning periods punctuating the traditionally "free" atmosphere of preschool classrooms is a promising modification of the idea that children should have freedom and play, rather than structure and work.

These early linguistically-oriented training sessions have been systematized and elaborated and are described in the Engleman and Bereiter text. [17] More detailed research projects with disadvantaged children as young as two years of age have been completed by the Bereiter group. The results in measured IQ and psycholinguistic abilities are most dramatic. [21]

Programing Concept Learning

Fowler [18, 19] attempted to stimulate conceptual development in culturally deprived black children and failed. Despite eight months of "personal warmth," small group learning, and use of play activity techniques in an experimental compensatory preschool program, he found no significant changes in cognitive functioning. Subsequent work led him to conclude that lack of systematic programing of stimuli will neutralize the effect of compensatory education. According to Fowler, "unless stimuli are ordered sequentially, it is difficult to regulate the flow of stimulation to conform to each child's rate, style, and level of acquisition." [20]

The key to programing stimuli for concept learning in preschoolers is for the teacher to master a model of concept teaching that he can apply to any situation or set of materials. Fowler's idea of programing is to provide a thorough sequence of stimuli to small groups of children at a very early age. The stimuli should be designed to teach the children to move from perceptual-motor manipulation of structures to abstractions (words or word sequences) that are manipulated (concepts).

To set up a stimulation program, the teacher selects a particular subject area. The selection of the subject depends upon the available materials or resources. If we recall the guidelines to building a preschool curriculum listed in Chapter Seven, relevance to reading in preprimers and first readers should be the first priority. Fowler goes so far as to claim that "Closeness of relation to the preschool child's interest in the dominant culture is secondary under the assumption that teaching techniques utilized are adequate to arouse and sustain interest in unfamiliar material. . . ." [18] After selecting the subject area, the teacher analyzes the subject into parts and subparts, and then analyzes the subject's relations to other subjects. For example, if the subject is "stores to shop in," the teacher analyzes the subject into types of stores, things in all stores, things in different types of stores, and so forth. There is no end to the analysis "within" that category. Then he "synthesizes" the store into part of a greater whole (buildings in the community, places to go, the community we live in). The analysis is expressed in both a teacher's guide and a concomitant collection of pictures, toys, objects, and list of trips to be taken.

The children's analyses follow a six-step scheme moving from simple to complex.

1. Gross perceptions of objects
2. The functions of each object
3. Salient features
4. Functions and relations to the whole
5. Relation of object, structure, and components to other structures and aspects of the environment
6. Classifying activities (sorting and grouping) according to functions and to abstractions (words)

To control for complexity, children start with objects or functions that are culturally close to them. Second, they move to simple structures; that is, gross attributes. Third, they move to objects and functions that have fewer parts, relationships, and mechanisms. They move from simple to complex in these dimensions.

Small groups can attack the concept learning sessions as a game or as a problem to be solved. The children perform three basic processes. On the easiest level, they *discriminate* and *identify*. This process may involve either verbal or motoric responses to a question such as, "Where is the drugstore?" The children may select the appropriate picture from a large group of pictures. The second process is for children operating on a more difficult level. They may have to *match* and *construct*. They may synthesize: "Put all the pictures about schools together," or "What goes with this?" (a picture of a wagon). When children can perform processes at the highest level, they are *grouping* and *classifying:* "Put all the pictures of things that will roll in one pile and of things that stand still in another."

These processes, Fowler reminds us, are embellished by pedagogical techniques that motivate the learner. Pictures can be put in boxes or pinned on walls as parts of murals. Simple tasks can be purposely complicated by requiring more or less verbalization or by requiring the children to hold concepts in their memory. A simple request, such as asking children to find a picture in a magazine at home of something that rolls, is a method of reinforcing concept formation at higher levels of complexity, for the child must maintain the concept over time and space. Fowler's model is an effective guide for planning concept learning training sessions in early childhood classrooms. The perceptive reader should have also noted the excellent opportunities for expanding oral language using John's model for labeling, sequencing, and categorizing.

Summary

Learning readiness involves two very practical—perhaps hardhearted, but also realistic—clusters of behaviors: classroom decorum or self-control and mastery of school routines. Because conformity to routine is the major criterion for judging pupil self-control in school, these factors are not necessarily separate. We must recognize that schools are restrictive and that preschools designed to prepare children to succeed in such a restrictive atmosphere must gradually impose enough external controls to make their children "acceptable" to the elementary school. Although it is sad to have to propose a program of control because of an institution's inability to tolerate reasonable but high levels of spontaneity, physical expression, and noise, it is simply true that most first-grade teachers look more favorably on the conforming child. Well-meaning educators responsible for educating disadvantaged children ought not to use them as wedges for innovations.

Wedges have a way of being scarred in the process of prying things open, and disadvantaged wedges have enough wounds to be healed without adding more. When innovation involves attacking basic psychosocial mores, such as conformity to school protocol, routine, and expectations of school behavior, less disadvantaged middle-class youngsters can serve as wedges.

The second two aspects of learning readiness—physiological readiness and language-concept development—are reasonable goals for the preschool. The former is relatively new to early childhood programs because so little was known about the development of cognition until the "age of Piaget." Now we know beyond question that the basis of intelligence or cognition as we measure it is visual motor and visual perceptual. It is time, however, to translate this knowledge into carefully structured programs at the preschool level. Language-concept development is the other half of the cognitive development process and is certainly old hat to early childhood specialists. What is relatively new is the introduction of carefully structured "academic" learning sequences to teach specific language patterns and specific concepts at the preschool level. This aspect is still new enough to be a controversial subject among early childhood teachers.

Finally, the category of learning readiness must be recognized as functionally separate from reading readiness. Too many early childhood teachers confuse the two. When children do not learn to read in first or second grade, these teachers advocate more readiness activities. The problem is that these activities still involve learning readiness behaviors, not reading readiness. Teachers must understand that learning readiness activities will not lead directly to success in reading. They may be necessary prerequisites to reading readiness, but unless the latter is taught, many children will not learn to read well. The next chapter describes what these reading readiness activities should be and how they differ from learning readiness.

References

1. L. J. Stone and J. Church, *Childhood and Adolescence,* 2nd edition (New York: Random House, 1968), p. 110.
2. J. McV. Hunt, *Intelligence and Experience* (New York: Ronald Press, 1961).
3. Carl Bereiter, *The Relative Importance of Verbal and Nonverbal Factors in Cultural Deprivation: Evidence from Children with Sensory Handicaps* (Urbana, Ill.: Center for Research on Exceptional Children, University of Illinois, 1965).
4. A. Gesell *et al., Vision, Its Development in Infant and Child* (New York: Hafner, 1967).
5. H. G. Birch and L. Belmont, "Auditory-Visual Integration in Normal and Retarded Readers," *American Journal of Orthopsychiatry,* 34 (1964), 852–61.
6. M. Blank and W. H. Bridger, "Deficiencies in Verbal Labeling in Retarded Readers," *American Journal of Orthopsychiatry,* 36 (1966), 840–47.
7. J. T. Goins, *Visual Perceptual Abilities and Early Reading Progress,* Supplementary Educational Monograph No. 87 (Chicago: University of Chicago Press, 1958), pp. 1–108.
8. D. L. Poling, *Auditory Deficiencies of Poor Readers,* Supplementary Educational Monograph No. 77 (Chicago: University of Chicago Press, 1953), pp. 107–11.
9. P. A. Katz and M. Deutsch, "Relation of Auditory-Visual Shifting to Reading Achievement," *Perceptual and Motor Skills,* 17 (1963), 327–32.
10. ――― and ―――, "Modality of Stimulus Presentation in Serial Learning for Retarded and Normal Readers," *Perceptual and Motor Skills,* 19 (1964), 627–33.
11. L. C. Lee and M. Loy, "Visual Retention Performance of Kindergarten Children as a Predictor for Reading Success in the First Grade Year" (Paper presented at the Social Research in Child Development Conference, Minneapolis, March 1965).
12. R. D. Hess and V. Shipman, *Cognitive Environments of Urban Preschool Children* (Progress Report, 1963, 1964, Urban Child Center, University of Chicago).
13. A. Hawkins and C. C. Spiker, "The Effect of Type and Amount of Preliminary Verbal Experience on a Subsequent Classification Task" (Unpublished monograph, 1964).

14. S. Salzinger, "Operant Conditioning of Continuous Speed in Young Children," *Child Development,* 33 (1962), 683–95.

15. Vera John and M. Deutsch, "The Role of Language in the Cognitive Processes of Middle-class and Lower-class Children" (Paper presented at American Association for Advancement of Science meeting, New York, December 1960).

16. ———— and ————, "The Intellectual Development of Slum Children: Some Preliminary Findings," *American Journal of Orthopsychiatry,* 43 (October 1963), 813–22.

17. Carl Bereiter *et al., An Academically Oriented Preschool for Culturally Deprived Children,* monograph (Urbana, Ill.: Center for Research on Exceptional Children, University of Illinois, 1965). Now elaborated as a full text: Carl Bereiter and S. Engelman, *Teaching Disadvantaged Children in the Preschool* (Englewood Cliffs, N.J.: Prentice-Hall, 1966).

18. A. Fowler, "A Study of Process and Learning in Three-year-old Identical Twins and Triplets Learning How to Read," *Genetic Psychology Monographs,* in press.

19. ————, "Cognitive Stimulation, IQ Changes, and Cognitive Learning in Three-year-old Identical Twins and Triplets," *American Psychologist,* 16 (1961), 373.

20. ————, "Concept Learning in Learning Children" (Paper presented at American Educational Research Association meeting, Chicago, February 12, 1965), p. 18.

21. C. Bereiter, *Acceleration of Intellectual Development in Early Childhood* (Washington, D.C.: U.S. Office of Education, 1967).

Chapter Nine

Teaching Reading Readiness

Present Methods of Assessing Reading Readiness

Two popular methods of assessing reading readiness are intelligence tests and reading readiness tests. Intelligence tests, however, are relatively weak predictors of reading readiness. Studies of relationships between IQ and reading are misleading because reported coefficients, more often than not, are correlations from studies of older children. For example, a study of relationships between Thurstone's *Primary Mental Abilities* tests [1] and reading comprehension scores of the *Iowa Tests of Basic Skills* [2] revealed coefficients of .70 and above. [3] Such high correlations were drawn from seventh- and eighth-graders. In kindergarten and first grade, the correlation coefficients between various measurements of intelligence and success in reading cluster around .45. [4, 5, 6] This low correlation is hardly adequate for predicting reading achievement for individuals.

For older children, the intelligence test becomes more verbal than for younger children. Thus, at the seventh-grade level, IQ and reading achievement tests appear to tap similar behaviors. This leads to higher correlations. But in the early grades, IQ tests are exceedingly weak at predicting reading success of individuals in grade 1. Over ten years ago, one well-constructed study reported a correlation coefficient of .23 between IQ and reading achievement in grade 2. [7] Since that time the same type of study has consistently turned up low correlations between IQ and reading in early elementary grades.

Reading readiness tests are only slightly more reliable than IQ tests in predicting reading success in the early grades. Berwick [8] found correlations of .13 to .49 on four subtests of the *Lee-Clark Reading Readiness Test*. [9] Other studies yielded coefficients of .26 to .50 between various readiness measurements and reading success in the first three grades. [10, 11] In ten different studies at Boston University, [12] the highest correlation between reading readiness tests and reading achievement was found on the *Gates Readiness Test,* which yielded a .55 coefficient. The other studies showed lower correlations.

Elsewhere the findings are consistent. Zingle and Hohol [13] reported a .40 coefficient between reading readiness tests and reading in a large Canadian population. Karlin reported a correlation of .36 between the *Metropolitan Reading Readiness Test* and reading achievement. When he factored out IQ and age, the correlation dropped to .25 with a test error measurement of .08. He concluded that it was "virtually impossible to predict from a reading readiness test score how well any child in the sample will do on the reading test." [14]

Three major reading readiness tests have undergone revision in recent years. Their predictive correlation coefficients have improved, but they are still relatively weak predictors. Nevertheless, these tests contain measurements of certain skills that, when combined with other learning readiness and psychosocial factors, are not only good predictors of reading success, but are probably causal factors as well. If these learning readiness and psychosocial factors were amenable to formal testing, the reading readiness test could be improved. In the meantime, factor analyses of reading readiness tests give us good clues to specific subskills that affect beginning reading. Before we consider these factors, let us look briefly at existing reading readiness programs.

Specific Behaviors in Published
Reading Readiness Programs

Reading readiness workbooks include nine types of skills. The most common exercise, called "language development," consists of a conglomeration of pictures that children are required to label. A second type of activity involves the child in matching pictures. This exercise consists of presenting the child with a stimulus picture and requiring him to match it with one of four choices. For example, if the picture is a toy sailboat and four pictures of various other toys are presented, only one of which is a sailboat, he must match sailboat to sailboat. Another visual matching task involves replacing the stimulus picture, like the sailboat in the above example, with triangles or other geometric shapes. A fourth type of exercise is called training in eye-hand-motor coordination. These exercises usually involve pencil and paper line drawings and include work in spatial orientation. Geometric shapes or drawings of meaningful figures (chairs, ladders, teddy bears, and so on) are arranged in rows with one facing the "wrong" way, and the child is required to select the one item that is different. Often, this exercise is presented as a matching task in which the child selects the response that is facing the same way as the stimulus picture.

Most programs include "ear training" in which the child is required to identify the nonword auditory stimulus presented by the teacher. Also, many reading readiness programs include some work with words near the end of the readiness sequence. Usually this includes three types of exercises: identifying initial consonant sounds, letter matching, and matching word outlines in which letters are replaced by word configurations.

Studies of specific behaviors found in reading readiness programs reveal low correlations between ability in most of these skills and success in reading. [4] Furthermore, a number of the skills found in reading readiness programs are not directly related to learning to read. They may be ingredients of a learning readiness program as described in Chapter Eight.

In addition to studies of predicting reading success, a number of longitudinal studies of good and poor readers have been completed in the past decade. [15, 16, 17] They give us some clues about the types of behaviors and experiences that produce good readers. These studies indicate that good readers come from homes where there are older siblings or parents who read to them, who value reading and books, in general, and who answer children's questions about words. From such homes come children who have a curiosity about words, are self-reliant, persistent, and have the ability to concentrate in school. They usually come into school with a knowledge of the alphabet, good auditory memory, ability to write their names, and the ability to copy from printed materials. Many of these children pretend to read even before they really can; they play with books and are very attentive to signs and symbols. In almost every case, these children have parents who are intensely interested in school and communicate this interest to their children. Many of these children come from economically disadvantaged homes, which is one reason for not being able to assume that all children from lower socioeconomic classes come to the school educationally disadvantaged.

To summarize, we know that both intelligence tests and reading readiness tests are weak predictors of reading success in early grades. But we also know from item analyses of reading readiness tests, as well as numerous studies of specific behaviors related to reading, that visual and auditory discrimination of words or word parts are good predictors of success in beginning reading. A careful analysis of these studies, using partial and multiple correlations, shows that visual and auditory discrimination of words or word elements, not of sounds or general shapes, are the two most crucial specific behaviors related to early reading success. For example, a child's ability to discriminate between the sound of a mooing cow and a quacking duck, or between numbers and geometric shapes, does not relate to reading significantly.

Alphabet knowledge appears to be the best single predictor of reading success in early grades. Perhaps the fact that all but two of the letters of the alphabet include one major sound of that letter in their names accounts for this relationship, and this may aid children in beginning phonics. The ability to discriminate letters is included in the larger skill of matching letters and reading them. These factors, plus the high predictive correlation, warrant the intelligent teaching of the alphabet in reading readiness, although this technique has not been in vogue for some years. If methods used to present these stimuli are consistent with the perceptual development of children, and if teachers desire to make letter sound and letter shape training as interesting as training in geometric shapes and general sounds, preschoolers will not be bored with their preschool.

The stress on visual discrimination of letters is further strengthened by research results from experimental psychology and later studies in beginning reading. Research indicates that higher animals do not discriminate by processing total shapes. Instead, they perceive fine details from which they induce the gestalt. This would suggest that fine discrimination of letters, *not whole words,* is the key to teaching visual discrimination of sight words. This fine discrimination of letter differences should be part of early childhood reading readiness training.

Finally, many commercially published reading readiness programs are overloaded with specific behaviors not directly related to learning to read. For example, these programs usually include exercises for developing eye-hand-motor coordination as a reading readiness skill even though this coordination is not specifically related to reading readiness. Poor eye-hand-motor coordination may be part of a perceptual dysfunction syndrome related to poor learning readiness in general. Of all the perceptual factors, eye-hand-motor coordination seems to be the best developed visual perceptual skill in socially disadvantaged underachievers, according to the study reported in Chapter Five.

A List of Basic Reading Readiness Skills and Perceptions

This list of seven core reading readiness skills and perceptions and of suggestions for teaching them in preschool, kindergarten, and early first grade is compiled according to the following three criteria.

First, research establishes high correlations between these factors and reading success in grade 1. The quality and quantity of these correlations, as well as empirical evidence, suggest a cause-and-effect relationship.

Second, this list is limited to specific types of activities that can be manipulated by the school. Preschool and kindergarten children need more than these seven areas of activity. Many socially disadvantaged children also need the activities described in the preceding chapter. All children need the enriching activities of the traditional preschool and kindergarten. It has already been pointed out, however, that most of these activities are present in the advantaged child's environment and that the middle class school's prereading programs are merely reinforcers of stimuli inherent in the environment. In certain deprived environments these stimuli are often not present to the degree that we would expect. As a result, the school's typical readiness program is relatively ineffective with deprived children. The purpose of focusing on these seven areas is to marshal the school's resources in the areas most likely to make a difference in the education of culturally deprived children.

Third, reading involves skills, attitudes, and general behaviors that permeate the total psychophysical organism. Because the task of making culturally deprived children ready to read is so great in relation to the limited facilities and time of the school, this list is restricted to seven specific behaviors most directly related to beginning reading instruction in the hope that schools will concentrate their resources in areas most likely to yield results. The seven reading readiness areas selected are:

1. Letter knowledge
2. Visual discrimination of letters and words
3. Auditory discrimination of sounds in words
4. Love of books and interest in printed symbols
5. Story sense and memory for sequence
6. Vocabulary for reading
7. Attention to the reading task

Subsequent research may eliminate one or more of these factors, may refine them to more specific operations, or may reveal additional factors. Some of the areas overlap because they contribute to the development of each other. The amount of space devoted to discussion of each area does not reflect its importance to the total reading readiness program. It reflects, instead, this overlap.

Ways to Teach Letter Knowledge

Knowledge of letters is, perhaps, the best single predictor of reading success in grade 1. This high correlation does not mean a cause-and-effect relationship between alphabet knowledge and ability to read. It may be that the preschool or kindergarten child who can recognize, write, and name letters, and is interested in them, is a product of an environment that has incidentally taught the child visual and auditory discrimination of letters and sounds and other skills and attitudes related to reading. Academically speaking, then, letter knowledge is probably not a cause, but an effect, of an environment that tends to produce children who are ready to read. Practically speaking, however, letter knowledge requires visual discrimination of letters and association of a grapheme with a specific sound. This association may establish a basis for the awareness of grapheme-phoneme relationships, and may orient the child toward reading and writing. For this reason it is included here as a "causal" factor.

How should letter knowledge be taught? Certainly not by dull drills. Alphabet jingles and songs with alphabet cards using a sing-along-and-point-with-me technique are fun for kindergarten children. Eventually, these children can point to the appropriate letters as they sing the jingle. Letter form boards are excellent methods for teaching visual discrimination of alphabet letters. One board, developed at the Institute for Developmental Studies in New York City, and another version, devised by Mobilization For Youth, were very successful in inner-city programs for preschoolers. Commercial companies have other versions (Creative Playthings, Inc., Playskool, and so forth). Of all the techniques I have used to teach alphabet knowledge, visual discrimination of letters and *p-b-d-q* reversals, the form board appears to be the most effective. By its very construction it applies the best principles of operant conditioning. Children waiting for their clinicians in the Reading Clinic of Yeshiva University's Reading Center begin to play with it informally. At first by trial and error and soon by visual matching, a child teaches himself by interacting with his environment. Each letter form fits its appropriate space so that the child is never able to complete the wrong match. He gets immediate feedback of either of two possibilities: (1) the task is not yet completed—the letter form is not yet in place; or (2) the letter form is in the correct place.

Magnetic plastic letters, letter templates for tracing, and play blocks with raised letters that can be used to imprint letters in soft clay are materials that fascinate children. All children love to see their names in print. The teacher can hold up a stimulus card and ask, "Who has this letter in his name?" Using this method, preschool and kindergarten children can compare names and find similar letters. This type of activity lends itself easily to many game variations. If letters are three dimensional, or are printed in large letters with contrasting figure-ground, they can be motorically or visually manipulated easily by children. The activities in auditory discrimination described below can be supported by displaying alphabet cards showing the grapheme for whatever phoneme is being taught.

Durrell's *Improving Reading Instruction* contains over twenty ideas for teaching letters. [18] Murphy and Durrell, in *Speech to Print Phonics,* offer ten systematic lessons on the alphabet that are particularly useful early in grade 1. [19] Lois Kalb, a member of Mobilization For Youth's Materials Development Unit, has outlined a number of alphabet games for the schoolyard and gameroom. She has found "Alphabet Hopscotch" a favorite children's game and has invented games involving large-muscle activities for learning letters.

By the beginning of grade 1, many children can alphabetize words and group words that begin or end with the same symbols. Younger children can do the same using large flash cards with big print and associated pictures. By placing letters or words in piles around the room and by placing bins or boxes labeled with large letters across the room, children can fetch and categorize to music. Phyllis Cerf describes interesting alphabet games in her manual to *Skilstarters* [20] that have been successfully tried in slum area preschools. In "Name Double Solitaire" a child uses a deck of alphabet cards in a pick-and-discard game. The object of the game is to get all the cards necessary for printing his name according to a model supplied by the teacher. In "Alphabet Pig," four decks of alphabet cards, each one a different color, are used in a pass-the-card version of "Hearts." Children build sets that consist of a single letter in four different colors. Versions of "Go Fish," "Alphabet Concentration," "Crazy Xs," "Alphabet Solitaire," and "Competitive Solitaire" are other alphabet games included in the materials and manual for *Skilstarters*. Children's games companies, such as Kenworthy, Milton Bradley, and Garrard Press, offer many manipulative alphabet games.

The early stages of Catherine Stern's *Structural Reading Program,* [21] Buchanan-Sullivan Associates' *Programmed Reading,* [22] and many other newer beginning reading programs using a phonic-linguistic approach have valuable techniques for teaching letters. In evaluating such programs, however, teachers must be certain that the activities are interesting to children, that they fit the large-muscle, gross-motor level of preschoolers, that children do not end up reciting alphabets, but are able to manipulate, discriminate among, and even print letters on large chalkboards with thick chunks of chalk. [23] It is imperative that methodology fit the developmental stage of the child. The problem is rarely *what* to teach as often as it is *how* to teach.

The orders of difficulty in learning letters vary according to the task required of the child. When the teacher calls out a letter and the child is asked to point to it, the order of letter difficulty is different from the situation in which the child names the letter directly. The research done by Dr. Helen Murphy on orders of difficulty is reported in Durrell's book. [18] In general, research in spelling at Boston University's Secondary Reading Clinic indicates that matching letters to other letters (matching) and finding letters in a series after a stimulus letter has been shown and removed (recognition) are the two easiest tasks for children. Finding the letter in a series after it is named by the teacher or pupil teammate, or naming a letter to which the teammate or teacher points (identification), is more difficult. More difficult still is writing a letter from dictation (reproduction). Ultimately, the objective is to use letters automatically in writing and reading without thinking about it (habituation).

1. Matching
2. Recognition
3. Identification
4. Reproduction
5. Habituation

The five orders of difficulty are an excellent guide to teaching other skills beyond letter knowledge. For example, the Reading

Clinic of Yeshiva University's Reading Center uses them as steps in skill mastery (easy to more difficult) to teach sight words and spelling.

Ways to Teach Visual Discrimination of Letters and Words

Research in visual discrimination in children still leaves many unanswered questions. We do know, however, that most young children beginning reading *do not recognize words by their total shapes.* Over half a century ago, one researcher found that children depended upon certain familiar letters within a word. [24] Arthur Gates [25] verified this twelve years later. More than forty years ago, another researcher not only verified these findings but isolated such letters as *i, ll, g, o,* and *k* within the context of words as principal cues to word recognition. [26] Over thirty years ago, Hill [27] pinpointed the same letters as the principal cues at the beginnings and ends of words. In reviewing all the research, Anderson and Dearborn [28] concluded that young children search out one or two letters or small groups of letters to recognize words. This research, along with abundant evidence that visual discrimination of letters and words is directly related to success in beginning reading, [29, 30, 31, 32, 33, 34] forces us to reemphasize the need to teach letters early and to teach them well. The best way to ensure good visual discrimination of letters and words is to teach letter knowledge thoroughly.

In addition to suggestions in the previous section, kindergarten children can be asked to match their name cards to large white envelopes with their names clearly lettered. Labeling two or three items in the room until most children recognize the words, then switching the labels so that they are mislabeled and challenging the children to seek the correct match, is a useful technique. Allen and Allen offer *Read Along with Me,* [35] a kit to be used in a 1-to-1 situation. It contains a number of letter games, as well as a beginning reading technique, for use by volunteers and nonprofessionals working with young children. Lowry's *The Basic Phonics Program* [36] has excellent alphabet cards and letter discrimination games and exercises for the early grades. Some of these activities can be used in kindergarten, whereas others need slight modification if they are to be tried below grade 1. Same-different games using flash cards of children's names, common sight words, or letters are effective. Copying words from charts or signs is an old standby that still works. Primer-size typewriters in preschool are exceedingly effective in teaching letter discrimination. There is an excellent series of tracing exercises on letters and numbers in the Getman and Kane *Physiology of Readiness* manual. [37]

One particularly effective game, called "Going Somewhere Solitaire," is included in Cerf's *Skilstarters*. [20] This game uses illustrated word cards in four decks of two-, three-, four-, and five-letter words, respectively. Children flip a fifth deck of alphabet cards and build the words, starting with two letters and moving to five. A number of tachistoscopes are available with exercises for early first grade. Some of these are described in the Appendix. A tachistoscope is an automatic device that flashes visual stimuli at controlled speeds. Teachers are cautioned against using tachistoscopic materials that present pictures, numbers, geometric shapes, or any nonletter or nonword stimuli. As discussed earlier, there is no substantial evidence to indicate that there are any causal relationships between visual discrimination of these stimuli and learning to read. Teachers are also cautioned about large-group instruction in visual discrimination or letter knowledge. These activities should be done with very small groups. Many of the activities described are self-directing and individual. Only those children who need the training at a level (steps in skill mastery) and a rate consistent with their needs should be involved.

Ways to Teach Auditory Discrimination of Sound in Words

The ability to notice the /b/ sound in *boy, bake, ball,* and *boat* and the ability to discriminate the separate sounds in the spoken word *baby* are auditory discrimination skills necessary for success in beginning reading. Ability to identify sounds in *general,* such as a tapping drum, a tinkling bell, mooing cows, and honking automobile horns, and the ability to pronounce words spoken by adults *are not causally related to reading.* These activities may entertain preschoolers and their teachers and visitors, but they are functionally unrelated to success in beginning reading. Pronunciation may be used as part of a technique for teaching auditory discrimination of sounds, but a child's ability to mimic words spoken by the teacher is no indication of his ability to hear separate sounds in words. Furthermore, auditory discrimination is not auditory acuity. Sharpness of hearing and sharpness of vision are not the same as auditory or visual discrimination. Hearing loss as measured on a decibel meter or by a whispering teacher does not tell us whether or not a child can discriminate sounds, just as the Snellen eye chart does not tell us how a child sees written symbols. Certainly severe losses of acuity may incapacitate the learner. But slight losses (and in many cases, severe losses) cause many children to overcompensate by perfecting hypersensitive discrimination skills. More important, perhaps, is the reverse of this statement. Good auditory or visual acuity in no way tells us whether or not a child can discriminate letters or sounds. In fact, the audiometer and the Snellen eye chart are two of the most useless tests administered in the school. Most teachers are adept at spotting children with acuity problems without them.

Auditory discrimination is adequate when a child can recognize spoken sounds at the beginning, middle, and end of words as being either the same or different. If he does not know his letters, the "same-different technique" is the only way to test this skill. If the child knows his letters and can already associate a letter with a sound, he is more than halfway to this crucial goal of auditory discrimination. A third way to test for auditory discrimination is the same-different technique in which, instead of presenting oral stimuli, the teacher uses pictures.

Phonic programs will usually fail unless children are thoroughly trained or have previously mastered auditory discrimination of sounds in words. Neither artificial orthographies, nor orthographic aids such as diacritical marks or color codes, nor phonic programs called "linguistic" will be successful with children who cannot hear the difference between, for example, /pit/ and /pet/. In general, plosives /p/, /b/, /t/ seem to be the easiest for children to discriminate with fricatives /f/, /v/, /s/ or /z/ as in /raise/ and nasal sounds /m/, /n/ next. Sibilants /s/ as in /sail/, /ch/, /sh/, /j/, /ge/ are more difficult, and short vowel sounds markedly harder to discriminate than long vowel sounds. The young child has difficulty when phonemes from the same group appear in close proximity; for example, /chalk/ is easier than /charge/ because /ch/ and /ge/ sounds are so close. Letter blends that form phonemes are difficult for young children, especially the most common blends that use *l* or *r*.

Durrell gives many valuable suggestions for teaching auditory discrimination in *Improving Reading Instruction.* [18] Reciting verses that emphasize repetitive sounds, listening to words in sound families and repeating them are commonly used techniques that are successful. Although Catherine Stern's *We Learn To Listen,* the first book in the Structural Reading Series, [21] has an excellent program for auditory discrimination, the Durrell, Sullivan, and Murphy workbook, *Building Word Power,* [38] is, even after twenty years, still one of the best programs in early word-attack skills training. Lyons and Carnahan in *Phonics We Use,* Book A [39] have some auditory discrimination of sounds in word exercises using picture stimuli. Teachers are cautioned to analyze carefully workbook exercises labeled "auditory discrimination," because many really contain visual, not auditory, tasks.

Singing along with children's records that emphasize specific sounds is an extremely valuable exercise in kindergarten. The *We Speak Through Music* series [40] of long-playing records was highly effective in auditory discrimination training for Puerto Rican and black children on New York City's Lower East Side. Kindergarten teachers can designate a letter and its sound for each week of the school year. During *M* Week, for example, children listen for and collect words that begin with the same sound as the beginning of /mom/, /make/, /mailman/, /Mike/, and so forth. Children look for pictures or report words they have heard with the sound of the week. During *M* Week both the teacher and children can overemphasize the initial /m/ sound when they pronounce such words.

Early childhood teachers can invent dozens of ways to integrate methods of teaching sounds in words with their usual pre-kindergarten and kindergarten program. For example, a standard technique for fostering visual memory in kindergarten is to place six or seven items on a felt board. After the children have studied the board, the teacher removes one item and the children must try to remember the missing item. During *M* Week the teacher might limit all items for this exercise to things with names beginning with the /m/ sound. The visual symbol *M* should be prominently displayed and printed by those children interested in such activities. Early association of phoneme with grapheme is valuable, and many children are ready and eager to play with letters. However, teachers must not confuse visual discrimination training with auditory discrimination training. They must be careful, too, not to isolate the sound but to present it always in words: Not /mmm/ in isolation and certainly not /muh/; but /mmmman/ in its entirety with overemphasis of the beginning sound is most effective. Teachers should also beware of confusing auditory input with oral output. Auditory discrimination of sounds in words is an input skill. It may or may not be related to output in an individual; that is, speech articulation problems in themselves do not cause auditory discrimination problems. Well-educated Puerto Ricans tend to drop the ends of their words in speaking both Spanish and English. Their short /a/ sound is pronounced as a Boston /au/ or /o/ as in /on/. In fact, /and/ sounds like Boston /on/ when pronounced by most Puerto Ricans who are highly literate in English. Yet they hear sounds of English accurately. Therefore, speech patterns do not necessarily have to be changed to teach auditory discrimination of sounds in words.

The most common method of teaching recognition of a particular sound in a word, however, is to train a child to articulate the sound in context of the word. This does not imply that an expressive behavior necessarily accompanies receptive behavior. The child is taught to articulate the sound in word context so he can hear it and associate it with a kinesthetic input. The teacher asks the child to feel what his mouth is doing: "What are your lips doing at the beginning of /man/?" Often she uses a mirror to show the child what his mouth is doing. Thus, oral articulation of the sound in the word provides auditory, visual, and kinesthetic inputs increasing the stimuli for learning purposes. But once the child recognizes the sound, it is no longer necessary for him to pronounce it in a dialect that is unnatural to him. To argue that Puerto Rican, black, and Mexican American children who speak English with ethnic dialects must be retrained in standard dialect is absurd on two counts: first, this assumes there is a standard dialect; second, most of us bred in Boston, Bayonne, Charlotte, the French Quarter of New Orleans, the Chinatown section of San

Francisco, or in any of a thousand other American neighborhoods are able to discriminate sounds in words adequately, in spite of our dialects. A Spanish American dialect (if there is *one*) is just one more regional and/or ethnic dialect and should be accepted as such. Children with such dialects have a right to them and a right to be proud of them. Lois Kalb, a former MFY staff member, has used dialect differences as a teaching asset in the urban classrooms populated with highly mobile ethnic minorities. She asks children with different dialects to pronounce the same word and uses this technique as a stepoff to lessons in auditory discrimination.

Finally, with older children so retarded in reading that they must go back to basic readiness skills, taped word pairs that are the same or different are presented through headsets. Sounds are taught by contrast (moving from maximal to minimal differences); the exercise requires the child to designate a simple response such as circling S (same) or D (different). Using these exercises with socially disadvantaged fourth-graders, we obtained learning curves that reached perfect discrimination scores in fifteen minutes or less for any specific pair of phonemes.

Ways to Teach Love of Books

Most children treasure books that they receive as gifts. The wilful destruction of schoolbooks cited by teachers of children in middle and upper grades usually expresses negative attitudes toward school and toward dull or outdated books, attitudes not unique to the lower class child. The best way to teach a love of books, therefore, is to purge every classroom of dull, worn textbooks, especially the traditional basal readers. At least 200 colorful storybooks should be in every prekindergarten and kindergarten classroom. In grades 1 through 3 the number should jump to 250 or 300. Although the books may be the property of the school library, they must be stored and used in the classroom. They must be distributed helter-skelter in bins or on long tables, not neatly placed on bookshelves that obscure the colorful, well-designed covers. Books must be available to the children; they must be used, used up, and replaced.

These books should include everything from *Cat in the Hat* to *Now We Are Six*. All the best sellers of children's literature should be purchased. American Library Association recommended lists are a good start, but more valuable are publishers' own lists of good sellers. The American Library Association lists reflect certain biases. For example, some of the books that have delighted and entertained children for years have never received professional librarians' endorsements, perhaps because librarians have tended to avoid books containing wild fantasy, sexual symbolism, and violence. But these are organic to all normal children and adults, and stories that deal with them should be included in the children's classroom library. Purchasing good children's books for every classroom is one of the most important priorities in expending federal government funds for disadvantaged achievers in the early grades.

One simple and effective use of funds from the Elementary and Secondary Education Act, Title I, is to purchase a book for each preschooler's birthday. A parent-school program in which parents or older siblings are given children's books to read to young children is an excellent technique. Preschoolers can discuss or report stories that have been read to them. A gift of one book for every five books read to him gives the disadvantaged child the opportunity to build his own library. By trading off some of his earned books for new ones, he can continue to hear new stories and expand his library. This is an effective technique through the elementary grades, especially when teachers plan weekly trading sessions or book fairs.

Reading sessions, using volunteers, upper-grade children, Neighborhood Youth Corps, and school dropouts, can introduce children to the world of literature. Weston Woods sells tapes, filmstrips, and books for read-to sessions. Schools can build their own libraries of read-to stories and utilize the inexpensive headset and coupler arrangements described in the Appendix.

Ways to Teach Story Sense
and Memory for Sequence

Using storybooks in each kindergarten and first-grade classroom will do more to develop good story sense in children than any drill or workbook. When children have a sense of the dramatic, when they retell the major sequences of a story line, and when they begin to invent their own story lines, a teacher knows they are developing story sense.

Children should have developed the basis for story sense before they begin formal education. Two major types of activities appear to contribute to this development between two and four years of age. First is the daily storytelling experience many children, both economically advantaged and disadvantaged, receive from their parents or older siblings. Initially, these sessions usually take the form of family folk tales, verses, and songs. Toddlers love repetition, particularly repetitive sequences: "First I knock at the door (forehead), then I ring the bell (nose), then I look in the window (eyes), and now I open the door (mouth)." "This little piggy went to market" is practically universal in one form or another. Children love their parents to repeat these over and over again.

Teachers should not assume that lower class minority group children miss these experiences. Although such children may be unable to demand enough parent attention, they may engage in these interactions with older siblings or other members of an extended family. Lower class children are more likely to miss the second stage of story sense development—read-to and read-along —simply because there are no books in the home. Special programs for disadvantaged preschoolers should, therefore, include heavy dosages of read-to sessions.

Random House publishes taped libraries called *Sights and Sounds,* which are sets of tapes and companion children's books. Preschoolers listen over headsets to stories read by professional actors. At the same time, the children follow the story in a book. All the children in a single classroom are able to hear and see different stories simultaneously. Children are not merely spectators in a read-to session. For example, in the *Sights and Sounds* taped library they follow the story in a copy of the appropriate book. In a teacher-directed read-to session, children participate even more. They anticipate events in the story: "What do you think happens next?" asks the reader at crucial points in the story. Children retell events in correct sequences. They discuss personal experiences related to the story: "Do any of you have a dog? Did he ever get lost?" Children love to dramatize events that were read to them in story form. Often these dramatizations are elaborated into productions with props, scenery, and costumes. Children enjoy retelling stories using puppets.

The third stage of development of story sense and sequence of events is the tell-me stage. From about four to ten years of age children need the opportunity to report personal happenings to others. Usually they jump about in their time sequences. They need adult guidance to help them to focus first, on the beginning ("What happened first?"); second, on the end ("What finally happened?"); and then on the steps in between. The dining table is an excellent place for developing "conversation." Schools miss this ideal setting for learning by separating teachers and children at lunchtime. Lunch should be served family style in small groups with adolescent leaders (particularly males) or adult volunteers specifically trained to foster this type of sequenced conversation.

One of the most discouraging tendencies observed in early childhood teachers is their discomfort with fantasy. Children learn early enough the difference between reality and fantasy; they do not need a formal anti-fantasy program waged by kindergarten and first-grade teachers. They need their fantasy and it should be encouraged. When a teacher asks Johnny what he keeps in the windowbox of his second-floor tenement room and Johnny answers, "An elephant!" he knows, as does everyone else, that this is not true. More important pedagogically is whether or not Johnny can invent a sequenced story to explain his elephant's presence in a windowbox. If Johnny really believes his story, he may be pre-psychotic, in which case no amount of teaching to discriminate reality from fantasy will help. If Johnny is merely engaging in healthy fantasy and a classmate tried to tear the story down, the teacher can simply say that "Johnny's elephant makes a good story and all stories do not have to be true."

Ways to Teach Vocabulary for Reading

When a child correctly associates an aural or written word or series of words with a personal experience, he has vocabulary. The quality of that association determines the quality of his vocabulary. This is true at the college level, as well as at the reading readiness stage. If the child associates the spoken word /cut/ with the incision on his finger, he has aural vocabulary. If he further associates /cut/ with pain, bleeding, and scabbing, the quality of his vocabulary is increased. If /cut/ is associated, in addition, with other *cut* concepts and experiences—of dividing into parts; of *cutting* glass; of taking a *cut* of the profits; of taking a *cut* in pay; of taking a *cut* at a baseball; of *cutting out,* in the sense of leaving; of *cut* glass; of choice *cuts* of beef; of *cutting down* on fatty foods; of *cutting up* in class; of *cutting down* the enemy; of *cutting* a diamond; of *cutting* prices; of *cutting* remarks; of *cutting* teeth; of *cutting* a deck of cards; of *cutting* across a vacant lot; of a newspaper *cut;* of a short*cut;* of *cutting* back production; of *cutting* in on the dance floor; of being *cut out,* or best suited, for the job; and on and on—then we say the child's vocabulary is enriched.

Although class trips and other enrichment activities can be valuable, unless they provide the experiences needed to teach specific vocabulary for reading, or to teach specific concepts and skills related to the curriculum, they are luxuries we cannot yet afford when we consider the limited time we have and the unlimited reservoir of needs of the children we teach. Most formal education will continue to take place in the schoolroom. Under these conditions, teachers of disadvantaged children must not confuse labeling and experiencing. They must recognize that vocabulary development must start with teaching, by sharpening and reinforcing labels for experiences children already have. These tasks do not require class trips. As discussed earlier, most disadvantaged children have sufficient experiences and enough oral-aural labels to learn how to read the published materials that presently exist in the schools. Vocabulary work should start with this repertoire. Basal words like *run, jump, look* should be sharpened by acting out the multimeaning variations. This can be supported by pictures, stories, and discussions within the four walls of the classroom.

The second step in vocabulary development is to analyze the words and concepts used in the beginning reading materials of each school system. Children should be tested to see if they have oral-aural labels for these concepts. Some teachers will be surprised to find that most disadvantaged children have all the concepts and most of the labels. Those labels (words) unknown to the children can be supplied by the teacher.

"Show me the *wagon.*"

"Which one is the *wagon?*"

"What is this?" (Answer: A *wagon.*)

The third step in vocabulary development is to preteach sight vocabulary that is already part of the child's oral-aural vocabulary and that he will need to read in the books the teacher plans to use. All basal reading systems provide materials and techniques for this.

The fourth step is to increase vocabulary by introducing trips, stories, and multimedia. But here, too, the reading material at sequentially higher levels must be the guide to which words and concepts to teach in the story or on the trip. Teachers should realize that vocabulary development of words *in general* tends to be ineffectual. Careful selection of words based on the published materials and curriculum content of the school is a much wiser criterion for selection of vocabulary.

Ways To Teach Attention to the Reading Task

The ability to stick to a page or to a book is a learned psychophysical process. Separating the cause of poor concentration into visual, perceptual, motor, and personality problems is futile because they appear to interact. The treatment of the problem or the development of the skills can be approached either way. For example, children who undergo successful visual perceptual training usually develop the skill to stay on a line, on the page, and in the book for acceptable time periods. On the other hand, story or picture books that are exciting or easy enough for children to succeed in offer less of a potential concentration problem than do dull textbooks.

The best technique available to the teacher for developing concentration is to use colorful picture books at the reading readiness level and very simple materials at the primer level. Good literature will draw children to the page and keep them there. Second, materials that are short and complete give children a sense of closure within a reasonable length of time. A collection of five picture stories in an anthology are better presented as five separate books, each self-contained. Third, things to do in connection with the printed page keep children interested. Marking pages, cutting out pieces, drawing lines, and filling in letters are good promoters of concentration.

Not unrelated to this technique is that of directed reading, which at the reading readiness stage consists merely of giving children a reason to attack a specific page:

"Can you find a mouse in the picture?"
"How many people on that page?"
"Who can find Michael's name on this page? It looks like this."

The Controlled Reader, described in the Appendix, is an excellent device for keeping children fixated on the reading source and, simultaneously, training them in smooth left-to-right eye movements. This filmstrip projector presents reading readiness materials by showing stimuli moving from left to right across the screen at controlled speeds. Other techniques for training in visual motility can be obtained from consulting optometrists specializing in visual perceptual training for children. They have developed a variety of interesting visual tracking and rotation exercises that can be used in the classroom. The tachistoscope (see earlier section on Visual Discrimination and the Appendix) is an excellent device for fostering attention to and concentration on visual symbols and pictures. Perhaps the best technique for promoting attention to the reading task is the stopwatch. By challenging children to perform a directed reading task against time, gradually increasing the difficulty of the task and the amount of time allotted, a teacher can increase children's concentration spans.

Summary

The last two chapters have stressed the concept of readiness as a repertoire of learned behaviors. In the first case, these behaviors are basic to cognition and to classroom "socialization"; in other words, they are related to *learning* readiness. In the second case, these behaviors are directly related to the reading act, and include letter knowledge, visual discrimination of letters and words, auditory discrimination of sounds in words, love of books and interest in the printed symbol, story sense and memory for sequence, vocabulary for reading, and attention to the reading task. These behaviors constitute *reading* readiness activities. The first major point proposed in these chapters is that both types of readiness are learned and, therefore, susceptible to manipulation. Schools can make children ready by providing specific training.

The second major point is that careful, sequential, thorough training in readiness activities at the prekindergarten through first-grade levels is not injurious to the psyches and somas of children unless, of course, unreasonably stressful stimuli are employed. What is unreasonable? Any stimulus that requires responses the organism is physiologically or intellectually unable to handle. A five-year-old may not be able to print the letter *A* in one box of an 8½ × 11 sheet of graph paper, but he may very well be able to trace a 1½-foot grooved template of the letter *A* with a 1½-inch chunk of chalk on a chalkboard on the floor. And he may very well enjoy himself.

The third major point is that teachers must know precisely what behaviors they are trying to shape in their children and why they are doing so. This is a prerequisite to good teaching at any level. The more precise this analysis, the more successful the teacher will be. That is why it is imperative for school people to recognize those behaviors that pay off in learning to read (reading readiness) and those behaviors that are valuable to cognitive development but that do not directly yield payoffs in reading achievement (learning readiness). Faced with disadvantaged preschoolers, educators must provide precise and effective programs that lead to observable results. These results may have to be limited to the specific behaviors most likely to pay off in school achievement in the early grades. In order to plan which behaviors to shape, teachers must make hard, realistic decisions, because their children's needs are greater than the school's ability to meet them. And teachers can make these decisions only when they recognize that learning readiness skills must be pared down to those essential for a foundation on which to build reading readiness skills. When disadvantaged children descend upon the schools with great deficits in learning, economy of time and effort are absolutely necessary if they are to survive the system. Provide the necessities, and a generation of slum children could enter the elementary grades ready to succeed in reading, the subject of the next chapter.

References

1. G. Thurstone, *Primary Mental Abilities* (Chicago: Science Research Associates, 1963).
2. ———, *Iowa Tests of Basic Skills* (Boston: Houghton Mifflin, 1964).
3. S. Alan Cohen, "A Study of the Relationships Among Reading, Intelligence and Vision Using a Dynamic Theory of Vision" (Unpublished doctoral dissertation, Boston University, 1965).
4. R. J. Allen *et al.,* "The Relationship of Reading Factors to January First-grade Reading Achievement" (Unpublished master's thesis, Boston University, 1959).
5. S. R. Gavel, "Patterns of Growth in First-grade Reading" (Unpublished doctoral dissertation, Boston University, 1957).
6. E. A. O'Sheasy, "The Predictive Value of Certain Pre-reading Tests Employed at the First-grade Level" (Unpublished master's thesis, Boston University, 1951).
7. Sister M. J. Harrington, "The Relationship of Certain Word Analysis Abilities and Reading Achievement of Second-grade Children" (Unpublished doctoral dissertation, Boston University, 1953).
8. M. M. Berwick, "An Evaluation of the Prognostic Value of Certain Pre-reading Tests for Reading Achievement" (Unpublished master's thesis, Boston University, 1947).
9. W. W. Clark and M. J. Lee, *Lee-Clark Reading Readiness Test* (New Cumberland, Pa.: California Test Bureau, 1962).
10. J. Dobston and K. Hopkins, "The Reliability and Predictive Validity of the Lee-Clark Reading Readiness Test," *Journal of Developmental Reading,* 6 (Summer 1963), 278–81.
11. M. Powell and K. M. Parsley, Jr., "The Relationship Between First-grade Reading Readiness and Second-grade Reading Achievement," *Journal of Educational Research,* 54 (February 1961), 229–33.
12. D. D. Durrell and H. Murphy, "Boston University Research in Elementary School Reading: 1933–1963," *Journal of Education,* 146 (December 1963).
13. H. W. Zingle and A. E. Hohol, "Predictive Validity of the Metropolitan Readiness Tests," *Alberta Journal of Educational Research,* 10 (June 1964).

14. R. Karlin, "The Prediction of Reading Success and Reading Readiness Tests," *Elementary English*, 34 (May 1957), 320–22.

15. D. Durkin, "Children Who Read Before Grade One," *The Reading Teacher*, 14 (January 1961), 163–66.

16. ———, "Earlier Start in Reading?" *Elementary School Journal*, 63 (December 1962), 146–51.

17. M. Sutton, "Readiness for Reading at the Kindergarten Level," *The Reading Teacher*, 17 (January 1964), 234–40.

18. D. D. Durrell, *Improving Reading Instruction* (New York: Harcourt, Brace & World, 1956), pp. 74–76.

19. ——— and H. Murphy, *Speech to Print Phonics* (New York: Harcourt, Brace & World, 1965).

20. Phyllis Cerf, *Skilstarters* (New York: Random House, 1967).

21. Catherine Stern *et al., We Learn to Listen*, Structural Reading Series (New York: Singer, 1963).

22. Buchanan-Sullivan Associates, *Programmed Reading* (New York: McGraw-Hill, 1964).

23. S. Alan Cohen, "Applying a Dynamic Theory of Vision to Teaching Reading," *Journal of Developmental Reading*, 6 (Autumn 1962), 15–25.

24. J. H. Bowden, "Learning to Read," *Elementary School Journal*, 12 (1911), 21–23.

25. A. Gates and E. Boeker, "A Study of the Initial Stages in Reading in Preschool Children," *Teachers College Record*, 24 (1923), 469–88.

26. L. H. Meek, *A Study of Learning and Retention in Young Children*, Teachers College Contributions to Education, No. 164 (New York: Bureau of Publications, Teachers College, Columbia University, 1925).

27. M. B. Hill, "A Study of the Process of Word Discrimination in Individuals Beginning to Read," *Journal of Educational Research*, 29 (1936), 487–500.

28. I. H. Anderson and W. F. Dearborn, *The Psychology of Teaching Reading* (New York: Ronald Press, 1952).

29. Sister M. J. Harrington and D. D. Durrell, "Mental Maturity vs. Perception Abilities in Primary Reading," *Journal of Educational Psychology*, 46 (October 1955), 375–80.

30. Sister M. Nila, "Foundations of a Successful Reading Program," *Education*, 73 (May 1953), 543–55.

31. S. R. Gavel, "June Reading Achievement of First-grade Children," *Journal of Education*, 140 (February 1958), 37–43.

32. A. V. Olson, "Growth in Word Perception Abilities As It Relates

to Success in Beginning Reading," *Journal of Education,* 140 (February 1958), 25–36.

33. E. B. Linehan, "Early Instruction in Letter Names and Sounds As Related to Success in Beginning Reading," *Journal of Education,* 140 (February 1958), 44–48.

34. A. Nicholson, "Background Abilities Related to Reading Success in First Grade," *Journal of Education,* 140 (February 1958), 7–24.

35. R. Allen and C. Allen, *Read Along with Me* (New York: Bureau of Publications, Teachers College, Columbia University, 1965).

36. M. A. Lowry, *The Basic Phonics Program* (Cleveland: Reardon, 1964).

37. G. N. Getman and Elmer Kane, *Program for Accelerated School Success* (Minneapolis: P.A.S.S., Inc., 1965).

38. D. D. Durrell, H. Sullivan, and H. Murphy, *Building Word Power* (New York: Harcourt, Brace & World, 1945).

39. M. Halvarsen *et al., Phonics We Use* (Chicago: Lyons and Carnahan, 1964).

40. *We Speak Through Music* (Valhalla, N.Y.: Stanbow Productions, Inc., 1960).

Chapter Ten

Reading in Elementary Schools

Introduction

What is the best way to teach children to read? Although general educationists, PTAs, and behavioral scientists debate the phonics versus sight controversy, most leading reading researchers agree that a combination of the two approaches is necessary for optimal learning. Recent research sponsored by the U.S. Office of Education tends to support this conclusion. A more detailed analysis and compilation of 27 research reports plus longitudinal studies now underway will eventually make available the specific qualities of optimal sight-phonics combinations. Most reading specialists suspect that different types of learners will need different combinations of sight-linguistic approaches, but all indications thus far point to the fact that a strong "code-busting" word-attack skills component in a sight approach to reading gives the best results. [1, 2]

Various methods and materials I have used that have proved to be successful to teach beginning reading to disadvantaged children in the primary grades are described in this chapter. Many of these children were from city slums; some were from small towns and cities in western Pennsylvania, upper New York State, western Florida, southern New Jersey, Long Island, and Kentucky; some were rural poor. The populations included black, white, Puerto Rican, and Chinese children. Some of these disadvantaged children entered first grade already reading or close to reading. The majority, however, were nonreaders from environments deprived of opportunities for learning those verbal behaviors expected by the American school. However, wherever teachers taught thoroughly and sequentially, most of these children did learn to read.

A familiarity with basic textbooks in reading is necessary for an understanding of some of the materials covered in this chapter. Nila Smith's *Reading Instruction for Today's Children* (Prentice-Hall, 1963) and Donald Durrell's *Improving Reading Instruction* (Harcourt, Brace & World, 1956) are especially valuable to novices.

Some Basic Problems in Teaching Beginning Reading

Most schools are not teaching disadvantaged children to read adequately in the first four grades. The published reading achievement scores from large cities are discouraging testimonials to this fact. More discouraging are the experiences of educators who work in the classrooms from which these reading achievement scores are drawn, for, in the flesh, these children look even worse than the statistics. Yet, when schools do the job they are supposed to do, using well-trained teachers, good materials, good methods involving persistent, thorough, well-defined instruction, most disadvantaged children *do* learn to read in the first four grades. Such schools exist, for example, in some of the worst slums, where surrounding schools continue to fail in their efforts to teach reading. Based on the success of these extraordinary schools and on the success of specific programs we have conducted, we can only conclude that the deprivations of disadvantaged beginning readers loom large when methods and materials for teaching reading are mediocre. The deprivations become insurmountable impediments when the methods and materials for teaching reading are less than mediocre.

The poor quality of teacher training in reading, an assessment based on thorough studies of classroom elementary teachers across the nation, is painfully evident. New York State, for example, does not require a reading methods course for elementary certification, and New Jersey requires only one undergraduate course. A single lecture course is obviously not enough to give teachers adequate training in the most important skill in the curriculum. Many first- and second-grade teachers do not know what the word-attack skills are; they lack knowledge of phonology, testing, reading subskills, materials, and children's literature. More serious, perhaps, is the question of the depth of actual knowledge of reading instruction of professional personnel who are called "supervisors of reading," "reading specialists," "corrective reading teachers," or "remedial reading specialists." Some of them are less knowledgeable about reading instruction than regular classroom teachers. For example, one New Jersey community uses a social worker to provide reading instruction to disadvantaged children. The superintendent was unable to secure a trained reading specialist. So serious has the shortage of trained reading specialists been that the Pennsylvania State Department of Education one year discouraged applications for federally funded projects that included programs requiring reading specialists.

In addition to poor training, weak or no licensing requirements, and inadequate supply of trained personnel, there is weak professional leadership in the area of reading. The International Reading Association has no prerequisites for membership. Except for the newly formed College Reading Association, there is no professional organization to recognize, license, and sanction competent reading specialists.

A second basic problem in teaching beginning reading to disadvantaged children is the tendency of teachers to cling to stereotyped expectations. All minority group children are not economically disadvantaged, and although most racial minority subgroups in the United States suffer social and cultural discrimination, many members of these groups enjoy and manifest the results of culturally and economically enriched environments. Yet, how often do school social workers or classroom teachers ask black and Puerto Rican parents who are professionals the question: "Do you have books and magazines in your house?"—a question they never ask white professional parents. Even when children come from economically and socially disadvantaged environments, they may not be culturally deprived in terms of the expectations of the school. Many referrals to the Yeshiva University Reading Clinic are from frustrated lower socioeconomic class black and Puerto Rican parents seeking documentation to present to the school that their offsprings are not cognitively or perceptually inferior. A number of these children have high IQs and excellent perceptual and cognitive skills. Many are reading or ready to read in kindergarten and first grade.

A third problem, which has been discussed in earlier chapters, is the tendency of teachers to overteach some learning readiness skills and underteach reading readiness skills. It should be recognized that kindergarten and early first-grade curriculums must emphasize reading rather than learning readiness skills. Unless the children are poorly developed, learning readiness skills may have to remain below optimal levels to make room for intensive reading readiness training, or first and second grade will come and go without children being able to read, and the reading disability pattern will be set.

A fourth problem in teaching beginning reading, especially to disadvantaged children, is the lack of sequential, thorough training in word-attack skills, especially phonic skills. In our observations of classrooms, many teachers who were providing phonics instruction were teaching incorrectly. For example, some were teaching phonic rules to first-graders still too young to apply them. Furthermore, many of the rules were not valid; teachers taught sounds in isolation instead of in words. Sounds in context are very different from sounds in isolation, and only the former is relevant to reading. Most teachers grouped phonics families according to grapheme instead of according to phoneme. This error leads to teaching the one-grapheme–one-phoneme fallacy that confuses children and leads to unnecessarily complex, artificial orthographies. Many teachers teach phonetic analysis of words out of context or without meaning. This, of course, is not reading; it is name calling.

Experimental psychologists and linguists, in particular, are confusing the analysis of language, psycholinguistics, and analysis of learning theory with how children learn to read. The results are tedious code-busting schemes—linguistically sound, but pedagogically absurd. The problem is not in their analyses, which are valuable to reading instruction, but in their attempts to apply these analyses to everyday pedagogy. For example, Woolman's accelerated progressive choice reading method in *Reading in High Gear* [3] offers an excellent model of teaching code busting based on his analysis of verbal learning. His "closing the meaning loop" method is not unfamiliar to competent teachers. Key words are pretaught on the aural-oral level, concepts are set, and then a synthetic method moving from visual discrimination through identification to auditory identification and blending is presented to teach the subject to unlock the code. The child closes the meaning loop when he breaks the visual code by turning it into the aural-oral symbol he originally learned. Except for the serious lack of an auditory discrimination step, the model is sound. But when Woolman translates the model into a reading program, the results are reading selections, which he labels "linguistic," that are not only artificial and obscure to pupils, but equally obscure to teachers.

Frustrated by the lack of success in teaching disadvantaged children to read, a few communities have had the courage to innovate. Unfortunately, they have adopted phonic systems long known to be inferior. Carden's phonic system is a good example of an ancient method that is linguistically and pedagogically unsound. Or they have resorted to new products in which some phonic code-busting systems have been renamed "linguistic methods." Some are, in fact, linguistic, but they are still inadequate as reading systems because they do not consider content equally important to code busting. The *SRA Basic Reading Series,* [4] *Let's Read,* [5] and the *Miami Linguistic Readers* [6] are three examples of such series. Some of these materials are exceedingly useful in reinforcing phonics learning in certain situations, but as basic reading programs, they were not successful in the projects in which we tested them.

A fifth problem, then, has been the flooding of the school market with new "linguistic" beginning reading programs. Most of them are excellent for very limited or specific needs (see discussion in subsequent sections of this chapter). A couple would make good beginning reading modules if they were used with other materials to teach literature. But the indiscriminate use of these "new" materials by frustrated and desperate educators of disadvantaged children has, in most cases, merely reintroduced some ineffective methods and materials discarded thirty years ago.

A sixth problem involves one major misassumption about traditional basal readers. Most teachers and curriculum supervisors assume that commercially published basal "sight" reader programs adequately cover the scope and sequence of skills needed to produce good readers. The MFY staff analyzed ten series of basal and word-attack skill books. We found that some skills are taught in the wrong sequence. For example, in one series children dealt with sound-symbol relationships before they had work in auditory discrimination. The latter obviously must precede the former, if it is worth teaching at all. Some skills, such as analyzing roots and affixes, are overtaught because they lend themselves to workbook exercises better than other skills. Some are undertaught, and still others are not taught at all. Another study, completed recently at the Yeshiva University Reading Clinic, involved a detailed behavioral analysis of the teacher manuals of three representative basal reading systems currently in wide use. Over 66 percent of the skills taught were unrelated to reading as defined in this book. For example, much of the manual was devoted to teaching hand puppetry, oral language development, enjoying movies, and so on. These are all valuable language arts activities, but teachers ought not to expect children to decode the printed page as a result of them. This analysis verified the previous finding of the MFY study. It added specific findings, demonstrating very poor sequencing of skills and inconsistent reinforcement of word-attack skills. Even the sight basal reader's *raison d'être*—controlled vocabulary—was very poorly done. Vocabulary control means careful sequencing and regular reinforcement of newly introduced sight words. Such sequencing and reinforcement were very weak after the first two primers. The argument that basal readers are valuable because they provide the inexperienced teacher with a sequential, thorough program is therefore untrue. The school must invent its own reading program by organizing published materials and training teachers to use these materials effectively. In this sense, the teacher becomes the key to effective instruction.

A seventh problem is the tendency of administrators under pressure to introduce dramatic but not particularly useful innovations. A talking typewriter, for example, can be a highly visible public relations gimmick to appease community action groups; it looks much better to the unprofessional eye than 200 storybooks (not texts) in each elementary classroom. But the books are far more useful to disadvantaged children who come from homes that cannot provide *Cat in the Hat.*

Finally, our observations of beginning reading classrooms for disadvantaged children reveal that they do not read enough *in* the classroom. Either the teacher talks too much or the children sit and listen while one child reads. The actual amount of time each child spends reading for pleasure and/or information is quite short. A recent study indicated that 47 to 49 percent of the classroom time designated as the reading period was spent by teachers talking to or at their pupils.

Developing Reading Skills in Five Levels

One of the persistent criticisms of an individualized reading program which uses storybooks supplemented by skills materials rather than basal readers is that the sequence of reading skills is not adequately covered. But we have found this to be true of all reading programs and recommend that the teacher keep her own checklist of reading subskills for each pupil. The checklist is a guide for ongoing diagnosis of each child and follows him through the elementary grades and into high school. Supplementary skills materials purchased for each classroom can be ordered to fulfill the needs for each skill.

Level I: Skills to be Taught
at the Preprimer Level

At Level I the reading readiness skills and a few learning readiness skills are reinforced by using the specific demands of the first readers as guides to skills development. For example, the learning readiness of concept development involving organizing and categorizing is reinforced using concepts drawn directly from the readers the children will get at Level II. Also introduced at Level I are some beginning word-attack skills and some practical skills such as word copying. These practical skills are needed to succeed at Level II. Traditionally, Level I was taught early in grade one, but in the modern schoolhouse where children are either officially or unofficially ungraded, Level I is introduced earlier to those children who can handle it and later to others who cannot.

1. *Visual skills:* Left to right progression is taught at the readiness level but must be continued at the preprimer level. The ability to coordinate vision by supplying exercise sheets requiring discriminations of fine shades of likenesses and differences in simple words must be presented no later than the preprimer level.

2. *Oral-aural vocabulary:* Enrichment of oral-aural vocabulary is necessary at all levels of education. Priority is always given to words and concepts that will appear in reading material in the early grades. Teachers must set the prepositional concepts and multimeanings of common words; that is, the fine shades of meaning between such concepts as *burst* and *pop, shove* and *push, pull* and *tug.*

3. *Organizational and categorizing skills:* These skills must be reinforced by oral response to objects or pictures. The child should be taught to classify things under such general headings as things to eat, places to visit, fruits and vegetables, soft things or hard things.

4. *Visual discrimination:* Discrimination of words and letters learned in reading readiness must be reinforced.

5. *Auditory discrimination:* Discrimination of word sounds learned in reading readiness must also be reinforced.

6. *Visual memory:* Visual memory training for both pictures and letters must be continued from the reading readiness stage for many children. Simple words can be introduced.

7. *Auditory memory:* Like visual memory, training in auditory memory for sounds in words, as well as for stories, must be continued.

8. *Language rhythm:* A child should have a sense of rhythm in language as a base for syllabication later on. Poems and humming exercises are effective games.

9. *Sentence sense:* The child at this level needs to be encouraged to express himself orally in simple, but complete, sentences. The tendency to use sentence fragments in spontaneous speech is not unique to the disadvantaged child. All children need to practice speaking in complete sentences.

10. *Interpretation and elaboration of ideas:* At this level of develop-

ment, the child should be able to interpret ideas through color and line drawings.

11. *Following directions:* This is a skill taught in preschool. At the preprimer level, the child should be given the chance to follow directions that require more sophisticated judgment and discrimination, such as making correct selections.

12. *Story sequencing:* At a more sophisticated level than the story sequencing exercises in kindergarten, the child should practice supplying the best ending to a story from a series of alternative endings. Inventing his own endings is another form of training for this ability.

13. *Book sense:* The child should have a book sense—he should know how to take care of his books, how to open and use them correctly, and how to turn pages.

14. *Letter and word transfer:* Copying words is an important basic skill. Copying from the chalkboard and from flashcards onto paper at his desk is the first step to transferring words from the chalkboard or flashcards to the printed page.

15. *Sight vocabulary:* Once a child can transfer words from the chalkboard and flashcards to his paper, it is time to teach him sight words. (For some children this occurs as early as kindergarten; for others it can occur as late as grade 2.)

16. *Sight phrases:* As soon as sight words are beginning to be taught, the child should be introduced to sight word phrases. He needs to be able to form his own phrases from sight words.

Level II: Skills to be Taught at Primer–First Level

The emphasis at Level II is on code busting or word analysis, but with a heavy dose of comprehension skills. The average child is well along in grade 1 and is struggling to master the basic skill of decoding the squiggles on a page. But as he masters the code, the teacher continuously emphasizes the reason for code busting—comprehending and feeling—for code busting itself is not reading. Some writing is introduced to reinforce code busting.

1. *Word-attack skills:* Formal instruction in word analysis must begin as early as possible. Starting with initial consonants and simple blends, the child should move quickly to recognition of special word parts.

2. *Mastery of alphabet:* A child should have been taught the alphabet before this level. Now he should be able to recognize and name all the letters in the alphabet in both upper and lower case. He should be able to answer such questions as: "What is the last letter in *walk?* Find it on your paper and circle it."

3. *Personalized phonics skills:* Each individual needs materials for self-directed instruction in whatever phonics skills he is lacking. Some skills are learned easily, whereas others take longer to learn. The type of skill and the schedule and rate of learning differ from child to child.

4. *Sight vocabulary:* Sight vocabulary taught at Level I is increased and training in rapid recognition is introduced. Depending upon his learning rate, each child needs a certain amount of new words daily.

5. *Word demons:* Common confusions, such as was—saw, kitchen— kitten, our—your, on—no, horse—house, how—now, must be worked on.

6. *Context clues:* The child must be taught to extract appropriate words from class lessons to fit into reading and writing in context.

7. *Transfer of sight skills to literature:* The child must learn to transfer new sight vocabulary learned in the basal program to material considered children's literature or "outside" reading.

8. *Voluntary reading:* By this level, a child should begin to browse through new books at his reading level for pure enjoyment. This is the beginning of voluntary reading.

9. *Interpretation of readings:* The child should read orally and draw pictures to show how he had interpreted what he has read. But oral reading should not be overemphasized since most reading later on will be silent reading.

10. *Independent word attack:* At this level, a child should start to acquire new words that have not been taught specifically as sight words in his reading material. He should be using, for example, his picture dictionaries.

11. *Phrasing:* Formal instruction in phrase reading, with a gradual approach to the inverted sentence, must be covered.

12. *Comprehension skills:* There must be constant emphasis on comprehension and the ability to read and to answer questions presented before reading. This is called directed reading and is a crucial study skill in the American school system.

13. *Reading to recall:* The child should be made to retell the stories he has read—first, with immediate recall, and later with delayed recall.

14. *Speed reading:* The first step in reading against time can be introduced through alphabetizing. The child can alphabetize words or categorize sight words against time.
15. *Silent reading:* A child must read independently as early as possible. As a larger sight vocabulary is established, the first-grader can increase his silent reading.
16. *Vocabulary growth:* Vocabulary development through new experiences, both real and vicarious, will help a child understand more new words set in context with already mastered sight vocabulary.
17. *Creative expression:* Dramatization, drawing, dancing, and other applied skills related to reading are necessary to build deeper levels of comprehension.

Level III: Skills to be Taught
in Grades 2–3

At Level III, instruction in word analysis is continued. A child's weaknesses in these behaviors are isolated and improved. But the emphasis now begins to swing toward the interpretive elements of reading. Traditionally, this level occurred in grades 2 or 3, but in the modern school, with individualized instruction, this stage will occur much earlier for some children and later for others.

1. *Word analysis skills:* By this level, a child should make more independent use of word recognition skills. He should be able to attack words through phonetic analysis and context clues and should be able to unlock new words independently.
2. *Context clues:* The child should be able to rely on context clues backed up by phonics as his principal method of word analysis.
3. *Eye-voice span:* The child should be practicing oral reading to get proper phrasing to improve fluency in reading. He should be aware that the eyes move ahead of the voice in oral reading. Regressive eye movements and repetitions should decrease with forms of controlled reading training.
4. *Speeded silent reading:* As fluency in oral reading increases, more silent reading must be introduced so that midway through this level, silent reading should become more rapid than oral reading. Further instruction and use of silent reading for studying will be an important part of the reading curriculum. Beginning silent reading instruction should lead to reading for details, specific informa-

tion, the main idea, following directions, summarizing a story for retelling, adding original endings, and writing short summaries.

5. *Spelling and writing skills:* Word analysis skills should be transferred to spelling and written recall. The child should be getting short dictation exercises.

6. *Word analysis in oral reading:* The child should begin to solve new words independently in oral reading without breaking down the phrasing.

7. *Reading texts of increased complexity:* Toward the end of this level, smaller type and longer sentences should be introduced.

8. *Poetry skills:* The child should be taught to read poetry aloud. The vocabulary load of the poems should be below the frustration level of the reader.

9. *Higher comprehension skills:* A child needs lots of silent reading practice. He should be giving evidence (through comments or responses to questions) that thinking has been going on during the process.

10. *Higher study skills:* More abstract material should be introduced. Such material as simple science and social studies stories should be used to pick out significant information needed. The beginning step in ability to choose relevant material and discriminate between major and minor points in reading material is introduced at this level.

11. *Reading for problem solving:* The child should be directed to specific reference books to find information to solve problems that arise in class.

12. *Associating personal experiences with reading:* The child must be encouraged to use his everyday experiences and associations to bring added interest and stimulation to the materials he reads.

13. *Overcoming reading crutches:* By improving basic skills, the child should be able to shed such symptoms of poor skills as lip reading, whispering, head movements, and mechanical mannerisms that are often found at Level I reading. Teachers should remember that such mannerisms are usually symptoms of basic problems and that they ought not to remove the crutches until they have solved the problems.

14. *Reading in content areas:* Reading should now be used to acquire more knowledge for other school subjects. Now reading begins to become a tool to be used to learn, rather than an end in itself.

15. *Vocabulary development:* As at every level, a child needs increased work in relating words to concepts in reading.

16. *Interpretive reading skills:* A child needs many opportunities to

interpret pictures, to use everyday experiences to support what he reads, to participate in plays and other activities of which reading is a part.

17. *Voluntary reading:* The real test of how successful a reading program can be is to observe the number of children who seek books to read "on their own." Teachers and librarians should devise programs beyond the basic reading curriculum that will entice children to take home books to read. At the elementary school level, this is the librarian's chief job. Books that the teacher knows the children can read and enjoy should be supplied to each classroom library as the preliminary step in the use of the public library and as a beginning in the development of permanent interest in reading.

Level IV: Skills to be Developed in Grades 3–4

By the intermediate grades, the average child has learned, more or less, to bust the code and is now reading for information, and if his teachers have been effective, for interest, enjoyment, and personal growth. Word-analysis skills are sharpened or improved where weak, but the emphasis is on comprehension, study skills, and functional reading. This is Level IV.

1. *Independent word-attack skills:* By this level, the child should have considerable independence in word analysis. He should be able to solve most new words he meets in reading quickly and without help.

2. *Expanded sight vocabulary:* By the end of grade 3, each child should have a large sight vocabulary. He should begin to add to his repertoire new words outside his classroom reading. About 700 words should have been formally taught by this time, but he should have, in addition, about 200 more "private" words in his sight vocabulary.

3. *Practical reading skills:* The child should be indicating some curiosity about reading street and bus signs, and posters and signs in general. The school has an obligation to foster this type of functional reading.

4. *Independent directed reading skills:* A child should receive plenty of practice in reading directions from the chalkboard or from printed sheets and carrying them out independently.

5. *Comprehension and appreciation of literary forms:* The child needs

a gradual introduction to a variety of content, such as surprise, humor, and conversation.

6. *Study skills:* Daily exercises in study skills and informational material is gradually introduced midway through this level.

7. *Reference skills:* Early at this level, the child is taught to use tables of contents and index material to help find sources to materials he needs in content areas.

8. *Functional reading skills:* At this level, the child learns to read orally and silently for different purposes:
   a. To find out how to make something
   b. To find answers to questions that have stimulated his curiosity
   c. To get an author's point of view
   d. To take notes to retell the content of material
   e. To give a report to his classmates
   f. To take a test

9. *Test-taking skills:* A child needs formal instruction and practice in taking tests, including practice in properly marking IBM answer sheets, in intelligent guessing on alternative-answer-type tests, and so on.

10. *Voluntary reading:* Class time must be allotted to allow each child to go to the classroom library corner. This requires 200 or more books in each classroom and requires a classroom atmosphere in which children are sufficiently self-directed to take the time to read from the library.

11. *Interpretive reading:* The child must be taught to draw deductions from his readings at home or in class and to discuss materials read in the light of his growing curiosity.

12. *Skills in reading publications:* The teacher must provide opportunities to use children's newspapers and magazines. Parts of the local newspaper, such as the weather report and sports section, should be introduced.

13. *Oral reading:* By this level, the child should be adept at oral reading. Except for special types of materials, such as poetry and drama, almost all reading should be done silently.

14. *Related literature:* The fourth-grader can begin to seek reading materials from outside sources that relate to class activities and outside assignments in which he is interested.

15. *Comprehension clues:* By now, the child is ready to practice reading by concentrating on key words so that silent reading becomes much more rapid than oral reading.

16. *Speeded reference skills:* Exercises in alphabetizing must become more rapid. Speeded exercises in classifying words by blends

should be used as background for dictionary work. More and more children should be made to perform these tasks against time.

17. *Special study skills:* Interpreting simple maps, tables, and graphs should be taught.
18. *Selective reading*: Practice in judging the appropriateness of materials for specific needs must be provided. This should lead to self-selection of materials.
19. *Vocabulary development and speeded reading comprehension:* As the child's reading becomes constantly more rapid and fluent and his phrasing of more involved sentences becomes easier, new vocabulary must be assimilated into new content without hesitancy. The ability to analyze new words should improve rapidly.
20. *Higher word analysis skills:* The child must be taught to use and understand synonyms, antonyms, and so on.
21. *Skill in finding major and minor ideas:* The child must be taught to discriminate between major and minor ideas in selections read.
22. *Recall of abstract materials:* The child must learn to work with materials that are more abstract than the simple narrative materials at the previous grade levels.
23. *Concentration:* Many children need formal training periods to learn to concentrate on longer units, to do concentrated study for longer periods of time.

Level V: Skills to be Improved in Middle and Upper Grades

By the time children have mastered most of the skills in Levels I through IV, they have become functional readers. Now reading is a tool for learning and a means of enjoyment. The use of reading in the content areas of the curriculum will be discussed in the next chapter. These skills must be taught or reinforced in each of the content areas. But there are also skills that must be continuously taught or reinforced as general reading skills in the middle and upper grades.

1. Following directions
2. Selecting the central thought
3. Noting details
4. Picking the relevant material from a unit
5. Judging values
6. Organizing ideas
7. Remembering personal characteristics in a unit
8. Locating specific information in a story from general reading

9. Skimming
10. Rereading articles for different purposes
11. Recognizing characters from descriptive words
12. Determining the type of story or literary form
13. Remembering details at later date from notes taken
14. Selecting proper titles for units
15. Drawing inferences
16. Recognizing comparisons, opposites, and so on, in word vocabulary
17. Outlining
18. Writing abstracts
19. Interpreting the author's meaning
20. Building individual associations around materials read
21. Using study guides
22. Interpreting graphs
23. Using reference books and indexes
24. Using card files correctly and rapidly
25. Visualizing scenes (mental imagery)
26. Selecting the theme in a story
27. Reading fluently and rapidly material that requires rapid reading
28. Checking comprehension with specific questions after speed test
29. Rapidly using the dictionary

These skills lists are useful starting points for *what* to teach. *How* to teach is the next problem to tackle. The following section starts with the area that is most poorly taught—word-attack skills.

Some Tips about Teaching Word-Attack Skills

This section and the rest of the chapter do not attempt to give a pedagogical set of procedures. Pupils and teachers have various needs and different schools have very different conditions. What is provided, however, are tips about pedagogy and materials that we have found successful in teaching beginning reading to disadvantaged and advantaged children.

Oral Language Development and Word Attack. Most words in beginning reading books, including storybooks, are well within the oral-aural vocabulary of most disadvantaged children. In fact, this problem is less prevalent than some educators realize. Children we have worked with, on the whole, understand the words used in basal readers and a sufficient number of words found in low-reading-level children's storybooks, such as the *I Can Read* series (Harper & Row) or the *Beginner Books* series (Random House). When a word or concept is strange to the disadvantaged or to the advantaged child, that word must be pretaught on the experience level at the beginning reading stage.

Context Clues as the Umbrella Skill. The attack skill whose role is least appreciated by many teachers is context clues. We use word-attack skills in combination. The sight word *cat* aids the child trying to unlock the new word *bat*. His phonic skills allow him to substitute a /b/ sound for /c/, and his word structure analysis helps him see *at*. Phonic skills come into play again when he associates *at* digraph with /at/ phonogram. But the ultimate skill that backs up all his word-attack skills is context. If his efforts result in a word that makes sense in context, he receives intrinsic reinforcement.

When a child's phonics, word structure, and sight skills lead him to words that do not make sense in context, something is wrong with the word-attack skills instruction. Usually, this occurs in classes where the teacher has fixated on phonics instruction at the expense of word meaning (comprehension). All word-attack skills must be taught within the overall skill of context clue—an umbrella word-attack skill—which requires continuous focus on meaning as the goal of reading. As the child applies his word-attack skills, he must be taught to ask himself, "Does it make sense?" Whatever skill he uses should lead to a word that makes sense in context.

Picture Clues. Children must learn to recognize words by sight. Adequate readers are sight readers who have, in addition to this word-attack skill, others in their repertoires to use when a word cannot be recognized by sight. At the very beginning of reading instruction, most basal reader programs advocate picture clues as an aid to unlocking key words not recognized by sight. Teachers should be aware, however, that many basal reader pictures are misleading; in some cases they do not relate to the text. Because most books beyond the basal reading stage rely on the text without pictures, the use of picture clues is a temporary aid. Reading specialists advocate it as an aid to getting children started. [7]

Our work with disadvantaged children suggests that teachers should not directly teach picture clues as an aid to word attack. Because the use of other word-attack skills appears to be more difficult for these children, we have trouble moving them beyond picture clues to the higher-level word-attack skills. Potential slow achievers tend toward the path of least resistance. Once they master picture clues, they tend to stick with it, rather than risk more difficult word-attack skills. Because almost all children discover without teacher prompting that the pictures in their basal readers give them clues, we have advocated a sort of neutral position—do not teach it, but do not discourage it.

Controlled Vocabulary. Limiting beginning readers to low-level vocabulary is an established tradition based on a half truth. A basic vocabulary of common words most often used in the language should be mastered as early as possible. We have used a basic remedial word count list rearranged according to grammatical function as a guide to teaching beginning reading (see Table 1). The list was originated under Dr. Mabel Noall at Boston University's Secondary Reading Clinic. Children should be quickly conditioned to these words. They are so basic to the language that they will appear with high frequency in any type of literature.

In our work with disadvantaged and advantaged children, we have used a different concept of controlled vocabulary. The number of different new words introduced is limited to ensure that a child has mastered each new word by sight. Too many new words at once can discourage the beginning reader. We try to increase the frequency of the appearance of new words to help reinforce them. The rate of introducing new words and the frequency of usage is controlled, but the grade level of the word is not. Practically any word, regardless of its official grade level, can be taught to any child if it is within his oral-aural vocabulary and if it is taught thoroughly by introducing it in context of known sight words and by reinforcing it regularly. This procedure allows us to use any beginning reading storybook, as well as the child's own experience stories, to teach him to read.

Using Picture Dictionaries. In addition to sight, phonics, and word structure, most reading specialists list dictionary usage as a third

word-attack skill. Some basal reader series provide picture dictionaries for their books. We have found *The Cat in The Hat Beginner
Books Dictionary* (Random House) the most colorful and interesting to children in our projects. It does not, however, cover all
the words children may encounter in their reading. So we back up
six to eight classroom copies of this dictionary with a copy of each
of the following picture dictionaries:

> *A Child's First Picture Dictionary* (Wonder Books)
> *Illustrated Golden Dictionary* (Simon and Schuster)
> *Picture Book Dictionary* (Children's Press)
> *A Picture Dictionary for Boys and Girls* (Garden City Publishers)
> *My First Dictionary* (Grosset and Dunlap)
> *Words I Like to Read and Write* (Harper & Row)
> *Young Reader's Color-Picture Dictionary for Reading, Writing
> and Spelling* (Grosset and Dunlap)

The Use of Printing. From the very first day of instruction we
encourage children to print words. After they have gone through a
learning and/or reading readiness program, they are encouraged to
print every new word they learn. Children with poor hand-eye
coordination use large sheets of paper or the chalkboard to utilize
large muscles. Some children need wooden or plastic letter templates to trace, because they are still poor in hand-eye coordination. Some children need extensive tracing exercises. No matter
what his level of development, every beginning reader keeps a file
of word cards or a notebook with all his sight words. Each word
has been printed with his own hand.

Preteaching Sight Vocabulary. The best way to ensure high meaning load is to arrange for applied word-attack skills to pay off for
the child by "closing the meaning loop," to use Woolman's term
This means that at the beginning reading stage the child should
read those words that are part of his oral-aural vocabulary.

In our projects in teaching beginning reading to disadvantaged
children, we have adopted this rule:

> The child reads only those words he already knows as
> part of his oral-aural language experience.

If a word he is about to read is not part of his oral-aural vocabulary, we teach it by explanation, demonstration, or definition on the

Table 1 Basic Remedial Word Count Lists

Level	Nouns	Pronouns	Adjectives	Verbs	Adverbs	Connectives
Pre-primer	can go will	all he his I it me one she that them they we what which you	a all big his little my one that the what which	are can do go have is see was went will	all not out there up	about at for in of on to up with
Low first grade	back boy call day down help house make man mean play saw say take time two water well	any him its many this us who	an any better good her just long many mean no old over some this two your	back be call came come could did get give had help house let's (v. + pron.) like long looked made make man mean must play please put ran running said saw say take tell thank time wanted water well were would	again away back better here how just now over so then too well when where why (inter.)	as but by down from into like over so then when where

Level	Nouns			Pronouns	Adjectives		Verbs		Adverbs	Connectives
High first grade	above	friends	nothing	another	another	most	asked	keep	alone	above
	bear	girl	oh (interj.)	both	best	mother	bear	know	along	after
	bed	gray	open	other	black	Mr.	bed	last	before	against
	bird	guess	pay	such	blue	near	been	laugh	best	before
	black	half	present		both	new	black	letter	close	between
	blue	hand	rabbit		brown	open	blue	live	even	if
	book	head	school		even	other	book	love	far	near
	brown	hope	sleep		fast	same	brown	matter	fast	or
	car	keep	still		fine	still	catch	meet	first	under
	catch	know	thing(s)		first	such	chair	might	gray	without
	chair	last	three		four	sure	close	milk	last	
	children	laugh	tree		gray	their	cover	mother	more	
	cover	letter	try		half	three	cut	named	most	
	cut	love	use		hard	very	does	open	much	
	dog	matter	vat		last	white	dog	pay	never	
	door	meet	walk		live	young	eat	present	off	
	eye	might	way		more		even	read	once	
	fast	milk	white				eye	school	soon	
	feel	more	wish				fast	seem	still	
	find	morning	work				feel	send	sure	
	fine	mother	year				find	sleep	under	
	first	near	yes (interj.)				fine	still	until	
	four	night	young				found	stopped	very	
							gave	think	walk	
							got	took	wish	
							guess	tree	without	
							hand	tried		
							has	try		
							head	use		
							hear	work		
							heard	write		
							hope			

Level	Nouns			Pronouns	Adjectives	Verbs		Adverbs	Connectives
Low second grade	animal	great	room	each	afraid	ate	miss	ago	around
	baby	green	round	our	ago	baby	need	almost	because
	bad	high	second	those	bad	ball	paper	always	either
	ball	hold	set		clean	began	part	around	than
	basket	home	show		cold	being	pass	bad	till
	being	hundred	sing		each	believe	people	each	upon
	birthday	land	six		either	boat	place	early	yet
	boat	lay	something		enough	bring	point	enough	
	buy	light	stand		evening	buy	pull	fair	
	care	line	street		every	care	reach	high	
	change	mind	summer		fair	carry	reason	late	
	city	miss	table		fall	change	remember	only	
	cold	month	talk		few	clean	rest	today	
	country	need	ten		glad	done	right	tougher	
	dinner	paper	till		great	egg	roll	yet	
	egg	part	today		green	end	room		
	end	pass	town		happy	evening	sat		
	enough	people	train		high	fall	second		
	evening	place	turn		late	farm	set		
	fair	point	wait		light	father	show		
	fall	pull	week		only	fire	sing		
	farm	reach	whole		our	going	stand		
	father	reason	word		right	green	started		
	few	rest	yellow		round	hold	summer		
	fire	right			second	kept	table		
	going	roll			several	land	talk		
					short	lay	till		
					six	learn	train		
					ten	light	turn		
					those	line	wait		
					true	mind			
					whole				

High second grade

			these	beautiful	strong	arm	garden	sit	already	behind
anything	field	piece		beautiful	strong	arm	garden	sit	already	behind
arm	fill	pig		bright	these	bag	gone	snow	also	through
bag	fish	poor		busy	third	bit	ground	speak	ever	while
barn	five	quiet		coming	warm	blow	grow	stay	often	
behind	floor	rain		company	watch	board	held	stone	sometimes	
bell	flower	ride		cry	wood	box	hide	suppose	tomorrow	
bit	fly	ring		dark		bread	hill	surprise		
blow	fun	road		different		cap	hit	thought		
board	game	shake		fell		coat	hole	told		
box	garden	shoe		five		coming	jumped	top		
bread	grass	side		floor		cost	knew	warm		
brother	ground	sister		flower		course	leave	watch		
cap	hill	snow		fly		cry	left	while		
child	hide	song		full		dance	leg	win		
coat	hit	stay		game		doll	lost	wind		
company	hole	stone		grass		don't	move	winter		
cost	horse	story		hot		draw	noise			
course	kind	sun		hungry		dress	number			
cry	kitty	surprise		kind		drink	picture			
dance	leave	third		large		duck	piece			
dark	left	thought		left		except	quiet			
doll	leg	tomorrow		lost		face	rain			
draw	lost	top		minute		feed	ready			
dress	lot	watch		Mrs.		fell	ride			
drink	men	wind		poor		field	ring			
duck	minute	window		pretty		fill	seen			
ear	money	winter		quiet		fish	sell			
everything	move	woman		ready		floor	shake			
face	noise	wood		side		flower	shall			
feed	number	yard		small		fly	shoe			
feet	party						should			
fell	picture						side			

203

Level	Nouns			Pronouns	Adjectives	Verbs		Adverbs	Connectives
Low third grade	address	fix	sea	mine	air	address	leg	afternoon	across
	afternoon	foot	seven	myself	clear	air	mail	east	except
	air	front	ship	whose	cross	beg	mark	else	instead
	body	hair	sign	yourself	dead	begin	mine	low	past
	break	hat	silk		deep	break	nest	next	though
	build	heart	sound		eight	brought	note	past	whether
	cake	lady	south		else	build	ought	quite	
	card	lead	spring		family	cake	page	rather	
	case	leg	step		front	can't	plant	south	
	cause	mail	stick		heavy	card	print	though	
	Christmas	mark	store		low	case	save	west	
	class	mile	suit		next	cause	ship	yesterday	
	color	mine	sweet		nice	class	sick		
	copy	music	thousand		quick	clear	sign		
	cross	next	touch		real	color	sold		
	dead	note	visit		seven	copy	sound		
	deep	page	wall		sick	cross	spring		
	die	past	war		silk	didn't	step		
	drive	plant	wash		sold	die	store		
	cast	print	weather		spring	dig	suit		
	eight	quick	west		sweet	drive	teach		
	family	real	window		thousand	dropped	touch		
	felt	river	wonder		wide	except	visit		
	finish	robin	wrong		wrong	felt	wall		
	fit	Santa Claus	yesterday			finish	war		
						fit	wash		
						fix	wear		
						foot	weather		
						forgot	wonder		
						front	wrong		
						goes	wrote		
						lead			

Pronouns

High third grade

act	farmer	middle	shoot	anybody	able	least
amount	fight	mistake	shot	everybody	alike	nine
apple	fold	mix	sir	nobody	alive	paid
bank	food	mountain	size	whom	all right	possible
beat	fruit	news	skin		angry	rich
bill	glass	nine	slip		awful	sad
bother	gold	nobody	smoke		bottom	safe
bottom	grade	north	son		broken	Saturday
bridge	handle	nose	spoil		business	slow
brush	hang	office	stamp		certain	soft
burn	horn	order	star		church	sorry
business	hour	paint	state		cloth	steel
button	hunt	pencil	station		cool	strange
candy	hurry	person	steel		decided	straight
cent	hurt	pick	stitch		dry	struck
chicken	idea	plan	study		fat	Sunday
church	inside	pound	Sunday		free	swimming
climb	iron	practice	supper		funny	tonight
cloth	I'm	price	swim		glass	understood
clothes	it's	push	teeth		gold	wet
college	kick	rich	throw		horn	written
cook	kill	rock	tie		interesting	
cool	knock	rubber	tire			
corn	least	rule	tonight			
count	lie	safe	toy			
cow	life	sail	trade			
cup	lift	sale	trip			
doctor	likes	Saturday	trouble			
dollar	measure	seat	wagon			
dry	meet	seed	wet			
excuse		sheep	wrap			
fat		shine				

Level	Verbs				Adverbs	Connectives
High third grade	absent	fed	lose	slow	ahead	although
	act	fight	measure	smoke	apart	among
	add	finger	meet	spend	asleep	apart
	amount	fold	mix	spoil	certain	during
	bank	follow	nose	stamp	hardly	inside
	beat	forget	order	star	inside	nor
	belong	free	paid	state	north	since
	bill	glass	paint	station	really	
	born	grade	pencil	steel	sad	
	bother	grew	pick	stitch	since	
	bottom	handle	plan	struck	sorry	
	bridge	hang	pound	study		
	brought	happened	pour	swim		
	brush	haven't	practice	swimming		
	burn	horn	price	take		
	button	hunt	push	threw		
	candy	hurry	received	throw		
	caught	hurt	rock	tie		
	choose	I'm	rule	tire		
	climb	interesting	sail	toy		
	cook	iron	seat	trade		
	cool	it's	seed	trip		
	corn	kick	sew	trouble		
	count	kill	shine	understood		
	cup	knock	shoot	weigh		
	decided	least	shot	wet		
	doctor	lie	shut	won't		
	doesn't	lift	size	wouldn't		
	dry	likes	skin	wrap		
	excuse	listen	slip	written		

Level	Nouns	Pronouns	Adjectives	Verbs	Adverbs	Connectives
Above third grade	cousin February goodbye Halloween January October squirrel stationery Thanksgiving writing		February January October teacher's Thanksgiving	getting suppose writing	sometimes	

Sources: E. W. Dolch, *Teaching Primary Reading* (Champaign, Ill.: Garrard Press, 1950), pp. 269 (95 nouns), 267 (Basic Sight Vocabulary). Donald D. Durrell, *Improving Reading Instruction* (New York: Harcourt, Brace & World, 1956), pp. 359–62. J. A. Fitzgerald, "Spelling Word Difficulties for Children in Grades II–VI," *Elementary School Journal*, LIII (February 1952), 221–28. "Garrison's 155 Spelling Demons," in Glenn Myers Blair, *Diagnostic and Remedial Teaching*, rev. ed. (New York: Macmillan, 1956), pp. 276–79.

oral-aural level. This does not restrict his vocabulary. His oral-aural vocabulary is expanded as his reading vocabulary demands, because every reading session begins with careful, extensive preteaching of concepts and their oral-aural symbols.

In the individualized reading classrooms that utilize storybooks at very early stages of instruction, we have designed flashcards and tachistoscopic exercises to preteach key words in each book. First, two or three words are presented and the child matches alphabet cards to each word, spelling out the model. Then he prints the word. Next the words are flashed at him on various tachistoscopes or by hand by the teacher or a classmate. When all the key words are recognized by sight and the child understands the concepts for each word, a second set of flashcards using the same words in phrases is flashed. Finally, a third set of longer phrases is flashed. These phrases are taken directly from the book or selection that he is to read. By this time he has mastered these pretaught sight words and phrases. The last step is to read the book or passage, which he certainly can do after this thorough preteaching.

A 50-word Sight Vocabulary. Some teachers still insist that children learn a 50, 100, or 150 word sight vocabulary before teaching phonics. Not only does research refute this, [8] but our experience with disadvantaged children has taught us to teach phonics early and well for the reasons discussed above. In addition, phonic analysis of words already in their sight repertoire is artificial and dull. Learning to read using phonic and structural cues is supposed to make visually strange words familiar to the reader. Phonics is the beginning reader's way of turning such words into sight vocabulary. To move in the opposite direction is to defeat our purpose and to subject the child to a meaningless phonic drill. He is the first to realize this and will tend to reject phonic skills applied to sight words because they really do not help him.

When to Teach Phonics and Structural Analysis. The same tendency to rely on one word-attack skill occurs with sight words as an aid to unlocking the written code. This is why we have begun phonics instruction and word structure analysis at the reading readiness stage and advocate that teachers put heavy emphasis on phonics and word structure analysis, as well as sight, from the very first day of formal beginning reading instruction.

Suggestions for Teaching Phonics. Phonics instruction is given with the assumption that children can hear sounds in words, just as sight vocabulary instruction assumes children can discriminate visual differences in words. Most phonics programs fail when the children cannot hear differences. Children who do not respond to beginning reading instruction usually lack these readiness skills and must be taken back to that level for instruction.

No evidence from controlled research indicates that beginning readers are confused by the multiphonic system of American English. The fact that a phoneme can be symbolized by more than one grapheme in our language appears to bother linguists, teachers, and professors of education more than it bothers children who are learning to read for the first time. As the child moves up the grades, he begins to assimilate this discomfort of his elders. In fact, they teach him the discomfort by giving him such gross misinformation as the *or* symbol representing the sound in /horse/ and then exposing him to the written code *work horse.* The *or* symbol may or may not represent the /or/ sound in /horse/. The sparse evidence from controlled research that is available indicates that when children are first introduced to the grapheme-phoneme relationship in a way that does not teach this misinformation, the multiphonic English language does not confuse them even when they are disadvantaged slum dwellers.

How do we avoid teaching this misinformation? By teaching phoneme word families instead of grapheme word families. We teach the sound in *bed, head, said, bread,* and *wed,* and show the children all the various graphemes for that particular phoneme. When using consonant substitution, we present the various spellings for a given sound. And we always present word families with meaning: "On a pillow we rest our———. The pillow is on the———. We put the butter on the———." We always present phonemes in words, rarely in isolation, because phonemes are influenced by context. The ability to hear, say, and print an isolated phoneme does not ensure the ability to hear, say, or print the symbol of the phoneme in word context. The phonemes should be taught to children in meaningful words, words they will see today or tomorrow in their reading selections. The day after tomorrow may be too far off to make phonics instruction functionally effective. When a child is struggling through a phonic attack on a word, we use two types of clues. First, we give him a phonically analogous word that he knows; then, we give him meaning clues to remind him that all word-attack skills go hand in hand with context clues. A phonic attack is successful when meaning or comprehension is achieved.

We have had marked success using two phonic programs to supplement sight basal reader programs, individualized reading programs using storybooks, and language experience programs. One is Murphy and Durrell's *Speech to Print Phonics* kit. [9] The other is Smith's *Michigan Language Program.* [10] These are alternates, not companions. Two short texts, Heilmann's *Phonics in Perspective,* [11] and Gray's *On Their Own in Reading* [12] are good surveys of phonics instruction for teachers who feel the need for self-instruction in phonics.

In addition to either the Murphy and Durrell or Smith programs, the beginning reading classroom needs a large variety of supplementary reinforcers. We have found selections in the Lippincott basal reader series [13] excellent phonics reinforcers. The Lippincott readers are a full reading program, but we have used it more often as a source of reading selections that reinforce various sounds. One or two copies of the early readers in each classroom gives the teacher a source of short selections built around key sounds. Two to five copies of Rasmussen and Goldberg's *SRA Basic Reading Series,* [4] Bloomfield and Barnhart's *Let's Read* readers, [5] and Wenkart's *Phonic Readers* [14] serve the same purpose. About five copies of each basal reader phonics or spelling workbook, or any phonics or spelling workbooks published independently of basal series, such as Lyons and Carnahan's *Phonics We Use,* [15] or Hildreth and LaCoste's *Spellingtime,* [16] or Lowry's *The Basic Phonics Program* [17] can supply a classroom with excellent resources for reinforcing phonics and other word-attack skills. Add to this one set each of the many phonics and word-attack skills games published by Parker, Dolch, Kenworthy, and other companies, and SRA's Word Games kit [18] by Parker and Scannell, and a classroom will be prepared to serve the phonic needs of its children.

How does the teacher use these materials? In addition to the basic developmental reading program (basal, individualized language experience), the teacher presents a structured phonics program (Murphy and Durrell or Smith). Each child moves along as efficiently as he can. By cataloging the content of the supplementary phonics readers, workbooks, games, and kits according to specific skill, the teacher can guide any child to activities reinforcing specific phonic skills he needs. Three children, who need more work than the Murphy and Durrell program provides in *bl* blends, play SRA word games with *bl* cards. Then they do worksheets on *bl* blends from various workbooks and finally read some stories from the *Let's Read* readers emphasizing *bl* words. Other children are simultaneously working in areas of their needs.

Providing each primary grade classroom with a few copies each of these supplementary materials is inexpensive. Most schools commit the error of ordering thirty copies of a workbook for each classroom. Thirty copies of five different workbooks will give six classrooms five different resources to help each teacher meet the individual phonics needs of her children. One SRA Word Games kit can cover three to four classrooms.

Using Commercial Basal Readers. Three basal reader series have given us the best results compared to other basals currently on the market. The Carillo *et al., Chandler Language Experience Readers* [19] have been the most successful sight basal readers with urban populations in our projects. Children seem to like the photographs, the short readers, the photo albums, the simple workbooks, and especially the collections of verse and poetry. Two Scott, Foresman series, Robinson *et al., The New Basic Readers,* Curriculum Foundation Series [20] and Bauer's *Health for All* in the Health and Safety Readers Series, [21] have also been relatively successful compared to most sight approaches in traditional basal reader form. Finally, Black's *The Bank Street Readers* [22] appear to be popular with New York City teachers and pupils. Whether or not other cities, suburbs, and rural areas find them as effective is still an unanswered question. All three programs need thorough correlate programs in phonics and word-attack skills. The prereading skills are poorly taught. But the preprimer, primer, and first readers, as well as the accompanying manuals, are very effective with teachers who are willing to introduce concomitant reading in children's storybooks.

Using Commercially Published Linguistic Programs. Particularly in the large cities, there is still formidable resistance to linguistic beginning reading programs. The cities tend to hold tenaciously to traditional sight basal approaches, in spite of the sagging reading achievement scores of their pupils. In the light of the serious reading retardation trend among disadvantaged children in the cities that have been using the sight basals for so long, we would expect the cities to have grasped for new approaches, especially for the new linguistic programs currently available. Unfortunately, city schools are slow to change in spite of the serious crises they face.

Three programs have been particularly successful in teaching beginning readers using a linguistic or phonic approach. Fries and Wilson *et al.* have developed linguistic readers [23] in the Philadelphia schools. These short, concise, sensible reading selections and excellent workbooks were very effective in our test of them with urban children and illiterate young adults. The *Structural Reading Series* by Catherine Stern *et al.* [24] was successful in some projects in Harlem and on the Lower East Side of New York, as well as in the Midwest and Northwest. The workbook-readers need lots of supplementary materials after Book A, but the games, phonic readers, and cards that accompany the program are very effective. For the early grades, *Programmed Reading* by Buchanan-Sullivan Associates [25] has been successful when teachers are willing to operate the program according to its design. For intermediate grades or junior and senior high schools dealing with illiterates, Sullivan has published another beginning program through Behavioral Research Laboratories [26] that is proving effective in some projects that I am currently involved in. The linguistic reading books that accompany the BRL program have been particularly effective.

Perhaps the "linguistic" program we found most successful with retarded readers and with beginning readers in a severely deprived urban area was Donald Smith's *Michigan Language Program.* [10] Unlike most colorful elementary school materials, this antiseptic-looking set of elaborate workbooks and teacher scripts is one of the most thorough code-busting programs on the market. Because of its experimental nature, the manuals are often incorrectly keyed, but this is a minor problem which, if anticipated, can easily be corrected by the classroom teacher.

Using Individualized Reading and Language Experience. When classrooms have 200 attractive storybooks, supplementary phonics and word-attack skills materials, a creative teacher who can teach children to teach each other, flashcards and check-out sheets for each storybook and some teacher aides, the individualized reading approach is the most effective technique we have ever seen. Unfortunately, most teachers are afraid to let their children do some of the teaching, and this fear perpetuates the rigid lock-step structure of one, two, or three reading groups in a classroom at any one time.

In addition to the materials suggested for phonics and word-attack skills in an earlier section of this chapter, the individualized reading center can use SRA *Reading Laboratories,* [27] *Spelling Word Power Laboratory* kits (in grade 2), [28] *Pilot Library,* [29] and a *Reading for Understanding,* junior edition, [30] to supplement the storybook library. Macmillan's *Spectrum of Skills* [31] and Xerox's *The Literature Sampler,* junior edition, [32] can be used in grades 3 and 4. Many of the skills materials listed in the Appendix must be available in small quantities in the individualized reading classroom.

Most important of all, the individualized reading classroom needs a teacher who is well trained in the teaching of reading. Such a teacher must perform ongoing diagnoses of his children to assign them to supplementary skills training. Even in the overcrowded school, individualized reading can turn an educational liability into an asset. In one project that I conducted, the school was on split sessions to accommodate the overload of pupils. First-graders attended class from 8 A.M. to 1 P.M. Second-graders attended the same class from 11:30 A.M. to 4:30 P.M. Three teachers were assigned across two classrooms to adjust to the extra-long day. During the hour and a half overlap when first- and second-graders were crowded into class together, the teachers conducted an ungraded reading period in which pupil learning teams taught each other to read. Second graders were able to act as teacher aides in each group and simultaneously receive reinforcement of their own reading skills. Slow second-graders were easily accommodated in this version of an ungraded class.

An Elementary School Reading Program

Homogeneous grouping on the basis of gross measurements, such as reading readiness, IQ, reading achievement, or any aptitude or achievement scores, has not proven effective with disadvantaged children. Research on homogeneous grouping with children in all socioeconomic and cultural settings consistently shows no significant differences in achievement compared to heterogeneously grouped children. The reason is obvious. Grouping is an administrative exercise that does not necessarily lead to effective instruction for individuals. [33, 34]

Grouping and Staffing for Instruction

The quality and quantity of instruction in the classroom, regardless of grouping, are the most important factors. The self-contained elementary school classroom does offer psychosocial benefits, but the most effective utilization of staff appears to be a modification that allows teachers to specialize in skills on one of the five levels described earlier. This should begin in grade 1. For any given skill, a child may be on any of the five levels, which means that one child is probably operating with a variety of skills on five levels. The only type of grouping that appears educationally sound and that has yielded excellent results is *skills* grouping. This requires a deployment of teaching staff into teams of six with each of four members of the staff specializing in one of the first four levels of skills (preprimer, primer-first, second, and third). Two members specialize in the fifth level (middle- and upper-grade skills). A child is temporarily placed in a group according to skills and moves from one level group to another as he masters each skill. At one time, he may be working under three different teachers depending upon the specific skills and level of skills he needs. The child still "belongs" to one of the teachers on the team, but benefits from a variety of instructional styles.

Even in traditional homogeneous grouping (based on gross

measurements of achievement and/or aptitude), if a school dares to look closely at the specific skills strengths and weaknesses in a group, it will observe the same spread of skills weaknesses as in a heterogeneous group. Furthermore, if a teacher attempts to meet the individual skills needs of a traditionally grouped class, he will find himself unable to teach all the necessary skills. He will have neither sufficient know-how, materials, nor time to meet the needs. We have no choice but to train each teacher in a delimited area of skills and to supply that teacher with a variety of materials to teach those skills.

Some Projects and Techniques That Have Proved Successful

Homework Helpers. Perhaps the first and most thoroughly researched program using older children to tutor younger children was conducted by Albert Deering of Mobilization For Youth. Called Homework Helpers, this program has taken various forms through the years. Deering used tenth-, eleventh-, and twelfth-graders to tutor third- to fifth-graders in special after-school centers. Each center was directed by a professional teacher who headed the staff of high school tutors and conducted "in-service" training programs for the tutors. Thus, the tutors were taught specific techniques for improving the school achievement of the elementary school children who came to the centers. Each tutor was assigned a child and was responsible for teaching him and escorting him back to his house. The tutor was paid by federal poverty funds or by foundation grants for both his tutorial and training sessions.

The tutors were from the slum area. In the early stages of the program, only high-achieving high school students were allowed to tutor. However, through the years Deering discovered that less able achievers were equally effective. Very careful data analyses using control and comparison groups over a four-year period revealed statistically significant gains in school achievement and attitudes toward school by both tutors and elementary school pupils. Some of the most gratifying results were the numbers of high school children who discovered that teaching was rewarding and exciting. Observers of the program were usually impressed with the quality of teaching displayed by the high school tutors.

Within the Homework Helpers structure we have experimented with many different variations. We have successfully tried the skills station technique, with tutors as skills specialists in a program similar to the one described in Chapter Eleven. We have also tried various types of grouping, using one tutor for two or three children. This also yielded results but was not as effective as the 1-to-1 treatment. Much of the information about specific children collected by the tutors was fed back to the schools for action. Tutors worked in teams in certain projects. We have experimented with tutor-pupil meetings twice weekly compared to three times weekly and found both schedules equally effective.

Using Dropouts. The use of aides and volunteers in the schools has opened a number of possibilities in methodology. Particularly effective have been school dropouts to read to beginning readers. These dropouts, as well as upper-grade children still in school, can be financed by Neighborhood Youth Corps funds granted by the U.S. Office of Economic Opportunity. These aides are particularly useful in modifying materials and producing "teacher-made" materials tailored for individualized instruction in the classrooms. One of the major conclusions we drew at the end of one extensive curriculum research project in teaching reading at all levels was that the introduction of one teacher aide to the classroom opened up a number of pedagogical possibilities to the teacher. [35]

Using Machines. Some machines have been found to be very effective in motivating children to read. Most of the reading machines we have used effectively will also be reviewed in the Appendix. The typewriter and tape recorder, which were discussed in Chapter Eight, are particularly good. A primer typewriter provides large print to help create teacher-made reading selections based on the children's language experience, and it is one of the most useful "toys" children can play with. Children love to hunt and peck their names and words they are learning. It provides excellent training in visual discrimination and visual memory, spelling, alphabet knowledge, and sight vocabulary. The tape recorder has many uses. Using inexpensive couplers and headsets, we have taught auditory discrimination of sounds in words, listening skills exercises, and story sequencing. We have tape-recorded children's stories for kindergarten and early first-graders, allowing more than one story to be told simultaneously in a classroom with only one teacher.

The Home. Another approach to influence beginning reading that lends itself to federally funded special projects involves the home directly with the school. In one project, I collected alphabet, word, and reading games. A social worker and teacher conducted a home visit program and after demonstrating the use of the games, left them with parents or with older siblings. We have done the same thing with children's books. In another version, a reading clinic met with the parents of the children learning to read once every two weeks and gave specific instructions with demonstrations to the parents. The parents carried out the instructions and reported back every two weeks for new instructions and/or materials. A thoroughly researched project entitled STAR is reported by Abraham Tannenbaum of Columbia University. [36] STAR was the final version of these home training experiments with the use of local volunteers as the home trainers rather than teachers or social workers.

Artificial Orthographies. One of the most controversial developments in beginning reading techniques has been the emergence of artificial orthographies. Two in particular have been developed and used to some extent. One is Cattegno's *Words in Color,* [37] which combines a writing-reading approach to code busting. Its major feature is, of course, its attempt to make the English language phonetically consistent. By color-coding most of the phonemes in the language, the system preserves the traditional orthography of the alphabet. The result is a complex color-coding system often as confusing as the color-coding system for resistors in electronics. In two applications, one with children and the other with school dropouts, I found the system to be unsuccessful.

Much more successful as an artificial orthography is the Pitman Initial Teaching Alphabet (i/t/a) [38] reading program. Once again, I must question the necessity of making English phonetically consistent for the beginning reader. It may be that the basic assumption of the i/t/a approach, that children are confused by the variable spellings of English phonemes, is a misassumption. Despite this cavil, however, the quality of the i/t/a program is outstanding. The reading materials are better than what is found in most sight basal readers. The phonics program is tight and sequential. The manuals provide an excellent writing-language-experience approach. The Initial Teaching Alphabet appears to be an effective approach to teaching beginning reading for both advantaged and disadvantaged children.

Paper Programs. The most common attack on reading retardation in urban schools has been to designate the entire curriculum as the reading curriculum. Every lesson all day is designed to teach or reinforce some sort of reading activity. Teaching content becomes teaching reading in content areas. This has been markedly successful only when each teacher in the school, regardless of content specialty, has had a thorough, extensive in-service training program in reading. Otherwise, such a program is effective only on paper. I have seen a number of such paper programs, but have observed only two schools where the program has truly been implemented. In both schools, the teachers had been thoroughly trained and the results were extraordinary.

Variations in Language Experience. One technique that I have piloted in a rural school was a variation of the language-experience approach to teaching beginning reading. Groups of ten children went on trips to local areas with a Polaroid camera. The pictures they took of themselves in various situations became the pictures for their own storybooks. Groups exchanged books and expanded their reading vocabularies.

Personal Book Libraries. The most effective "innovation" that I tried in a number of communities is not an innovation at all. It is simply the supplying of each first grade with sets of multilevel fifty-book classroom libraries with a series of methods to get the children and books together. The books are colorful storybooks. Each child gets one book to keep as a start for his personal library. For every five books he reads or has read to him, he gets a book bonus; that is, another free book for his personal home library.

Once a week children peddle their books. This involves small bargaining groups in which children trade their books to get a new book to read. The children know that for every five books read, they get a free book for their personal collections. It is important to make storybooks available in the classroom. The library habit can be built later. In the early grades, books in the classroom are far more important than books in the library. The library should control the flow and supply of books to classroom libraries, but the librarian should be a supplementary reading teacher concentrating on making books attractive to the children. The elementary school librarian should spend more time in each classroom than in the library. The librarian's major responsibility should be to get books into children's hands and into their homes.

Summary

Thorough and well-taught reading programs that use quality materials tend to be successful with disadvantaged beginning readers. In fact, research indicates that even if disadvantaged children start with a deficit, as measured by reading readiness tests and clinical evaluations, but are thoroughly and sequentially taught to read with good materials, they will make adequate reading achievement scores at the end of grade 1. [39] In other words, compared to middle class advantaged children who have higher reading readiness scores to begin with, the disadvantaged children show greater growth over the same period of time. In a study of one school populated by severely disadvantaged children, with five first grades, only ten children were reading on grade level at the end of grade 1. That left 90 percent of the children already retarded. Each child was individually tested with the *Durrell Analysis of Reading Difficulty.* We found the usual patterns we see in all severely retarded readers. Visual memory for words was poor, but auditory discrimination of sounds in words was worse. The children had a few sight words but no other word-attack skills. Everything was low except one score that was, in fact, above average for the school—listening comprehension. This suggested to us that if the children had the skills to unlock the written symbol, they certainly had the ability to comprehend the material. Here was proof on the oral-aural level that severely disadvantaged city children were intellectually capable of comprehending written material. The problem was obviously in the decoding process, because when the written word was decoded into oral-aural symbols, the children were able to comprehend.

It appears, then, that thorough, sequential reading instruction with a strong code-busting component is successful in teaching disadvantaged children to read. The question of methodology is not a phonics versus sight debate. A combination of word-attack skills is necessary to become a good reader. There is nothing new about such a conclusion.

The question of materials should not be a this-not-that debate. No beginning reading program currently available is good enough to do the job. Adverse criticisms of certain materials in this and subsequent chapters must be interpreted in light of the specific applications referred to in the discussion. So, for example, a linguistic code-busting program is weak because of such defects as poor literary quality, artificiality, and slow payoff in functional reading. But it is an excellent program to reinforce certain phonic skills that must be taught. In reading programs for disadvantaged children we end up designing our own elaborate learning centers utilizing a large variety of materials and pedagogies ranging from Dick, Sally, and Spot to linguistic tongue twisters and from teacher lectures to programed instruction. Experienced educators must understand that the tradition of purchasing one class set of a program with its teacher's manual and a few supplementary storybooks to provide an adequate reading program for disadvantaged children is no longer valid. Instead, teachers must select varieties of materials, programs, and pieces of programs to cover the skills listed in this chapter. The teachers themselves will have to integrate these into sequences and modules and then dispense them according to individually diagnosed needs. The next chapter will describe this approach in the middle and upper grades.

One overriding conclusion emerging from four years of intensive research in teaching beginning reading to disadvantaged children bears repeating:

Intensive, thorough instruction that meets individual needs teaches disadvantaged children to read adequately. Such instruction appears to counterbalance the effects of environmental deprivation when we use reading achievement scores as a criterion for growth.

If this is true for disadvantaged children, is it not equally valid for advantaged children? I think it is. Consider this point as the individualized reading program is discussed in the next chapter and the applied reading program is described in Chapter Twelve.

References

1. J. Chall and S. Feldman, *Beginning Reading Study*, Cooperative Research Project (Washington, D.C.: U.S. Office of Education, 1966).
2. E. P. Bleismer and B. H. Yarborough, "A Comparison of Ten Different Beginning Reading Programs in First Grade," *Phi Delta Kappan,* 6 (June 1965), 500–5.
3. M. Woolman, *Reading in High Gear* (Chicago: Science Research Associates, 1964).
4. D. Rasmussen and L. Goldberg, *SRA Basic Reading Series* (Chicago: Science Research Associates, 1965).
5. L. Bloomfield and C. I. Barnhart, *Let's Read* (Detroit: Wayne State University Press, 1961).
6. R. F. Robinett *et al.*, *Miami Linguistic Readers* (Miami, Fla.: Dade County Public Schools, and Boston: D. C. Heath, 1965).
7. N. B. Smith, *Reading for Today's Children* (Englewood Cliffs, N.J.: Prentice-Hall, 1962).
8. D. D. Durrell *et al.*, "Success in First-grade Reading," *Journal of Education,* 140 (February 1958), 5.
9. ——— and H. Murphy, *Speech to Print Phonics* (New York: Harcourt, Brace & World, 1964).
10. Donald E. Smith, *Michigan Language Program* (Ann Arbor, Mich.: Ann Arbor Publishers, 1966).
11. A. Heilmann, *Phonics in Perspective* (Columbus, O.: Merrill, 1964).
12. W. S. Gray, *On Their Own in Reading* (Chicago: Scott, Foresman, 1960).
13. Glenn McCracken and Charles Walcutt, *Basic Reading* (Philadelphia: Lippincott, 1966).
14. H. Wenkart, *Phonic Readers* (Cambridge, Mass.: Wenkart, 1962).

15. M. Halvarsen *et al., Phonics We Use* (Chicago: Lyons and Carnahan, 1964).
16. G. Hildreth and R. LaCoste, *Spellingtime* (New York: Singer, 1964).
17. M. A. Lowry, *The Basic Phonics Program* (Cleveland: Reardon, 1964).
18. D. Parker and G. Scannell, *Reading Laboratory I: Word Games* (Chicago: Science Research Associates, 1961).
19. L. Carillo (ed.) *et al., Chandler Language Experience Readers* (San Francisco: Chandler, 1965, 1966).
20. H. Robinson *et al., The New Basic Readers,* Curriculum Foundation Series (Chicago: Scott, Foresman, 1965).
21. W. W. Bauer *et al., Health for All,* Health and Safety Readers Series (Chicago: Scott, Foresman, 1962).
22. I. S. Black, *The Bank Street Readers* (New York: Macmillan, 1966).
23. R. G. Wilson and C. C. Fries, *Basic Reading Series* (Columbus, O.: Merrill, 1966).
24. Catherine Stern *et al., Structural Reading Series* (New York: Singer, 1964).
25. Buchanan-Sullivan Associates, *Programmed Reading* (New York: McGraw-Hill, 1963).
26. M. W. Sullivan, *Reading* (Palo Alto, Calif.: Behavioral Research Laboratories, 1966).
27. D. Parker *et al., Reading Laboratories* (Chicago: Science Research Associates, 1960).
28. ———— *et al., Spelling Word Power Laboratory, IIc* (Chicago: Science Research Associates, 1966).
29. A. Holl *et al., Pilot Library* (Chicago: Science Research Associates, 1963).
30. T. G. Thurstone, *Reading for Understanding,* junior ed. (Chicago: Science Research Associates, 1964).
31. *Spectrum of Skills* (New York: Macmillan, 1964).
32. D. Betler, *The Literature Sampler,* junior ed. (New York: Xerox Educational Division, 1967).
33. S. Alan Cohen, "Individualized Reading and Programed Instruction," *Programed Instruction,* 3 (April 1964), 2–6.
34. ————, "A Psychology of Teaching Reading to Individuals," in M. J. Weiss (ed.), *Reading in the Elementary School* (New York: Odyssey Press, in press).
35. ————, *Report on Summer Reading School* (New York: Mobilization For Youth, 1964).

36. Abraham Tannenbaum, "Research Report on Preschool Reading Program—STAR" (New York: Mobilization For Youth, 1967, unpublished).
37. C. Cattegno, *Words in Color* (New York: Xerox Educational Division, 1965).
38. H. Tanyzer and A. J. Mazurkiewicz, *Early to Read i/t/a Program* (New York: Pitman, 1963).
39. A. J. Harris and B. L. Server, *Comparing Reading Approaches in First-grade Teaching with Disadvantaged Children,* Cooperative Research Project No. 2677 (Washington, D.C.: U.S. Office of Education, March 1966).

Chapter Eleven

Skills Centers

Introduction

To develop a technology for teaching disadvantaged children and youth, *we must learn how to educate individuals within a system of mass education.* Individualized learning, desirable for all children at all levels of achievement, is imperative for culturally disadvantaged underachievers. The War on Poverty, with its emphasis on educating disadvantaged children, has suddenly forced educators to try to put into practice all the theories of individualized instruction developed over the past half century. Lacking methods for realizing the theories and unwilling to settle for the unsatisfactory status quo, specialists in experimental programs, such as those set up by Mobilization For Youth, are at present developing a technology for individualized learning with a 30 to 1 pupil-teacher ratio.

The skills centers program is one such method of individualizing instruction using learning centers rather than traditional teacher-directed classrooms. The program described in this chapter is merely a beginning, an attempt to stop talking and start doing. In five years of experimenting with the program, I have watched teachers modify and vary the basic scheme to fit specific content areas or to fit unique situations. Once teachers were convinced that an individualized learning technology could be applied to the classroom, they were able to innovate in this direction on their own. Perhaps this chapter can do the same for other teachers who apply skills centers.

A History of Skills Centers

In 1962, the skills centers program's self-directing, self-correcting technique for teaching basic reading skills was piloted at a Massachusetts reform school for disadvantaged adolescent delinquents. In the summer of 1963, it was demonstrated in the Secondary Reading Clinic of the Boston University summer school. From 1963 to 1965, the techniques were tested in a number of settings at Mobilization For Youth's Demonstration Experimental Reading School. A version of the technique was implemented the following year in a joint community and school effort called the Two Bridges Project in Lower Manhattan under funds from the U.S. Office of Economic Opportunity. This program was planned and staffed by participants in the previous MFY program and was patterned after the summer experiment of 1964.

The skills centers program was implemented in a number of schools under varied conditions of time, pupil-teacher ratios, physical plant, available materials, and so forth It was further tested in a junior high school attended by severely retarded disadvantaged children under a Ford Foundation grant. It has been modified and demonstrated for three years at the Yeshiva University Ferkauf Graduate School, NDEA Institute for Disadvantaged Children. It is the basis of a federally funded experiment for teaching emotionally disturbed disadvantaged children in New York City. Variations extending the technique to other content areas, such as writing, science, and math, are underway. The skills centers program has been used from grade 4 through secondary school and in two Job Corps camps. In every project, this program resulted in marked gains in the reading achievement of participating students. One variation of a skills centers program, which was conducted in a public junior high school north of New York City, is described below.

An Example of Skills Centers

Among the blighted smaller cities struggling to survive on the periphery of Manhattan is a town of 55,000 people that once had the finest shopping center north of Fifth Avenue. Here, the school superintendent, a friend of the mayor, lacks the qualifications established by the school committee that appointed him. Staff morale is low. School plants are outdated by half a century except for two new school buildings used by the town elite. The state has designated this town a "critical area," which qualifies it for state and federal poverty funds, but these funds have somehow managed to become part of a political porkbarrel.

The principal of one junior high school was born in the town and educated in its schools. He is committed to the education of a "new population." But over 600 children, grades 6 through 9, spill over into the auditorium of an eighty-five-year-old building built for less than 500 children. Slightly more than 50 percent come from bilingual homes, with about nine percent speaking a language other than English. About 31 percent of this school's population is black; 20 percent is Puerto Rican. Over 50 percent of the children come from families with average incomes below $3,500 per year. About 30 percent of the school population is known to the local police and Youth Board for delinquent behavior.

Figure 1 shows the average achievement scores for this school as measured on the *Iowa Test of Basic Skills,* (ITBS). The scores have been steadily declining through the years, correlating to change in school population. The trend has been toward an increase in nonwhite, lower socioeconomic level families moving into the school district.

With achievement scores declining, delinquency increasing, and no increases in services or expenditures to meet the critical educational needs of the new population, the principal sought help at a local university, where he found an education department with foundation money to experiment with a curriculum for socially disadvantaged children.

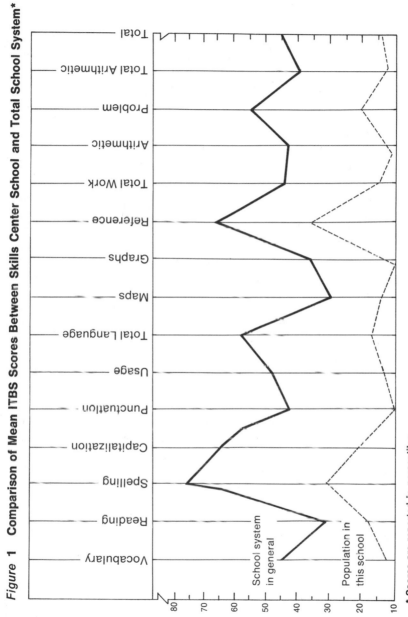

Figure 1 Comparison of Mean ITBS Scores Between Skills Center School and Total School System*

Vocabulary
Reading
Spelling
Capitalization
Punctuation
Usage
Total Language
Maps
Graphs
Reference
Total Work
Arithmetic
Problem
Total Arithmetic
Total

School system in general

Population in this school

80
70
60
50
40
30
20
10

* Scores are reported in percentiles.
Source: S. Alan Cohen, "Individualized Reading and Programed Instruction," *Programed Instruction*, 3 (April 1964).

Reforming the Curriculum

The problem of reforming the curriculum in such a setting was increased by the rigidity of the class schedule, physical plant, teacher-pupil ratio, and staff morale. These problems were further increased by traditional perceptions of classroom methodology— that is, a teacher's job is "to teach"; learning has second priority.

The university team, in attempting to solve these problems, had to structure an environment conducive to learning with under-achievers who were burdened by serious psychosocial pressures, and to do this within the limitations described. Most of these pupils had a history of school failure and delinquency. The university team's first job was to make learning the primary goal. Learning is an activity of the learner: *He* acts. If the primary goal is to teach, then the tendency is for the teacher to act—the pupil may or may not learn. The second job was to delimit the specific behaviors to be learned. With this particular population, basic reading skills were selected as most crucial to their needs. The third job was to define guidelines to learning; that is, what principles of education are most likely to meet the first priority?

The principal of the school agreed to give free reign to the experimenter and the teachers who volunteered to develop a program that would alleviate these educational problems. Three teachers, who expressed interest in attempting a new approach, met for two weeks in late August with the vice principal to rewrite the syllabus and to evaluate new materials that had been published recently. After four days with the experimenter, the teachers decided to ignore the syllabus and start from scratch. By the end of the two-week planning session the teachers agreed to meet the first priority: Emphasize learning, rather than teaching. Second, they agreed to delimit learning goals to basic reading skills and to include other aspects of literature, language, and social studies *only* if they aided the priority of "improving basic reading skills." This limitation was a sharp departure from the official teaching syllabus issued by the curriculum specialists of the central board of education. The decision had the consent of the principal, but did not carry the endorsement and approval of the central board of education administration. The state department of education, however, was willing to go along with the program even if it did not meet certain state requirements for the amount of time allotted for various content areas. This type of decision can be made by central administrative boards to encourage educational innovation.

By meeting the first two priorities the experiment was setting up an effective curriculum for severely retarded achievers in slum schools.

1. Emphasis on *learning* rather than *teaching*.
2. Emphasis on basic reading skills as the first educational objective.

The third priority was to draw up guidelines that would promote learning and that would guide the staff in the selection of materials and methods. The teachers agreed that effective learning usually occurs under self-direction. Therefore, the guidelines selected should lead to a reduction of teacher-directed activities in which the teacher lectures, explains, or addresses the entire class, and to more self-directing, differentiated learning by individuals or by small learning teams of pupils.

The following criteria, similar to those outlined by Durrell and discussed in various other publications, [1, 2, 3, 4, 5] were adopted as guides to methodology:

1. *High-intensity learning:* Pupils work individually or in small teams on self-directing materials that present a series of programed stimuli to which each individual responds. Learning is active and continuous. The individual does not have to wait his turn "to recite"; he is always "reciting"; he is always responding.
2. *Individualized content:* Based on diagnostic testing, children are assigned materials that match their needs. A child works on materials with subgroups of peers who have similar needs; he does not waste time working on skills he has already mastered.
3. *Individualized rate:* Because most of the materials are self-directing and self-correcting, a child moves at his own speed.
4. *Individualized level:* Reading selections are varied and individualized so that children read materials closer to their interest and ability levels.

Principles Underlying Skills Centers

The skills centers program is based on seven valid laws of learning. A concise list of these laws can be found in Hilgard's *Theories of Learning*. [6] A discussion of each law is presented here.

Laws of Learning

1. *When to teach what depends upon the individual's capacity.* For decades, American schools have predetermined the content of curriculum and the timetable and rate for teaching that content. Those who could not meet the timetable and rate and those who could not accept the content for various reasons usually ended up as dropouts. Now, with a focus on the disadvantaged, schools can no longer defend this method. Accumulated evidence shows that capacity is largely a learned "perceptual set" influenced primarily by early environmental opportunity in the form of incidental and formal learning. Content must be adjusted to this capacity and to individual need. Defending any content as being absolutely necessary to the education of disadvantaged children—with three exceptions: reading, writing, and arithmetic—would be difficult.

2. *A motivated learner acquires what he learns more readily than one who is not motivated.* In the skills centers program, motivation is handled according to valid laws of learning. Motivation that is too intense (pain, fear, or extreme anxiety) may introduce distracting emotional states. Every youngster has strengths and weaknesses. In an individualized, self-directing program each youngster moves at his own pace in a direction dictated by his own diagnosed strengths and weaknesses. In such a program, a youngster recognizes that two other classmates working on another skill, in another part of the room, do not have the same weaknesses. Their problems are different. Individual differences are obvious not only to the teacher, but to the pupils as well. Instead of punishing a youngster for his weaknesses, the self-directing program rewards him for helping discover his own weakness and for remediating that weakness. Ego defense is unnecessary. Finally, the system provides a floating teacher who can boost the ego of the threatened child and control the level of motivation.

Learning under intrinsic motivation is preferable to learning under extrinsic motivation. The entire program is built on achievement success rewards. Not grades or candy, but successful achievement of a skill is the basic motivation. Research indicates that achievement success feeds on itself and drives the subject to further achievement. Although research also shows that target behaviors in the laboratory tend to be learned equally well with either positive or negative reinforcers, most learning specialists agree that side effects or "social by-products" (nontarget behaviors) are more favorable when learning is reinforced positively. Failure or lack of success is a temporary state. The goal is success; the methodology offers each individual the chance to succeed.

Tolerance for failure is best taught through providing a backlog of success that compensates for experienced failure. By focusing on strengths and weaknesses and on specific operations, the skills centers program matches materials to strengths to ensure success, and to weaknesses to ensure growth. Learning goals are defined operationally in very specific subskills. Individuals move step by step through a complex pattern with a built-in high incidence of success.

3. *Individuals need practice in setting goals for themselves, goals neither so low as to elicit little effort nor so high as to foreordain failure. Realistic goal setting leads to more satisfactory improvement than unrealistic goal setting.* In the skills centers program, instruction is largely self-directing. The individual pupil is making decisions, constantly checking and pacing himself. His teacher is a consultant who offers suggestions for goals and for means.

4. *Active participation by a learner is preferable to passive reception.* The program's primary feature is high-intensity learning. Frequency of response is high because instruction is individualized. The program incorporates this feature of a tutorial system while preserving the advantages of a group experience by using self-teaching materials that can be used either individually or in learning teams. The student does the teaching in conjunction with materials, classmates, and a supervising teacher.

5. *Meaningful tasks are learned more efficiently than tasks not understood by the learner.* In the skills centers program, this learning principle is fulfilled through the following principle.

6. *Information about the nature of a good performance, knowledge of his own mistakes, and knowledge of successful results aid the learner.* Many educators insist that all materials should relate directly to the student's needs or interests. They argue, for example, that basal reader content is relatively meaningless to culturally deprived youngsters who cannot relate to the middle class content. This is an excellent guide: The materials and task of a program should conform to the student's needs or interests. However, there are other types of meaning. This is implied in research that indicates, for example, that basal readers are as effective as "high-interest" literature in teaching reading. Knowledge of goals, knowledge of results of drill exercises, and the chance to succeed give these tasks and materials tremendous meaning for individuals who want to succeed regardless of actual literary content.

7. *The personal history of an individual—his reaction to authority, for example—may hamper or enhance his ability to learn from a given teacher.* The day may come when teachers and administrators are psychologically secure enough to recognize individual differences of temperament and perception and are willing to transfer youngsters in order to best match teacher-student personalities. Meanwhile, a teaching program that allows both maximum and minimum contact between teacher and student will help us adjust to this problem. In a skills centers program, a youngster who cannot relate to his teacher (or vice versa) benefits from the self-teaching program and from close personal interaction with classmates in learning teams.

Principles of Psychosocial Development

Social Responsibility. Team learning techniques to teach skills and content thrust youngsters into situations in which they must depend upon each other. Our preliminary research with team learning indicated that when youngsters chose to work on a skill, they quickly recognized the necessity of interdependence. Excellent research in team learning at Boston University shows higher achievement on many tasks and in content units that are self-taught in teams of two, three, five, or ten compared to achievement when taught in groups of thirty or individually. To teach social responsibility, *real* experience is more potent than vicarious experience. In the skills centers program, social responsibility is necessary to teach individual goals. It is taught by the subtle and potent technique of incidental learning.

Personal Responsibility. A self-directing, self-correcting learning experience requires the individual to make decisions. He must teach himself. This situation is not unstructured; like most areas of our daily lives, it is a highly structured environment. But within the structure is the provision for adequate amounts of self-direction. Positive self-direction and decision making are two characteristics of maturity. Producing mature individuals is one of the school's goals. Yet, under present methodology, education contributes to the "social prolongation of infancy" by spoon-feedings, tight schedules, restrictions, dormitory curfews, and so on. From kindergarten through graduate and professional school, students are told what, when, how much, and by what means to read. Like their more fortunate "advantaged" peers, socially disadvantaged children quickly learn to wait for directions. Teachers spend energy and time training children to be educational robots.

Social-Personal Development. In a program geared to individual needs, the youngster perceives himself as successful. Each step fits his level and rate, and probability of success is increased. Furthermore, he recognizes around him the variability of strengths and weaknesses. The student experiences his own worth; materials and methods are matched to him, not he to them. With everyone working at his own pace on his own needs, he can devote time to some of his special interests—to what we call "pupil specialities." They become part of the classroom routine. Suddenly, his interests are important to the school, which is the power culture's agent. It is as if the power culture were saying to the individual, "We recognize and respect your uniqueness."

Rewards and Satisfactions. The focus of the experimental program is on intrinsic rewards. Although teachers talk abundantly about the evils of materialism, these same teachers hold extrinsic rewards over their students' heads as enticements to achieve: grades, honors, prizes, and special privileges. In skills centers success is its own reward.

General Hostility and Negative Behaviors. If theories of individual and social behaviors are valid, negatively reinforced behaviors affect the total personality in areas beyond the specific behavior being learned. The "social by-products" of constant negative reinforcements are hostility and, in general, negative behaviors throughout the entire personality. The skills centers program uses positive reinforcement and avoids these social by-products.

Frustration Tolerance. When the classroom provides an atmosphere in which a youngster succeeds, it builds into the personality a backlog of success to compensate for occasional failures. In culturally deprived areas the public school could become, if it adopted a skills centers program, the only major social force dedicated to the building of success reserves in a population that usually experiences failures, rejection, and disapproval. The juvenile delinquency that concerns us in disadvantaged areas is the end result of this frustration.

Control of Destiny. One characteristic of the culturally deprived is the attitude of futility. Puerto Ricans on East 2nd Street or blacks on 125th Street in Manhattan tend to see themselves as helpless victims of contemporary conditions. In a self-directing learning process, the individual becomes partial master of his educational destiny.

Operation of Skills Centers

In the skills centers program for the junior high school discussed earlier, a team of three teachers was assigned 180 children, 90 in the morning, 90 in the afternoon, for three consecutive class hours. The team and pupils were allotted three adjoining rooms. Because the traditional schedule called for a period of language arts, one of literature, and one of social studies, the scheduling for the program was not a problem. One teacher, thirty pupils, one room per hour was no tax on the principal's scheduling ingenuity. A skills centers program merely replaced the language arts, literature, and social studies block.

Each teacher became a specialist in one skills center. In this example the three centers (see floor plans and materials, pp. 241–245) were:

Skills center 1: vocabulary—word attack
Skills center 2: general comprehension
Skills center 3: work-study skills

In this particular program, each set of 90 pupils was grouped into three classes according to IQ and reading achievement. Grade 7 and 8 designations were eliminated; pupils were ungraded. The basis for grouping, however, was strictly arbitrary; the groups were not really homogeneous, but as in many school systems, the guidance office went through the complicated hocus-pocus of "grouping homogeneously" into Groups A, B, and C.

Group A started the three-class hour block in skills center 1, group B in center 2, and group C in center 3. The groups rotated for the second hour and again for the third. Each day, each group received intensive work in each of the centers except for individual students who needed more or less work in any of the three areas. Because the three rooms adjoined and the three teachers operated as a team, an individual pupil could remain at any center as long as necessary.

Each center offered self-directing, self-correcting materials to match individual or small group needs. Each center was also further broken down into skills stations. All pupils were pretested on diagnostic tests. According to the diagnostic patterns, each pupil was given a weekly schedule of daily activities listing materials he was to use and approximate time allotment. The individual schedules were modified daily as the pupil mastered subskills. A weekly schedule for a pupil in work-study skills center would appear on page 236.

Three or four pupils who had the same schedule formed a team and worked together. Teams and team positions in the room were posted weekly. During the week, however, a pupil might be shifted from one team to another if his individual schedule were modified. For example, Peter Smith might be able to eliminate dictionary skills from his schedule in the third week. He would then be assigned to another skill that his diagnostic pattern indicated was necessary, such as outlining from workbooks. Occa-

Work-Study Skills Station
Tentative Weekly Schedule

Name _*Peter Smith*_

Materials	Approximate time in minutes
English 2200 Frames 72–200	10
Gates-Peardon Main ideas	15
World history workbook	15
Dictionary skills	15

sionally, one pupil would have a unique schedule that fit no other pupil; he would work individually. Each pupil worked on self-directing materials, which he obtained and returned after he had checked himself. During a 55-minute class, a pupil participated in a variety of activities, moving about the room and pacing himself. When he felt ready to give up a skill, he would ask for a check-out test that would be administered by another pupil or by the teacher.

Less than half the materials used were published as programed instruction, and the remainder were materials modified under the staff's direction. However, the actual work of modifying materials was done by volunteer pupils and PTA members. The teacher team had the first and last class hours free for planning together and for directing volunteer materials modifiers. The teacher in charge of skills center 2 (general comprehension) used SRA Reading Labs as ongoing diagnostic checks. Although the first set of exercises on each SRA card helps train for comprehension skills, the rest of the exercises are less valuable as teaching stimuli and more valuable as testing stimuli. By analyzing patterns of errors in the SRA Lab Pupil Handbooks, the teacher was able to advise his team of individual weaknesses. Pupils ran listening centers, controlled reading centers, and tachistoscopic training exercises themselves. Listening skill exercises were recorded on tape. Seven individual listening stations were set up inexpensively using one tape recorder, two Koss T-4 couplers, and seven inexpensive headsets. A Speed-I-O-Scope (Graflex, Inc.) was mounted in front of a standard filmstrip projector to make an inexpensive tachistoscope. The same attachment was used in front of an Educational Development Laboratories (EDL) Controlled Reader to use it as a tachistoscope as well. All pupils kept extensive progress plotters that showed how well they were progressing. Many progress plotters were simple histograms and bar graphs, and this was thus an effective method of teaching graph-reading skills. Answers were provided for all exercises either with the worksheet or in one corner of the room designated as the "answer corner." Students always checked themselves, even on progress tests. The need to cheat quickly disappeared when pupils realized that all evaluation was self-evaluation. This realization occurred after approximately three to five weeks.

The Teacher's Role

The skills centers program stresses learning and redefines the traditional role of the teacher. When pupils are self-directed or when they operate in pupil learning teams, the teacher's role is drastically changed. The program described here, as well as other skills centers program projects, suggests that the new role may be unusually traumatic and difficult for most teachers. The most crucial variable in planning self-directed learning programs for schoolchildren may be the teacher's ability to assume a new role.

In a skills centers program, the teacher's responsibilities, in the order of priority, arc as follows:

1. *Arrange conditions conducive to learning by structuring a "therapeutic classroom."* A therapeutic classroom is free of punitive reinforcement for behaviors related to learning. If necessary, punishment may be sparingly used as a response to delinquent social behavior. But it is never used to negatively reinforce incorrect pupil responses to a learning stimulus.

The human organism tends to resist change, because change is risky business. When we perceive our environment as safe, we are more willing to risk trying a new behavior. If the pupil is presented a stimulus, the response to which may be reinforced negatively by a "red mark against him," a "flunk," or a look of disapproval from his teacher, the risk involves censure. There is danger. In danger, the organism flees or fights; it rigidifies— tightens up. Perception and resulting behavior become less flexible. Behavior variations are reduced. Research in psychology, neurophysiology, and stress has demonstrated this phenomenon. A therapeutic classroom accepts the wrong answer without threat of punishment or disapproval. The wrong answer signals an opportunity to learn. The correct answer symbolizes the termination of opportunity to learn—the child has *already learned*. In a therapeutic classroom, the teacher does not sit in judgment of his pupils. The judge is personal—*I*. Grades are deemphasized. Ideally, teacher-given tests are the bases of self-evaluation. The teacher helps the pupil interpret the tests and plan activities for learning, but the teacher preserves the individual's right to judge himself. Maintaining this therapeutic climate is the most important role of the teacher.

2. *Teach pupils how to teach themselves.* The largest amount of time in this new role is spent in teaching pupils how to direct themselves; how to select material appropriate to their needs; how to use the materials correctly; how to evaluate, record, and interpret progress charts. This activity requires the greatest investment of teacher time, but the results pay off in areas more basic than reading, writing, and arithmetic—in the form of independence, confidence, and general maturity.

3. *Ensure success by carefully matching materials to needs.* The pupil is not a professional. He is neither an expert in diagnosis nor a specialist in educational methodology or materials. The teacher has the responsibility to aid him in diagnosing his needs and to determine what goals are most important to his needs. Furthermore, the teacher must select the self-directing materials to

match the pupil's needs, and then change the pupil's schedule accordingly.

4. *Diagnose, guide, interpret, and evaluate growth.* These activities are always done in conjunction with the pupil as service to him, *not* as a judgment.

5. *Supply on-the-spot first aid when materials do not work or when they are unavailable.* Careful diagnosis can uncover so many possible needs, and no teacher in the skills centers program can always have at his fingertips ready-made, self-directing materials to meet these needs. Most published materials are designed for traditional teacher-directed methods. Although this situation will change, teachers conducting a self-directing learning classroom now will find this job most demanding, along with the following task.

6. *Develop new materials to solve the problem in the future.* Obviously, great quantities of preparation time would be involved here. One technique for increasing production of teacher-made, self-directing learning materials is to utilize the pupils themselves. In a number of skills centers programs, pupils were recruited from "work periods" to produce materials under the teacher's direction. More recently, I have used special corps recruited under U.S. Office of Economic Opportunity funds, such as VISTA and Neighborhood Youth Corps, to produce materials for various self-directing education programs.

7. *Personally interact with individuals and small groups.* No other teaching technique, except the 1-to-1 tutorial method, provides as much teacher-pupil interaction as the self-directing classroom. This technique provides adequately for individual attention. It is the face-to-face interaction that allows, for example, the sensitive male teacher to meet the psychological needs of the occasional disadvantaged child who tends to lack satisfying relationships with adult males, which seems to be a pet observation of educational sociologists.

8. *Group, and continuously regroup, small learning teams.*
Progress is swift in a self-directing learning program, and children
are moving at various paces in various directions. Diagnosis
should be ongoing. Pupil learning teams based on needs should be
continuously modified at least weekly, and often daily.

9. *Introduce lectures and other full group activities.* There is
nothing inherently bad about teaching thirty children at once.
Some activities are effectively presented to a full class—a film,
trip, discussion, and so forth. Thus, although the basic method is
individualized instruction and small pupil-team learning units, the
full class, teacher-directed technique is one minor variation in the
teacher's repertoire. This method, however, is used only when it is
the most effective means of learning for the pupils.

Three Skills Centers

What do skills centers look like? What kinds of materials do
they use? Following is a partial list of materials and a description
with floor plans of the three skills centers conducted in the junior
high school described above.

Word-Attack Vocabulary Skills Center. The teacher in charge of
the word-attack vocabulary skills center was responsible for matching the materials and methods to the diagnosed needs of each
pupil. In addition to information about vocabulary from standardized tests, the pupils were given a diagnostic word-attack
skills test developed by the staff. As pupils moved through the
center, the teacher in charge also gave spot clinical tests when he
needed additional information about a particular child. This
teacher concentrated on inventing many self-directing or pupil
team-learning techniques and on gathering materials for teaching
code busting, word analysis, and vocabulary development. In these
skill areas, a number of discarded workbooks were collected,
modified into self-directed exercise cards with accompanying answer keys and structured answer sheets. Individual exercises were
filed according to skill and level, resulting in a formidable supply
of reinforcement exercises in kit form. Included in this center were
spelling materials which were used to help teach word analysis and
vocabulary. Figure 2 shows the floor plan.

Figure **2   Floor Plan for Word-Attack Vocabulary Center**

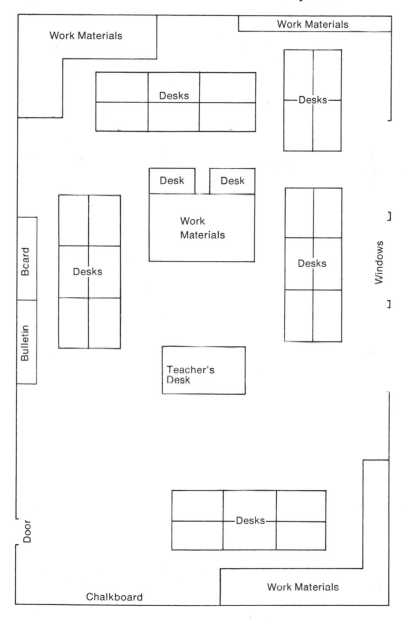

Materials:

Spectrum Word Analysis (Macmillan)
Spectrum Vocabulary (Macmillan)
Word Games Kit (SRA games with Mobilization For Youth Manual)
Spelling Kit (SRA)
Turner-Livingston Reading Series (Follett)
Learning How to Use the Dictionary (Macmillan)
Eye Span Trainer (AVR)
Word Analysis Cards (Harcourt, Brace & World)
Reader's Digest Skill Builders
Word Film Strips (EDL)
Programmed Vocabulary (Lyons and Carnahan)
Mystery Series (Harr Wagner)
Basic Reading Skills J.H.S. (Scott, Foresman)
Scope (Scholastic weekly magazine)
Specific Skills Series (Barnell Loft)
Tachistoscope (Graflex)
Botel's Writing Skills (Follett)
Basic Phonics Program (Reardon)
Phonics We Use (Lyons and Carnahan)
Spellingtime (Singer)
Games (Hammett, Kenworthy, Garrard)
Teacher-made materials
Word wheels
RSL Kit (Houghton Mifflin)
Key Lab (Houghton Mifflin)
Phonics with Write and See (Appleton-Century)
Landon Program (Chandler)
T-Matic 150 (Psychotechnics)

Comprehension Skills Center. Like the other centers, the comprehension center was entirely self-directing with large group instruction limited to demonstrations of how to use the self-teaching materials. The comprehension center focused on three techniques: reading in laboratories and the classroom library, training on a reading machine, and training in listening comprehension.

Listening comprehension exercises were drawn from SRA Reading Lab Teacher Manuals and recorded on magnetic tape. Six to eight headsets were plugged into Koss T-4 couplers that were

Figure **3** **Floor Plan for Comprehension Center**

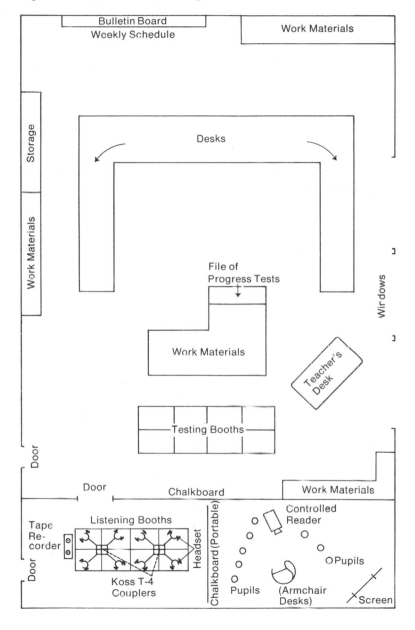

connected to a tape recorder. Pupils sat at a long oak table converted into small learning booths with Masonite partitions built by the pupils in the school workshop. Since the original skills centers, other listening programs have been tried with equal success. Figure 3 shows the floor plan.

Materials:

Spectrum Comprehension Skills (Macmillan)
Reading Lab IIa (SRA)
Reading Lab IIc (SRA)
Reading Lab IIIb (SRA)
Pilot Library IIa (SRA)
Pilot Library IIc (SRA)
Controlled Reader (EDL)
Films and workbooks (EDL)
Scope (Scholastic weekly magazine)
Phonics We Use (Lyons and Carnahan)
Classroom library (paperbacks as well as hard covers)
Tape recorder
Literature Sampler (Xerox)
Variety of comprehension workbooks
Koss T-4 couplers
Headsets
Specific Skills Series (Barnell Loft)
People to People (Random House)
Literature Sampler, junior edition (Xerox)
New Practice Readers (Webster)
Reading Attainment System (Grolier)
RSL Kit (Houghton Mifflin)
Reading Development Kit (Addison Wesley)

Work-Study Skills Center. In the work-study skills center every pupil worked on self-teaching self-correcting materials. As the program progressed, more traditional techniques were reintroduced as supplements to self-direction. Such activities as a lecture, a film, or a trip were used when they were the most effective technique for presenting a specific skill or information. Figure 4 shows the floor plan.

Figure **4   Floor Plan for Work-Study Skills Center**

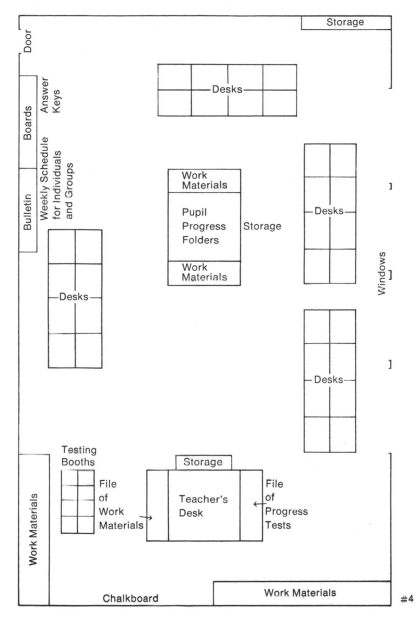

#4

Materials:

English 2200 (Harcourt, Brace & World)
Programed Geography (Macmillan)
Reader's Digest Skill Builders
World History Study Lessons (Follett)
Scope (Scholastic weekly magazine)
Reading Improvement Skill Texts (Merrill)
Turner-Livingston Reading Series (Follett)
Practice Readers Book 4 (Webster)
Basic Reading Skills J.H.S. (Scott, Foresman)
Adventure Series (Harr Wagner)
Gates-Peardon Practice Exercises (Bureau of Publications, Teachers College)
Basic Education Series (Follett)
Miscellaneous workbook exercises
McCall-Crabbe Reading Exercises (Bureau of Publications, Teachers College)
Tactics (Scott, Foresman)
RSL Kit (Houghton Mifflin)

Summary

Culturally deprived low achievers can become self-directed learners if we teach them how. Individualized instruction can be achieved with a 30-to-1 pupil-teacher ratio, if schools are willing to innovate. Delinquents, low achievers, and high achievers appear to learn well in skills centers. Learning increases and behavior problems decrease. In every experiment that used a variation of the skills centers program with all types of pupil populations, teachers reported a reduction of classroom discipline problems.

There are difficulties, however. One major problem involves teaching style. Even when teachers volunteer and become ego-involved, they have great difficulty shifting from traditional teacher-directed, large-group instruction to self-directed learning by individual pupils and small pupil teams. In the program described, teachers felt guilty and inadequate about their new roles. This feeling lasted through the first month in most cases. Another problem is the teacher's need for direction. As a consultant, I had to continuously fight off pressure by teachers and administrators to have me directly administer the program. In every case, however, when the principal displayed faith in his own staff, teachers were eventually willing to assume full responsibility for curriculum change and for pilot experiments in teaching.

Still another problem has been the paucity of self-directing school materials. Publishers, however, are beginning to recognize the need for individualized instruction and to produce materials in a more self-directing format. Furthermore, a little labor and ingenuity can easily modify traditional materials into self-directing materials. Not so easily overcome is the problem of high-interest, low-vocabulary materials for grades 6 through 9. Teachers cannot get enough of these materials, and publishers, alas, cannot find enough people who are able to write them.

The skills centers program intensifies the problem of report cards, which has always plagued teachers. The therapeutic atmosphere of self-directed learning inherently conflicts with a traditional school's orientation toward judging children. The solution to this problem is simple enough when schools have the desire to change. We replaced report cards with diagnostic graphs plotting each child's status in each area in September and plotting progress at intervals throughout the year. Contrary to some teachers' fears, this system has not been too difficult for parents to understand. They are delighted to receive detailed analyses usually plotted against national norms. Another problem, one that ultimately becomes an asset, is the focus on diagnosed needs out of which the parent report form emerges and out of which the skills centers program curriculum develops. Most teachers are unable to diagnose these needs. But when the problem is faced, when teachers must operate skills centers and fill out diagnostic reports, when teachers commit themselves to this type of pedagogy, they show no difficulty in learning diagnostic techniques.

On the average, skills centers have been yielding 2.0 to 2.5 months' growth in reading achievement scores per month of operation. For severely retarded readers in grades 4 through 9 this gain may not be sufficient to allow them to catch up with on-grade achievers, who tend to accelerate even faster with skills centers. Add to this the very limited areas of the curriculum now covered by skills centers, and we are left with a great deal of work yet to be done in the education of disadvantaged children.

How much more will be done? The facts are that an atmosphere of fear and distrust of anything *really* new prevails in schools, in general, and particularly in inner city schools. The innovations presented in this and the next chapter, which describes innovation in content areas and the use of paperback books in the classroom, are limited to practical and conservative suggestions in the hope that they will provide the interested, committed educator with the resources to launch a program with some hope of success.

References

1. S. Alan Cohen, "Reading Instruction—Beating the 50-year Lag," *Pressures That Disorganize in Secondary Schools* (31st Yearbook, New Jersey Secondary School Teachers Association, 1966).
2. ————, *A Curriculum Demonstration Project for Teaching Literacy Skills to Disadvantaged Seventh and Eighth Graders* (Conference Proceedings, Research Planning Conference on Language Development in Disadvantaged Children, Yeshiva University, 1967).
3. ————, "A Psychology of Teaching Reading to Individuals," in M. J. Weiss (ed.), *Reading in the Elementary School* (New York: Odyssey Press, in press).
4. ————, "Reading: Large Issues, Specific Problems, Possible Solutions," in A. Reiss (ed.), *Schools in a Changing Society* (New York: Free Press, 1966), 121–152.
5. ————, "Individualized Reading and Programed Instruction," *Programed Instruction,* 3 (April 1964), 2–4.
6. Ernest Hilgard, *Theories of Learning* (New York: Appleton-Century-Crofts, 1965), pp. 486–87.

Chapter Twelve

Reading in Content Areas

Introduction

"Reading in content areas" is current educational jargon for what most people consider "reading in general." We read literature, history, science, current events, and mathematics, but we also read road signs, do-it-yourself directions, maps, recipes, and personal letters. The goal of curriculums concerned with "reading in content areas" is to teach children these functional reading skills. The term would never have been invented if the schools had been teaching functional reading. They have not and they do not; teachers expect children to use reading functionally, but very few teach them how. Most children teach themselves.

For example, in the first three or four grades, reading instruction is a "subject" taught for fifty minutes, two hours, or any specified length of time per day. Instruction consists of training in code busting and in other more sophisticated skills, such as those outlined in Chapter Ten. It is not uncommon for a fourth-grade teacher to teach reading from 9:30 to 10:30 A.M. to slow learners, using a second-grade basal reader that is, perhaps, suitable to their reading level if not their interest level. From 10:30 to 11:15 A.M. that same teacher will assign the same children a geography lesson from a fourth-grade geography textbook and expect the children to learn their geography. Thus, the need to focus on reading in content areas stems from two related problems: (1) the tendency to separate reading and writing from the rest of the curriculum; (2) the tendency to assign reading in content areas unrelated to reading levels and needs. Let us consider two examples.

Some Problems and Solutions

Example One—Math

Robert is an eight-year-old who attends an elementary school in a Midwestern industrial town of 60,000. We observed a staff conference in which his third-grade teacher described how Robert was barely beyond a preprimer reading level. According to the teacher, Robert's problem was "low general learning aptitude" because his arithmetic achievement scores were also below his grade placement. Her reasoning was based on research which indicated that many retarded readers with high learning potential show this potential in relatively high arithmetic achievement contrasted to low reading achievement.

We observed Robert later that same day working in Eicholz' *Elementary School Mathematics.* [1] When the teacher explained that segment *A* was longer than segment *B,* Robert understood her. But when Robert had to work his problems from his workbook, or when he had to learn a new math concept from his textbook, he was lost. When I sat with Robert and read the workbook and textbook to him, he was able to compute correct answers. Robert could not read the words *segment* and *longer.* As a result of this discovery, the school decided to move Robert back to a first-grade arithmetic book. But Robert was obviously capable of mastering third-grade arithmetic. To move him back would adjust the textbook to his reading level, but would deprive him of cashing in on his arithmetic abilities. We regrouped Robert's class into learning groups to preteach key vocabulary in arithmetic books to those who needed it. In this way, Robert's arithmetic text and workbook became, in a sense, reading books. Robert, and others like him, were taught to read their arithmetic books the same way they were taught to read Dick, Sally, and Spot. How could the teacher do this?

In a class of 28 third-graders, 10 children were reading at first-grade level, but were able to handle math concepts and arithmetic computation at third-grade level. Another 7 were less fortunate; they were retarded in both reading and math concepts. In his explanation of a new math concept, the teacher presented the full class with a verbal explanation and with computation on the chalkboard. Key terms were printed on the chalkboard and taught to the poorer readers. It took only a few seconds for the teacher to say and print a key term, such as *segment*.

The class was then divided into three groups—group one, consisting of those who needed further training in the math concept, as well as reading instruction; group two, those who needed help in reading the workbooks, but who understood the math concept (Robert's group); and group three, those who could work independently, having both adequate reading and math ability. The teacher taught a reading lesson using flashcards and writing reinforcement to groups one and two, while group three worked alone. To keep the independent group involved, the teacher built a self-directing, high-intensity pedagogy, as described in the skills centers method in Chapter Eleven. This method required immediate feedback, self-evaluation, and self-pacing. Once the members of group two had grasped the key terms as sight words, they joined group three in independent work. Thus, the teacher was free to concentrate on group one; they needed both reading and math instruction. Occasionally, Robert still fumbled with a word. However, rather than interrupt the teacher, who was working with group one, he asked a designated teacher-helper in group three for assistance.

This method requires a flexible classroom and a flexible teacher who can tolerate a reasonable amount of traffic and noise in a busy, pupil-directed classroom. The technique works successfully with a 30-to-1 pupil-teacher ratio when both furniture and teacher are movable. Another effective method is to use the traditional study guide to aid comprehension. A reading teacher might mimeograph a study guide for use with a story or reading selection. The study guide is a list of selected questions formulated to call the reader's attention to important ideas as he reads. The reader first reads the guide questions, which parallel the reading selection, and uses them to guide his reading. This technique aids comprehension, but, of course, is not the unique methodological property of reading teachers. It is equally effective when used by math teachers to aid children to comprehend their math books.

Example Two—English, Science, and Social Studies

Mr. Mackey is chairman of the science department of an urban junior-senior high school. "General science" is taken for four consecutive years by 66 percent of the students. "That's punishment duty for uncooperative teachers, or initiation for novices," says Mr. Mackey confidentially. General science is a pseudonym for *war*—war between disgruntled teachers and illiterate or semi-literate adolescents who cannot read the dull, tattered texts bulging with information they would find irrelevant to their personal needs even if they were able to read them.

"These kids can't read," says Mr. Mackey. "I don't know what their elementary schools have been doing and I can't get anywhere with our English department." So Mr. Mackey's teachers resort to fifty minutes of busywork, coercion, and brute force to restrain each class.

"We are lucky," says Mrs. Greene, chairman of the English and language arts department in the same junior-senior high school. "We have three reading teachers, three more than other schools have, who see about 50 percent of our pupils twice a week. But this is a drop in the bucket. Most of these pupils need more than one hundred minutes a week of intensive remediation. Besides, 66 percent of our pupils read at fourth-grade level or below."

The English, science, and social studies teachers in this school attempt to teach literature and grammar, biology, chemistry, physics and general science, world history, civics, geography, and American history to all pupils. All the textbooks are at grade placement level. Despite the fact that 66 percent of the pupils are semi- or totally illiterate, the school purchases classroom sets of useless textbooks far above the reading levels of the pupils.

The battle wages from September through June. Both sides regroup and mend their wounds during July and August to begin again the fall and winter campaigns. Ostensibly, the teachers win.

Some children break and conform, or survive and get their high school certificates. Many others surrender by leaving as dropouts.

Pedagogically, the problem boils down to predetermined content, much of which is irrelevant; poorly trained teachers caught in a bind; and illiterate or semiliterate pupils who cannot handle the content because they do not have the skills. All of this occurs in a tradition-bound system that resists change in both overt and subtle ways. How can they break this bind?

Human Obstacles to Change. First, some of the teachers cannot be salvaged—but the majority want to do a good job and can change. In every curriculum experiment or innovation we have implemented, most of the teachers responded. Whenever they saw the possibility of success they not only cooperated, but they began to innovate. A few teachers refused to admit that predicate nominatives were useless to a child who cannot read, or that knowledge of combustion engines was unimportant, because unless he can read, the young adult will be unable to fill out a job application to become a mechanic. But these teachers were exceptions; most of the staff recognized literacy as a basic goal of the school and were anxious to cooperate with the new program.

In Mrs. Greene's and Mr. Mackey's school, we introduced sensitivity training. Biweekly therapy groups were formed and met on school time. Their focus was on two group-dynamics problems: first, the individual's sensitivity to self; second, the individual's sensitivity to others in order to understand the dynamics of change. We have found sensitivity training for key school administrators and teachers an excellent backup to curriculum change. Coupled with curriculum changes and teacher workshops focusing on methods and materials, the T-groups facilitated change by opening communications among key administrators (particularly the principal) and teachers.

Frank communication was needed, for example, between Mrs. Greene and Mr. Mackey. There was obviously little communication among the separate academic disciplines. An administrative decree eliminating departments would have been a mere paper change—and far more than this was necessary. The science teachers needed to realize that the science books were not only useless to most of these children, but that the English teachers were no more prepared to teach reading than were they. All teachers had to understand that three reading teachers could not handle severe reading problems in such large numbers. Everyone, including the reading teachers, had to understand that teaching reading to semiliterate and illiterate children in the upper middle and secondary grades requires much more than two periods. It requires five full school days if we expect significant results in a reasonably short period of time. Finally, almost every staff member at every level had to confront his own perceptions of pupils, most of whom were disadvantaged black children from low socioeconomic backgrounds.

Solution: All Teachers Teach Reading. The three reading teachers were taken out of Mrs. Greene's English department to form a task force that was directed by an assistant principal. They were responsible to the principal, not to the department. Meanwhile, the principal agreed to make clear to all teachers that basic literacy would take precedence over content. This meant that an English, science, social studies, math, music, art, or physical education teacher could not escape his responsibility to upgrade reading and writing skills. This did not preclude content; each subject area teacher was expected to use his subject as reading material.

The task force conducted daily workshops for teachers on methods of teaching reading in content areas. Teachers agreed to spend one preparation period daily at a materials preparation center in a room adjoining the library. Soon after its implementation, teachers recruited students and eventually parents to help prepare materials for teaching reading through the content areas. Each department made an exhaustive study of vocabulary in the content area. The materials preparation center invented flashcard games, tachistoscopes, vocabulary exercises in structural analysis, and even phonics exercises with content area words.

Two teachers from each department formed a team headed by the librarian. Using lists and contacting publishers' representatives, they began to build classroom libraries that consisted of high-interest, low-vocabulary "general reading" books in content areas. Unfortunately, many of the books were not listed by the board of education. In addition, the principal could not get permission to spend textbook funds on other kinds of books, and the project had to be abandoned. Had this administrative impediment been overcome, teachers could have combined textbook and library funds and could have built packages of classroom libraries at various reading levels. Each package of thirty or forty different books could have covered an aspect of science, social studies, English, or math. Supplementary materials from the materials preparation center could preteach key vocabulary and reinforce comprehension. Teachers would teach from many books and children would supply most of the information.

Reading in Content Areas for High Achievers

The typical history homework assignment is to read pages 67 to 74 and to answer questions 1 to 6 on page 93 (in ink, of course). A "smart" student knows he can get the answers to the questions from Tom during homeroom period before class. During the history period the teacher will merely repeat what is on pages 67 to 74, or if he is "progressive," he will "elicit" responses from students to leading questions that repeat the information. Good listening skills and some guts will get a "smart" student through his history courses.

Especially in math, teachers rarely expect their students to understand what they read. The typical math class begins with a thorough discussion of a theorem, for example, that is explained on page 42. Nevertheless, the teacher explains the theorem. If the explanation is successful ten minutes short of the bell, the children begin to do the 30 exercises on page 43. (This reinforces the theorem on page 42.) The homework assignment, of course, is to do the 30 exercises on page 43 and then read and study the new theorem on page 44. The next day's lesson involves checking the exercises, and explaining the new theorem on page 44, which everyone was supposed to have read but not really to have learned. Most students peruse the theorem but do not spend enough time to think out its implications, because they know the teacher will explain it tomorrow. The teacher feels compelled to explain the theorem—what else is he good for? This teacher, incidentally, may be the first to be replaced by computers.

From the early grades reading is not real. Learning is supposed to come out of discussion but not really out of reading. So pupils learn not to use reading in content areas; they do not really need to. Therefore, the first rule of effective teaching of reading in content areas is: *make reading real.* The classroom is a place to share insights and information, to interact, and to create. But it is not a replacement for reading nor should it be a checkpoint. A history teacher can pose a problem. Children reading many sources can use their information to solve the problem. A math teacher can pose a problem; his pupils can apply what they have read to solve the problem. The teacher can add information not available to the pupils in their books.

The content area teacher must collect appropriate reading material for his pupils, appropriate in reading level and content. Then he must expect his pupils who are adequate readers to glean the important points from their reading. He must provide them with opportunities to use what they have read. This technique may require a science teacher's showing his students how to use contextual cues, how to take notes from course texts, how to use references, how to read tables and measurements, how to interpret graphs, how to use a table of contents, how to analyze scientific terms. It is the science teacher's job to teach these skills, not the English teacher's. After he teaches these skills, the science teacher must allow students to use their reading by applying it to problems.

An Example of Applied Reading

An average-achieving, ninth-grade English class was studying some short stories by Nathaniel Hawthorne. The children decided to study Hawthorne's writing in some depth as a class project. (The English language arts class was a double period.) In this urban school, ninth grade was the last year in a junior high school. To prepare her students for the academically oriented high school, the teacher decided to build the project around the goal of teaching lecture note-taking, listening skills, reading improvement, and test-taking. In other words, she was concerned with both content (Hawthorne as literature) and reading skills (study skills).

The description that follows is a one-week *diary* of what occurred in the classroom. It is *not* a lesson plan. In general, careful records of what occurs in a classroom are better guides to planning lessons than the traditional lesson plan. The latter is usually a brief set of notes based on the diary. In this way we achieve sequence and continuity.

Monday. Problem: How to take lecture notes. How to listen critically.

I. Students compare notes they took during Friday's lecture on Nathaniel Hawthorne.
   A. Dispute over one main point, but there is some universal agreement.
   B. Each student's notes differ in form and, in some cases, content. This is discussed.
   C. Students share pet techniques and discuss ways of improving note-taking.
   D. Teacher offers suggestions.
   E. Teacher distributes mimeographed copy of her own lecture notes at end of class. At home students compare them to their notes, and decide for themselves how efficient their note-taking was.

II. Discussion shifts to content of lecture.
   A. Was Hawthorne mentally ill and how does it show in his writings? Each student has been reading Hawthorne biographies or some of his works, or something related to mid-nineteenth-century American literature.
   B. Hot debate: "Yes, he was crazy" versus "No, he was not."
   C. Teacher cuts off debate: "Anyone who cares to may write me a comment on this problem. Be sure you substantiate your argument with good evidence."

III. Speed reading check: Students use any textbook reading selection they choose to. Most use materials needed in other classes, for example, a chemistry chapter or a history passage.

Tuesday. Problem: Discussion of Hawthorne's works, plus historical background.

I. Writings.
   A. Over 66 percent of the class have written short papers (one to five pages) on the question of Hawthorne's sanity. These papers are discussed. The teacher collects and critiques them.
   B. Four pupils decide to resolve the role of Mrs. Hawthorne's relationship to Hawthorne's mental health. They have been

reading history and biographies and agree to present a paper on Mrs. Hawthorne's role at the beginning of the next week.

II. Readings.
   A. Children have been reading from a classroom library of about 40 books on Hawthorne, Brook Farm, Jacksonian politics, transcendentalism. Each has read a different selection. Some have read stories, others a novel, some a chapter of a non-fiction book.
   B. Teacher divides class into three groups: readers of novels and stories, readers of biographies, readers of history and related materials. The fiction readers initiate discussion. The nonfiction readers critique and check on the fiction readers.

III. Skills checks.
   A. Students compare notes on their readings. They discuss the best way to take notes and find that different people find different styles best suited to them.
   B. The four students researching Mrs. Hawthorne (Sophia Peabody) begin to write their report.
   C. During the last 20 minutes, teacher conducts a speed reading drill with 15 children who use one of their texts as reading material. Each student checks his reading speed and plots it on a graph that records his previous speeds. Then each child writes a one-paragraph synopsis of what he has read using a topic sentence to state the central controlling idea and not more than 100 words to support that idea. Teacher collects these papers for critique.

Wednesday. Problem: How to listen and take lecture notes. Guest lecturer from history department.

   I. Students are given one chapter from a set of Amherst College series: *Problems in American Civilization* ("difficult" reading for students).

   II. Students must read chapter in 15 minutes. The object is to read for ideas—to pick out the author's main point.

   III. Guest lecturer presents talk based on the reading: "Hawthorne and American Transcendentalism's Role in American Nineteenth-Century Politics."

Thursday. Problem: How different lecturers present information. Improve note-taking. How to prepare for tests.

I. Group compares notes on previous day's reading.

II. Group compares lecture notes. (Same types of comments and discussion of techniques as on Monday.)

III. Discussion and demonstration of how different students read the chapter the day before. Teacher joins students in suggesting how to read effectively.
   A. Use of introductions.
   B. Reading for ideas.
   C. Use of topic sentence and contextual cues.

IV. Discussion of the effect of attitudes on comprehension; for example, "What effect did my feelings for the guest lecturer have on my ability to read the chapter?" "Does my dislike of history affect my reading?"

V. Discussion of how to integrate readings and lecture notes for exam to be given next day.

Friday. Problem: Taking an exam.

I. Speed reading check, 3–5 minutes on lecture notes and/or chapter. "Do I regress to bad reading habits when I study 'for keeps' (lips moving, regression, slow down or freeze, unable to concentrate, and so on)?"

II. Discussion of what kind of test the guest lecturer is likely to give.
   A. Types of questions to be expected: objective, essay, short answer, and so on.
   B. Material that is important and likely to be included in the test.

III. Guest lecturer's test is administered.

Paperbacks—One Key to Teaching Reading Through Content Areas

Perhaps the greatest boon to the teaching of reading in content areas has been the evolution of paperback books. [2] Ever since Frank Merriwell dashed across the lurid pages of nineteenth-century dime novels, the American paperback has been big business. Almost 1 million copies a day are sold in the United States. Not until the mid-twentieth century, however, has literary quality kept pace with quantity. Today, dealers' bookshelves bulge with

30,000 different paperback editions. One-third to one-half of these paperbacks claim literary status above the gaudy, the sensational, the "noneducational."

Availability

David Moscow estimates the number of inexpensive paperback books available and appropriate for school use at 7,500. He publishes, for example, a list of ten quality paperbacks covering basic literary forms. [3] In the same volume, Sohn describes a 225-book classroom library. [4] Morris Gall has compiled at least four different paperback book lists in the content areas suitable for high school students. [5] The American Association for the Advancement of Science sells an annotated book list of paperbacks in science. Butman, Reis, and Sohn mention well over 100 articles and specially prepared book lists on the use of paperbacks in the schools. [7] Bowker's *Paperbound Books in Print* has increased its list almost 400 percent in a dozen years. Bowker also publishes a selective list for secondary schools and colleges. [8] Lee's *Paperbacks for High Schools* lists 500 titles available for high school use. [9] The NEA lists 2,400 titles that they have screened in *The Paperback Goes to School*. [10] Scholastic Magazines publishes *Readers' Choice*. [11] New American Library offers *Good Reading*, a quality book list for secondary school and college students. [12] Washington Square Press sells *The College and Adult Reading List of Books in Literature and the Fine Arts*. [13] The American Association for the Advancement of Science and The National Science Foundation have published an *Inexpensive Science Library* through 1961. *A Guide to Science Reading* has succeeded it. [6] The *Saturday Review*, the early January issues of the Sunday edition of *The New York Times*, and the December issue of *Studies in the Mass Media* [14] offer extensive lists of paperback books.

Certainly, there is no dearth of titles. Quality is high, and availability is as complicated as stopping at the corner candy store, the bus station, or even the student store. Some sophisticates prefer The Arrow, Teen Age, or Campus Book Clubs. Whatever the source, students and their parents will buy over 300 million paperback books this year. Paperbacks offer quality literature on every level of difficulty and interest at inexpensive rates. How has the classroom teacher reacted to this educator's windfall?

Research on Use of Paperbacks

In a survey on the use of paperbound books, the NCTE covered 48 states, kindergarten through grade 12, English teachers and librarians only, in 1959. [15] Of NCTE replies, 75 percent agreed that students were reading more because of paperback editions. Yet, the survey reported that most English teachers and librarians did not know where to get information about available paperbacks for high school use. Although most teachers have access to paperback catalogs, very few reported being familiar with Bowker's *Paperback Books in Print.* Of the California schools surveyed, 64 percent reported using paperbacks in classroom libraries, but only a few other states reported using paperbacks in school or community libraries. Yet, libraries reported being in favor of paperbacks on the library shelves, especially in schools with limited library budgets. Evidently, at the time of the survey, these sentiments had not been translated into action.

Most shocking is the list of 88 titles and 5 famous authors that teachers said they would most "like to see made available in paperbound editions." At the time of the survey, 41 of the 88 titles and all 5 of the authors already had been published in paperback form. Teachers asked for more classics, nonfiction, current authors, and more historical fiction, all of which were already in paperback editions at the time of the survey.

Landau surveyed an extensive stratified sample of 33 percent of the total public and parochial secondary schools of New England. [16] Size, type, and location of school and community were controlled. Data were based on a 56.3 percent return of questionnaires representing 17.8 percent of all secondary schools in the six-state area. The sampling technique was well structured and the survey dug into all content area classrooms. Landau reported that 72 percent of public and 76 percent of private schools make some use of paperbacks. Variations between schools are considerable, so these figures obscure the fact that in one area, one large school may use paperbacks extensively, whereas another school may use none at all. Schools in Maine, for example, report using paperbacks only 66 percent as often as do schools in Connecticut, Massachusetts, and Vermont. The proportion of classrooms in rural schools using paperbacks is half again as great as in urban schools. Only 33 percent of New England secondary school classrooms use paperbacks. Most frequently, these are English and social studies classes. A smattering of usage by math and science classes is reported, but business education and foreign language teachers report practically no use of paperbacks in their courses.

As in the NCTE survey, Landau's data report that "free reading" and book reports are the major uses of paperbacks. Half of the science classes who use them at all do so as reference tools. When paperbacks are used, the most usual source of stimulus is teacher recommendation. According to the data, English teachers "recommend" four times, and social studies teachers twice as frequently as all other teachers combined. Landau's report lists local stores, school libraries, and book clubs in that order as sources of paperback supply. Paperbacks were rarely secured from public libraries, classroom libraries, or book fairs. Both the Landau and NCTE surveys conclude that classroom teachers need more information about paperbacks and more distribution of them in the schools. Most of all, both studies agree teachers should explore the special advantages of paperbacks as aids to more effective teaching of reading in the content areas.

Unusual Ways to Use Paperbacks

Joseph Mersand's "Bibliography: The Use of Paperbacks in the Schools," [7] offers a guide to 105 references in professional literature discussing uses of paperback books in the classroom. This section [17] supplements the literature, and in doing so makes five assumptions:

1. Paperbacks are cheaper than hard covers.
2. Paperbacks are compact and convenient to store and handle.
3. Paperbacks are up to date.
4. Paperbacks cover a wide range of content and levels of difficulty.

5. Paperbacks are convenient for book reports and "free reading," but have greater value as core reading in content areas.

One more major assumption underlying this section is that the teacher has at least three jobs unique to his profession: motivate, teach skills, teach content. The following suggestions attempt to show the teacher how paperbacks can help him meet these obligations.

Motivate. Every teacher has an obligation to get his students reading books—books in general and books specific to a content area. This requires making many books a crucial part of the teaching of content. As long as a single textbook and a loquacious teacher are the core of the class, students will tend not to read. They do not need to; the teacher tells them what they need to know for the test. Between the teacher and the bland text, most students who care enough can squeeze by Friday's weekly inquisition. Worse yet, students easily slip into passivity. A major teaching obligation is to motivate, which means to teach students how to learn. When a student himself searches and seeks to discover content, the teacher is successful.

Field trips. One way to get students and books together is to take students to paperback bookstores. We once bused 53 high school juniors to an off-Broadway production of *Our Town*. For two hours before the play, a famous Greenwich Village paperback bookstore opened its doors exclusively to the browsing teen-agers, fed them tea and cookies, and chatted with them about books. Two teachers and two store employees walked through the stacks and demonstrated the joys of browsing. The owner sat in a corner and read selections from Dylan Thomas to a group of enraptured students. In another corner, one student read selections from Jules Feiffer to a group of his classmates. All over the store, groups of students shared found treasures of humor and tragedy. We had not planned it, but 87 paperback books were sold to those students in two hours.

Another teacher spent a full morning (before regular shop hours) with her class of low reading achievers in a paperback bookstore, where the proprietor joined her in helping youngsters choose books. He showed old Charlie Chaplin films right in the shop and discussed movies and literature. Every student purchased at least one book that he subsequently read and discussed in class. One paperback bookstore in the Boston area doubles as a first-rate art gallery and seems to be a natural for a paperback book browsing trip. Browsing is an art and pleasure that leads to other values associated with reading. It is an experience most urban and rural youngsters rarely have, and one that schools should consider as an exciting educational adventure. For enterprising science teachers, it is an effective way to build a classroom library. Every student "who cares to" may buy a science paperback. When he finishes reading it, the student can make a report to the class and donate the book to the classroom library.

Classroom libraries. Light, compact inexpensive paperbacks in the classroom can help promote learning. The science or social studies teacher can flood his classroom with literature in his content area. With books on the spot, each student can read and contribute a different phase to a common subject. In this way, a single text and one teacher become only two minor sources of information; books and the students become active participants in the learning experience. A simple, quick way to promote reading is to entice students with good books. For $100 to $200 per classroom, students can be deluged with colorful quality books. Allowing students 10 minutes per week to browse is enough to make a difference in the reading habits of students and in the quality and quantity of learning.

Classroom library committees. A number of effective teaching possibilities are offered by using committees:

1. Students run the library, classify, and learn library skills. They skim the books to write descriptive blurbs on the catalog cards.
2. Student committees evaluate books. Here again, they read, skim, and make reports to committees or to the entire class.
3. Student library committees build learning units by reviewing books and grouping them according to content, themes, countries, and so on. Committees build their own study guides to

each unit. If students go on a paperback book browsing expedition, they can search for books to fit specific units.

4. Committees build vocabulary glossaries for groups of paperbacks. Much content in science and social studies is, in essence, vocabulary study.
5. Library committees read a unit, discuss the books, and make a report, as a group, to the entire class.
6. (Committees design book jackets for the classroom library bulletin board. They design illustrations for specific chapters.
7. Committees redesign covers to correspond more closely with content, and demonstrate how some covers can mislead the buyer.

Teach Content. The suggestions for classroom library committees certainly apply to content area classrooms. In addition, consider the following possibilities:

1. Science experiments in paperbacks are cut up and remounted, leaving spaces between sections. Students keep their books and save the time of having to write out the entire experiment.
2. Maps, charts, and graphs are cut out of paperbacks and used to teach students how to interpret this material.
3. Each chapter is removed from a book and given to a different student to read for a report. In one day, an entire book can be reported. On this one day, one book per week schedule, a class can easily cover 30 extra books a year. Compare this to the history teacher who spends ten months on a single history text.
4. Groups of students read different views of the same subject and discuss them in teams, or before the entire class. A Southern interpretation of the Civil War may be profoundly different from a Northern version.
5. New paperbacks of programed instruction in arithmetic and mathematics allow slow students to review and fast students to accelerate.
6. Student-owned paperbacks give every content area teacher the chance to show students how to mark their texts—to annotate margins, underline important ideas, and so on.
7. From Shakespeare to the best of modern drama, great plays are available in paperback for classroom use. One or two weeks a year are set aside in English or social studies classes for a drama festival. Four or five groups of students perform scenes

from plays related to course content. A drama contest can increase the incentive to prepare creative presentations.

Teach Skills.

Testing. Consider the following uses of paperbacks for testing:

1. Cut up pages for testing saccadic eye movements and regressions using the "peep-hole" test. Veteran clinicians will discover that content will affect left-to-right eye sweep in reading.
2. Use a variety of clippings to test an entire class for main ideas, paragraph structure, and meaning from content.
3. Use pages from paperbacks for hand tachistoscopes to test (and train) speed of perception, word analysis, and visual memory.
4. Any reading evaluation that the tester feels can be affected by content can be tested by using selections from a variety of paperback books.

Teaching organizational skills. Paperbacks can be used to teach organizational skills. Consider the following suggestions:

1. Cut up individual paragraphs and ask students to find topic sentences, main ideas, chronologicial order, and so on.
2. Students skim a variety of paperback books. The teacher presents excerpts from the books and students match them to the correct book.
3. Small groups of students read parts of a book, or an entire essay, and underline important parts or specific sections that appeal to them. Students then compare what they have underlined and discuss similarities and differences of choice.
4. Pairs of students read two different books in a content area. In class, they exchange books and each uses the contents page and contextual cues to skim the other's book. Each student sees how much he can glean from a book in 20 minutes while his partner checks on his success. Students question each other about content on the basis of their skimming.
5. The teacher removes contents pages from paperback books and students supply new ones based on their own skimming. They compare their own efforts with the original.

Teaching general study skills. Consider the following suggestions for using paperbacks to teach general study skills:

1. The teacher has personal perceptions, appreciations, and tastes in which students want to share. (One teacher read most of the books in the classroom paperback library, underlined important and aesthetically pleasing passages, and as he did with his own books, wrote personal reactions and comments in the margins, then returned the books to the shelves. Any student who read a book could share the views, and this led to fascinating discussions. Some of the teacher's comments were critical and amusing, and the students were intrigued by his reactions. It offered them a personalized study guide as well as an "inside" look at their teacher.)

2. With many paperbacks available, students compare poorly written passages with good writing.

3. In a seventh-grade civics class, five avid readers formed a survey committee. They read over 50 books from the classroom paperback library and selected the sections of each book they felt most worth reading. They did this as a service to their classmates, who then had merely to read the selected passages catalogued on the inside cover and contents page of each book.

4. The teacher removes the end of a book or a story and students "anticipate" the ending. For writing practice, students write an ending, compare it with the original, and analyze the differences.

5. A similar technique is used after transitional words to teach students to anticipate meaning from context.

6. Some ninth-graders decided that all chapters should begin with a summary. They wrote summaries to chapters and glued them into the books in the classroom paperback library.

7. These same students were dissatisfied with some chapter titles in many of the classics. They added subtitles, all of which were accurate, if unorthodox. Chapter 2 of *The Scarlet Letter,* "The Market-Place," was awarded the subtitle "Or, The Tattooed Lady." Chapter XXII of *The Iliad,* which includes the death of Hector and the desecration of his body by Achilles, was subtitled, "Achilles the Heel." At least two other students plus the teacher had to pass judgment on each subtitle. This led to spontaneous reading teams banding together to ensure that at least two other students would be available as judges.

8. Students write guide questions in the top margin of each page for practice in reading with purpose.
9. Students build files of sample styles of writing. Each student pastes a page from a paperback on one side of oaktag, and on the other side pastes a copy of his own attempt in the same style. He thus builds a style notebook.
10. Students do the same thing with organizational patterns of paragraphs.
11. Paperbacks are cut up and scrambled. Students reconstruct paragraphs, essays, or chapters to discover subordination, coordination, logical sequence, or chronological order in good writing.

Teaching vocabulary, word-attack skills, word parts, and grammar. Paperbacks can be used for teaching vocabulary, word-attack skills, word parts, and grammar as follows:

1. Students circle passages containing unfamiliar words and present them to the class in context. They explain the use of the word in the particular books they read and, in this way, share their reading with others.
2. After a student reads a book, he cuts up a page of words and sorts them according to parts of speech as a grammar exercise. Students will discover that many words depend upon usage for their classification as a part of speech.
3. Each student takes a chapter from a well-worn paperback and finds good synonyms for weak words; for example, pretty.
4. In a paperback classroom library, a student circles each unfamiliar word and writes a definition or synonym in the margin to help the next reader of the book.
5. Students study the effect of different types of words in writing by crossing out all the adjectives on a page, all the nouns, and so on.

Summary

The standard textbook is not sacrosanct. There is no intrinsic superiority in a single text approach to teaching over an individualized approach in any content area in which paperbacks are available. And paperbacks are certainly available. They are also inexpensive and offer great variety. They are of superior literary quality because teachers can select the best from 30,000 titles.

They meet almost all reading levels and all content areas. They meet individual needs and interests, and they are flexible. In short, they can do anything the hardcover can do, plus more.

Despite a wealth of professional literature on their use in the classroom, paperbacks are still limited to book reports and "free reading." According to the NCTE and Landau surveys, they enjoy limited use "qualitatively," as well as quantitatively. These surveys indicate that teachers do not know what is available, where, and at what cost. Perhaps this demonstrates the cliché that fifty years must pass before an educational innovation works its way into the classroom. If so, I recommend Schick's *Paperbound Books in America,* [18] and *Hooked on Books: Program and Proof,* [19] which presents adequate documentation that the initiation period has been served.

Meanwhile, all teachers must begin to assume responsibility for teaching children how to read in content areas. Math teachers must teach their children how to read and study math. Social studies teachers must recognize that they are responsible for teaching children how to read in the social sciences. Finally, all teachers must recognize that English teachers also have an obligation to teach their children to read in their content area. But English teachers cannot be expected to prepare children to read in content areas of social studies, math, and science.

The paperback boom is one way schools can individualize teaching content at the same time they use content to improve literacy. Paperbacks replacing the usual classroom set of watered-down texts in English, social studies, and science are not so radical an innovation that schools could not move quickly in this direction. Nor are they materials that imply a technique peculiar to a specific class of children. They are appropriate for low or high achievers, for advantaged or disadvantaged children. [20]

References
---

1. R. D. Eicholz, *Elementary School Mathematics,* Book 2 (Palo Alto, Calif.: Addison-Wesley, 1963).
2. S. Alan Cohen, "Using Paperbacks in the Secondary School," *Journal of Education,* 46 (April 1964), 19–26. (Author using a revised version in text.)
3. David Moscow, "Individualizing Classroom Reading," in A. Butman, D. Reis, and D. Sohn (eds.), *Paperbacks in the Schools* (New York: Bantam Books, 1963), p. 47.
4. David Sohn, "The Stimulation of Reading Through Paperback Books: The Classroom Library," in Butman, Reis, and Sohn, *op. cit.,* pp. 23–38.
5. Morris Gall, *Social Education,* vols. 22, 23, 24 (1958–1960). See also: "Using Paperback Classics in the Social Studies Classroom," *Social Education,* 27 (March 1963).
6. Hilary Deason, *A Guide to Science Reading* (New York: Signet Science Library, 1963), p. 2283.
7. Butman, Reis, and Sohn, *op. cit.*
8. R. R. Bowker, *Paperbound Books in Print,* published quarterly. See also: *Paperbound Book Guide for High School* and *Paperbound Book Guide for College.* All available from R. R. Bowker Co., New York.
9. Norman R. Lee, *Paperbacks for High Schools* (Syracuse, N.Y.: Reading Center, Syracuse University, or Champaign, Ill.: NCTE).
10. NEA, *The Paperback Goes to School* (New York: Bureau of Independent Publishers and Distributors, or Washington, D.C.: National Education Association).
11. *Readers' Choice* (New York: Scholastic Magazines).
12. The Committee on College Reading, *Good Reading* (New York: New American Library).
13. *The College and Adult Reading List of Books in Literature and the Fine Arts* (New York: Washington Square Press).
14. NCTE, *Studies in the Mass Media* (Champaign, Ill.: March 1961, December 1961, December 1963).
15. "Paperbacks in School: A Survey by Teachers of English," *Publisher's Weekly,* 176 (December 28, 1959), 37–39.
16. Hanan Landau, "A Survey of Use of Paperback Pocket-sized Books in New England Secondary Schools" (Unpublished master's thesis, Boston University, 1960).

17. Some of these suggestions come from a brainstorming session of 30 teachers under Dr. Mable S. Noall, Director of Boston University Secondary Reading Clinic, 1964.

18. George Schick, *Paperbound Books in America* (New York: Bowker, 1958).

19. D. N. Fader and E. B. McNeil, *Hooked on Books: Program and Proof* (New York: Berkeley Publishing, 1968).

20. For an up-to-date review of the use of paperbacks in schools see: S. Alan Cohen, "The Use of Paperbacks in the Classroom: Research and Implications," *Journal of Reading*, January, 1969.

Appendix

Materials for Teaching Reading

Introduction

For most educators, the Elementary and Secondary Education Act, the National Defense Education Act, and the Economic Opportunity Act have eliminated the timeworn excuse for lack of materials in the classroom—no money. As the first half decade of plenty comes to a close in education, a new problem emerges—poor spending. Huge amounts of money are being squandered on machines and surplus materials. The problem appears to be two-fold:

1. Many reading specialists, as well as administrators, do not know what materials are available to help them increase the quantity and quality of learning to read, especially in classrooms of disadvantaged children.
2. Many educators do not know how to purchase materials wisely according to the economics of the market and according to effective methodology.

This Appendix is devoted to helping resolve the first problem. A review of these materials and suggestions for using them effectively are included. Before presenting that list, however, we should try to alleviate the second problem.

How to Purchase Materials Wisely

Most educational equipment salesmen are exceedingly knowledgeable about techniques and resources, often more knowledgeable than the educators to whom they sell. Educators should take advantage of this knowledge. For example, the school and library salesman is an excellent judge of the books most likely to attract reluctant readers. But his knowledge is, of course, limited to his own publishing house, and no single publishing house has a monopoly on all good children's books. In addition, some educational salesmen are particularly overzealous. For example, in one Midwestern high school the reading specialist purchased 15 Craig Readers at a cost of hundreds of dollars each, plus films and supplementary material. The Craig Reader looks like a television screen on which speeded reading selections are presented. This expenditure represented the total amount of money allotted that school under ESEA, Title I, to remediate reading problems of disadvantaged youth. The Craig Reader is an attractive and an effective machine for improving reading, but it is not a remedial reading program, and it is certainly not the type of equipment one needs in quantity. A New Jersey elementary school spent over $10,000 on EDL (Educational Development Labs) Controlled Readers, learning booths, and supplementary equipment. This was the sum total of their reading center—they had no books! One or two Controlled Reader Juniors are excellent machines for any reading center. But like the Craig Reader, an EDL Controlled Reader and Tach-X setup in quantities of 15 or more is not an adequately equipped reading center. As a matter of fact, $10,000 is enough to equip three or four complete reading centers in any school system. Educators must understand that no single company, regardless of its claims, can adequately supply a reading center with its material needs. Most companies do, however, offer excellent materials, kits, and machines that, in correct quantities, increase the effectiveness of qualified reading specialists. What are the correct quantities? Eight guidelines for maximizing variety by minimizing quantity follow:

1. One or two of each machine is maximum per reading center.
2. Small machines for use with small groups are better than large machines for large-group instruction.
3. Five copies of any single workbook should be a maximum order. This allows teachers to call on a variety of materials to meet individual needs and helps prevent teachers from forcing thirty children into the same mold. Buying five copies of six different workbooks is wiser than buying thirty copies of one workbook—the same expenditure yields five times the variety.
4. One each of three or four different reading machines that are designed to do the same thing is better than four of the same machine. The value of most machines lies in their use in motivating the child, so that four different machines doing the same thing give four different tools to use to motivate.
5. Storybooks and workbooks, usually more effective than machines, should be purchased first.
6. Isolated learning booths can be built inexpensively out of discarded desks or tables and Masonite or plywood. School woodworking shops can do this job. Expensive learning carrels are still luxuries.
7. Any administrator who finds spending federally granted funds difficult or who is in danger of ending a fiscal year with surplus funds should buy classroom libraries of children's books from various publishers. On the secondary level, collections of paperback books for each classroom organized by level and content areas are sound educational investments. A good rule is: When in doubt, buy classroom libraries of storybooks and paperback books; try to avoid machines, textbooks, anthologies, basal reader series, and workbooks unless other books have already been adequately supplied. By all means stay away from 30 copies of any one thing.
8. Federal funds under ESEA or NDEA come in lump sums and must be spent before a specified deadline. But this is no reason to spend the allotments all at once. Save some of the funds. The educational market is booming and publishers are continuously producing new materials. Before a fiscal year is over, reading specialists will see new materials that should be purchased. Remember, the surplus can always be well spent at the last minute for more nontextbooks.

Criteria for Selection of Materials Reviewed

Many recently published materials were piloted, demonstrated, and/or evaluated in various reading projects. Some were tried in clinics, others were piloted in schools and special projects. I used over twenty-five new materials in one experimental summer reading project. A number of kits and remedial materials were tested by teachers in schools on New York City's Lower East Side and in a special school for delinquent adolescents. An exhaustive analysis of materials and methods was made for school dropout populations and tested in various "second chance" programs, including Job Corps. Some materials were tested with adult illiterates and literate Spanish-speaking adults, both in MFY projects and New York City Board of Education's Operation Second Chance. Other materials listed were tried in school systems involved in special programs for socially disadvantaged youth for which I am a consultant. The list also includes the most promising materials tested and reviewed by the staff at the Reading Center, Ferkauf Graduate School, Yeshiva University.

In every case, evaluation of materials was made in relation to both the quantity and quality of learning and to the reactions of the teachers, clinicians, tutors, or volunteer teacher aides. We have found that effect on pupil learning is not a sufficient criterion for evaluating materials and methods in the schools. Teachers or nonprofessionals functioning as teachers, as well as administrators, make the final decisions for adoption. Often, ease of handling materials, degree of difficulty of learning to use new materials, and, alas, personal prejudices overrule the objective measurements of learning growth in children and youth. For example, the Structural Reading Series (L. W. Singer) for beginning reading was piloted in Harlem schools and was judged successful by teachers and principals working with the program. They felt it was more successful than the basal readers usually used in the classrooms. Further piloting was done in an experimental summer school with similar results; all the teachers and evaluators were high in the appraisal of the program. The program was further tested in a controlled experiment with severely retarded socially disadvantaged Puerto Rican and black children in a school where it proved more promising than the traditional basal reader. The final authorities for adoption, administrators in the central board of education, still found reasons not to list the materials for school adoption. It was not until more than a year after it had proved itself that the Structural Reading Series was finally listed as an approved material for the New York City school system.

A list of materials with brief evaluations for use in teaching reading to socially disadvantaged children and youth follows. Only those materials that proved valuable are included. It was impossible to have reviewed and field-tested all existing materials, so that exclusion from the list may indicate the author's lack of experience with the materials rather than disapproval of them. For the materials that were field-tested with disadvantaged populations, the following questions were asked:

1. Were the materials effective with socially disadvantaged children?
2. What adaptations, if any, can be made in these materials to make them more amenable to learning for socially disadvantaged children?
3. Will these materials contribute to the overall goal of an effective reading program in the schools, that is, to diagnose and teach to specific skills weaknesses of each individual? This means that self-teaching materials which can be used in small pupil teams with a minimum of constant teacher supervision are needed if we are to meet the needs of individuals in the classroom.
4. Will such materials help the teacher adjust to a self-directed classroom in which the teacher's role is to teach individuals first and the group second?
5. Are teachers able to learn how to use these new materials quickly?

Materials for Prereading Levels

The materials listed below were found to be particularly effective in preschool projects or research experiments with urban disadvantaged children.

Perceptual Training Materials

Chapter Six listed published materials for perceptual training. In one experiment involving Montessori preschools for disadvantaged children, we were most impressed with the standard Montessori equipment. It is expensive and can only be purchased from Dutch and Indian companies through national or international Montessori Society offices. Copies and other versions of the materials (equally expensive) are now beginning to be made by American companies that supply preschool materials, such as Creative Playthings, Inc.

Program for Accelerated School Success (P.A.S.S., Inc., Minneapolis, Minn.). A detailed, step-by-step teacher's manual and supplementary materials including templates for basic forms, tracing board with patterns, and 35-mm tachistoscopic slides, P.A.S.S. is the most thorough program available in visual perceptual training on the early levels of development. The manual refers to other "homemade" devices that should be used as part of the program (chalkboard, walking rail, and so on).

The program is an outgrowth of Getman's work with the Optometric Extension Program and with educators operating within the theoretical framework of Gesell, Piaget, and modern theories of visual-perceptual and cognitive development for early childhood programs. Along with Marianne Frostig's *Test of Visual Perception Development* (Follett, Chicago), Frostig's *Program for the Development of Visual Perception* (Follett, Chicago), and Kephart's *The Slow Learner in the Classroom* (Merrill, Columbus, O.), the Getman program provides a complete program for prekindergarten through grade 3. These programs require a teacher-helper in the classroom for maximum effectiveness. The smaller the teacher-pupil ratio, the easier it is to supervise and correct the children. School dropouts, pupils from upper grades, or mothers have been effective as aides in some programs using these materials.

Balance Board. For basic perceptual training development on the kinesthetic-motor level, the balance board has been an effective device used by the Gesell Institute for Child Development and clinicians trained through the Optometric Extension Program. Boards can be built simply by using 2-foot square, ½- to ¾-inch plywood on a 4-inch block approximately 3½ inches thick.

Children learn to balance on the board and eventually manipulate it forward, backward, or sideways on cue. Cues can be visual, auditory, or tactual depending upon the need of the child. Eventually, the child should be able to integrate complex cues of various combinations while moving in time with a metronome or drumbeat. Balance-board training is an excellent body balance technique that helps increase the child's awareness of his body in space.

Walking Rail. Like the balance board, the walking rail has long been an effective technique for teaching kinesthetic awareness of the body in space. It can be combined with various exercises for integrating multiple stimuli. The board is simple to construct: Traditionally a length of 2 × 4 is used as a rail. However, a modern adaptation by Lowman presents the board as a 20-degree sloping surface for each foot separated by a small rail. The walking surface is approximately 5 inches. Walking rails designed by the author are 3 to 4 feet long and notched for joining in tandem. Sections of 12 feet were found to be effective for most exercises. Discussion of the use of balance board and walking rail is included in Chapter Six. The P.A.S.S. manual, mentioned above, also describes methods of using the walking rail.

Frostig Program for the Development of Visual Perception (Follett, Chicago). The kit provides rexograph masters of exercises in five areas of perceptual development as measured in Marianne Frostig's *Test of Visual Perception*. A manual of directions with a short rationale explaining the program is included. Skills cover training from the simplest activities in discriminating body positions through complex problems of higher perception.

The assets and liabilities of the program are discussed in Chapter Six. With other materials currently being published and developed in this area of remediation, the Frostig program is valuable, especially in the early childhood programs currently underway in projects for the socially disadvantaged. In general, we found first- and second-grade retarded readers in the MFY area so deficient in visual perception development that this material was too advanced for them. Although the manual covers directions for teaching earlier skills on the motor-tactual-kinesthetic levels, it is presented too sketchily; that is, it depends too much on the teacher's ability to expand on the theory and examples presented by Frostig. A better program at this earliest level is presented in Getman and Kane's *Program for Accelerated School Success* materials and manual. Together with the Frostig kit, it is an effective program in visual perceptual development.

Perceptual Motor Materials (Teaching Resources, Boston, Mass.). This company markets a half dozen or more perceptual materials for various skills. Getman's *Eye-hand Coordination Exercises* kit, Dub-noff's *Directional-Spatial-Pattern Board Exercises* and *Sequential Per-ceptual-Motor Exercises,* the Fairbanks-Robinson *Perceptual Motor Development,* the Erie *Perceptual-Motor Teaching Materials* program and Ruth Cheves' *Visual-Motor Perception. Teaching Materials* among others are offered in sturdy hard and software packages at reasonable prices. These are discreet, separate programs, each one designed to shape specific visual motor and visual perceptual behaviors.

Spatial Organization Series (Allied Education Council, Galien, Michi-gan). Three workbooks for higher level, pencil-paper activities in shape matching, figure completion, shape identification. The program is part of the *Fitzhugh PLUS Program* and is more appropriate for first or second graders than for preschoolers.

Language and Concept Development

A number of photograph albums have been marketed to be used as concept builders and to foster language development at the learning readiness stage. The earliest one on the market was *Urban Education Studies* (John Day, New York). A series of large photograph albums, each one centers on a specific city (New York, Detroit, Washington). Each album is edited by an educator who is a native of that city. Also available are companion albums built around themes (*Growing Is* . . . , *A Family Is* . . . , *Renewal Is* . . . , and so on). A companion teacher's manual is really an elaborate short text on concept and language develop-ment in preschool with specific suggestions for each album. The only adverse criticism involves the quality of some of the pictures and the art and design. The selection of pictures could have been better, more exciting, and more esthetic without sacrificing peda-gogical content. But this drawback does not seriously reduce the value of the program.

The Chandler language-experience program, reviewed in the next section, has a reading readiness component built around collections of photographs of urban subjects. The manual is excellent and the pictures feed directly into the Chandler beginning reading program, which I consider one of the best sight basals available for urban children. These picture portfolios can be purchased separately from the program.

Another good picture album for language development is published by *The Encyclopaedia Britannica*. New kits for concept and language development are just being marketed by Behavioral Research Laboratories (Palo Alto, Calif.), Webster (New York), and Peabody College (Tennessee).

Materials for Beginning Reading for Old and Young

Chapter Ten discussed beginning reading and referred to some materials we have found successful at the early reading stage. Listed below alphabetically are reviews of these programs and/or materials for beginning reading. Included are only the programs we have tried and found effective. The reader is cautioned against skimming the list; although some full reading programs are listed, the review often focuses on the *limited* or *specific* uses of these programs or on those segments that were successful with disadvantaged children. Also included are suggestions for beginning reading programs for older illiterates. The major basal readers are omitted on the assumption that they are already in wide use throughout the country and are therefore familiar to most teachers. These include the basals published by American Book (Cincinnati), Allyn and Bacon (Boston), Ginn (Waltham, Mass.), Harper & Row (New York), Heath (Boston), Holt, Rinehart and Winston (New York), Houghton Mifflin (Boston), Lyons and Carnahan (Chicago), Macmillan (New York), and Scott, Foresman (Chicago).

Bank Street Readers (Macmillan, New York) Grades 1–3. This basal series appears to be one of the few teaching programs constructed according to pedagogical theory and research findings, as well as according to the nature of the school using it. Regarding the development of reading skills, the manual stresses auditory discrimination, phonics, and structural analysis, rather than word configuration or picture matching. Regarding content, the readers have discarded the "Look, Jane, look" story level and contain higher-level stories built upon colorful pictures of an urban environment with multi-ethnic dwellers. The series is designed for readiness and primer to third-grade level. This series should be of high interest to all urban children; it may, however, seem strange to children in some Midwestern and most Western cities. These readers give me a strong New York feeling, and educators in San Francisco, Denver, and other cities have corroborated this impression. Whether or not this is an advantage remains to be seen. All in all, the readers are a notch above the usual basal reader fare.

Basic Reading Series (Lippincott, Philadelphia). The publishers make two misassumptions about this basal series—first, that it initiated the move to linguistic readers, and second, that this is a linguistic reader. The series evolved from a conservative wing of the educational establishment and was an attempt to reintroduce a grossly traditional phonics approach to beginning reading. It has little claim to linguistics. The literary quality of the selections is worse than what we usually find in traditional sight basals. The Lippincott readers also contain the unpardonable pedagogical mistake of teaching phonic rules to first- and second-graders—an ineffective practice on two counts: (1) most children at this age do not apply the rules; (2) many rules just do not apply. "Two vowels together—the first takes its name and the second is silent"—applies in less than one-third the cases. With all these flaws, why include it here as a recommended piece of material? Because the readers provide excellent pattern drills. Like most of the "linguistic" readers, this phonics program provides effective phonic pattern drills to reinforce instruction in the classroom. A few sets of readers per classroom increase the teacher's resources. Add to the readers one set of Lippincott's new *Talking Teacher* tapes, two or three copies each of the basal workbooks, and the *Basic Keys to Spelling* series, and the classroom has an excellent store of reinforcement exercises in word-attack skills.

Chandler Language-experience Readers (Chandler, San Francisco). For the socially disadvantaged population, this is the most promising beginning reader using a whole-word approach. The series includes excellent teacher's guides and a separate manual guide, *Informal Reading-Readiness Experiences,* by Lawrence Carillo, which is a sane, authoritative, practical guide that escapes the rubrics of traditional misassumptions about reading readiness. The individual pupil workbooks are useful. The most outstanding feature of the series is the set of 5½- by 8-inch, 24-page paperback experience readers, such as *Trucks and Cars to Ride, Slides, Supermarket,* and *Bikes.* Content consists of large, clear photographs of black, white, Oriental, and what appear to be Mexican American (could be Puerto Rican) children at play with appropriate, simple text on the basal reading level. Preliminary field testing with retarded-reading intermediate-grade children and with beginning readers in early intervention programs indicated that the readers are most attractive to Puerto Rican, black, and white children in slum areas. Further field testing with retarded children and normal preschoolers also provided favorable feedback. Of particular value are the picture portfolios designed for oral language development and reading readiness. Many of the activities and children in the photographs will be met again in the basal readers. Accompanying single loop films with good teacher manuals round out an excellent beginning reading series. Because these basal readers are built around photographs of urban children, they are different enough from all other basals to be used with retarded readers in intermediate grades. In fact, the Chandler series is one of our favorite "last tries" with sixth- and seventh-graders too old for "Look, Jane, look!" and too illiterate or "phonic-deaf" for anything else.

Form Boards (lowercase letters). A set of wooden form boards, one upper and one lower case, these materials are used for teaching letter perception on a tactual-kinesthetic level to preschool and elementary school children. Preliminary research at MFY clinics indicated that these boards are effective. The wooden form board consists of replicas of each lowercase letter. The forms are easily removed from the board and replaced. They are sturdy, large, and clearly recognizable when in the proper direction. The wooden letters were used to reinforce the learning of the alphabet through the manipulation of forms. The form board was extremely useful as an additional teaching device, and individual children were pleased to work with it themselves. A number of toy manufacturers market letter form boards. Houghton Mifflin markets one for under $50.

Health for All, The New Basic Health and Safety Program (Scott, Foresman, Chicago). A complete program of eight readers, grades 1–8, a junior primer, and a set of kindergarten charts with teacher guides, this is the first basal reader that truly teaches subject matter. The readers are cleverly and subtly illustrated with racially integrated children. For school systems that insist on a traditional basal reading approach to teaching reading to socially disadvantaged urban children, this may be the least of all evils. There are excellent poems, pictures, and, on higher levels, stories that teach principles of health and safety. If the schools must use this system of reading instruction, this high-quality series at least teaches "Wash! Wash! Wash!" instead of "Look! Look! Look!"

Lift-off to Reading (Science Research Associates, Chicago). Grades 1–6. Long before anyone else dared to produce a "linguistic" programed instruction series in beginning reading for socially disadvantaged youth, Myron Woolman applied a theory called the progressive choice reading method to the development of such a program in the

Washington slums. That series is now published by SRA as *Reading in High Gear*. Its intent far outstrips its effectiveness. It suffers from the worst ills of traditional phonics and programed instruction. Deadly boring, it artificially isolates sounds, and sacrifices meaning for symbol rather than sound consistency to such an extent that even teachers cannot make the "correct" responses to the comprehension questions. But the progressive choice theory is attractive. Ann O'Keefe, a staff member of Woolman's Institute in Washington, used the theory to develop a lower-level program for retarded six-year-olds and came up with what SRA has published as *Lift-off to Reading*. Is it useful? It suffers, although not so drastically, from the same ills as the older edition. Ann O'Keefe knows children and has included valuable suggestions in the manual. It is included in this recommended list for this purpose: if nothing else works with a severely retarded achiever in the early grades, it is worth a try.

Merrill Linguistic Readers (Merrill, Columbus, O.). A series of linguistic readers in paperback for levels 1–3 and clothbound for levels 4–6, ranging from 50 to 130 pages *without pictures,* the series includes accompanying workbooks, also with a minimum of pictures. Lack of pictures forces the reader to "bust the code" using phonics rather than picture cues. The readers are built around basic sounds carefully controlled for phonic consistency. They progressively teach basic sounds in words, with formal reading introduced directly in *My First Reader.* The stories are clever and culturally close to urban children, but not obtrusively so. They are equally usable with nonurban children. One feature of the series is the absence of childish stories. Although it was not specifically designed for young adults, the series has been useful for illiterate adolescents and adults. I have used this program with remedial cases, and they responded well. The Yeshiva University Reading Clinic staff feels that the program has great promise for use with socially disadvantaged children. Most of the time the series was used as a supplement to instruction in traditional sight approaches to teaching beginning reading. Two projects in Harlem used the material with fifth-grade nonreaders and found it effective. A "quick review" series, which is a short form of this program, is also available from the publisher.

The Michigan Language Program (Ann Arbor Publishers, Ann Arbor, Mich.). For severely retarded readers or very difficult cases we have used Donald Smith's series of programed manuals in writing, spelling, listening, letters, words, phrases, sentences, and paragraphs. The series of 17 programed workbooks, plus teacher's script and manual, are a carefully designed behavioral analysis approach to reading. They appear to be the most thoroughly worked out program yet devised in reading and have been our last resort in very difficult cases. With adolescents who have failed at every other attempt to read, we have found this program relatively successful. It is radically different from the usual school materials. The workbooks are plain, offset black and white, rather technical or "special" looking in their almost antiseptic austerity. Traditionalists might consider this a liability; we find it an asset. The Michigan Word Attack and Comprehension program described in the next section (see p. 294) can also "plug in" to this series.

Programmed Reading (Buchanan-Sullivan Associates and Webster Division, McGraw-Hill, New York). A series of books printed as linear programs with constructed responses, this is a complete beginning reading program for elementary school. Books are colorful, and supplementary material, although limited, is attractive. At MFY, the program was used in a clinic with a 4-to-1 pupil-clinician ratio. Subjects were disadvantaged Puerto Ricans and blacks who appeared to be headed for reading problems. These children learned their letters and some associative sounds. They mastered left-to-right progression and learned how to follow directions. The program is an orderly and sequential linguistic approach to code busting. According to clinicians' reports, the pace was flexible. The program assures some measure of success for every child. Immediate satisfaction is provided for every correct response, and there is ample opportunity for reinforcement. The program provides the groundwork for some essential reading skills, particularly in phonics.

In the initial stages, the program tends to limit associative processes to visual stimulation and rote recall of letter. More manual manipulation, pictures, writing, and verbal imagery would be helpful for a multisensory approach. It was found that teaching the recognition and writing of all letters of the alphabet was a long, laborious process, particularly with culturally disadvantaged and slow learning children. It was felt that there were not enough motivating factors to sustain the children's interest. The form used for capital *I* in the primer was easily confused with the lower case *i*. *M* and *n* are taught simultaneously and create a great deal of auditory and visual confusion. The word *a* taught in isolation is confusing when the children have been taught the letter /a/ sound as in /man/. This material and other programs like it may be most effective in tutorial or small-group instruction. We suspect that the childish drawings would restrict the use of this program to children, but the Job Corps has used it with some success with young adult illiterates.

Sights and Sounds (Random House, New York). Random House has packaged some of its best children's books (including those by Pantheon and Knopf) into *Sights and Sounds* units. Each unit contains a 8 station portable listening station (optional), 8 copies of each of 10 books, and a taped reading of each book. The readings are done by professional actors, with tasteful background music and sound effects. Prereading children relax with headsets (which cuts down extraneous stimuli), listen to the dramatic reading, and follow along in a copy of the book. In one classroom we are experimenting with inexpensive plug-in tape cartridge units, so simple and so rugged that preschoolers, on their own, can select a book and cartridge and enjoy literature.

Skilstarters (Random House, New York). Eliminate the myriad of preschool, kindergarten, and first-grade activities that have been erroneously called reading readiness and extract only those activities that research demonstrates will pay off in success in beginning reading; build a diagnostic scheme to assess each child's achievement in these activities; design highly motivating individualized learning activities in the form of individual and/or small group games that teach to these diagnosed reading readiness activities; provide a classroom management scheme that allows one teacher to keep track of each child's diagnosed needs and subsequent game schedule; build the entire program in such a way that the child finally begins to read in established, high-quality, children's literature but is simultaneously able to handle the basic primer and preprimer standard basals—the result is *Skilstarters,* a personalized, diagnostic, game-oriented program of reading readiness that leads the child, at his own pace, to three beginner readers: *Go, Dog, Go!, Ten Apples up on Top,* and *Green Eggs and Ham.* The program was under development for six years in preschool to first-grade classrooms in disadvantaged areas.

Spice (Educational Service, Benton Harbor, Mich.). This handbook is a collection of enjoyable activities that teachers can use in giving pupils practice in phonetic analysis, structural analysis, reading for meaning, and creative writing while they (pupils) are at their seats, playing games, or engaged in independent work activities. It is an old standby that is still valuable for teaching reading and the language arts.

SRA Basic Reading Series and Satellites (Science Research Associates, Chicago). A "linguistic" beginning reading series, the BRS covers grades 1–6. The Satellites material offers a box of 190 four-page reading selections in a kit supplementing the BRS. Also available are diagnostic tests, alphabet cards, wall charts, elaborate manuals and guides. Like so many "linguistic" readers, this series is really phonic rather than linguistic, in the sense that it stresses phonic families and careful control of symbols rather than careful control of sounds and natural language. A truly linguistic system in the reviewer's sense would not use such artificial language as "a pig can jig." Because of its artificial language and its attempts to control symbols rather than sounds, it falls into the same trap as the Bloomfield-Barnhart, Merrill, Behavioral Research Laboratories, Buchanan-Sullivan, and Woolman "linguistic" readers—they are all better-devised phonic systems with all the latter's flaws. They are, however, excellent drills for reinforcing phonics instruction. We have used the readers, in particular, as pattern drills in word families.

Structural Reading Series (L. W. Singer, New York). A series of five workbooks (A–E), picture dictionary, vocabulary development booklets, and letter dominoes designed to teach beginning reading, this series is one of the best "linguistic" approaches available to elementary classrooms. It is *not* a language-arts program, but a beginning code-busting program and is valuable at the kindergarten through grade 3 levels. There are some weaknesses in the size of type and spacing and amount of reinforcement exercises, but it is the best self-contained code-busting program we have used in grades 1 and 2. Unfortunately, we have found it less useful with older children after grade 4. When disadvantaged underachievers are making no headway with conventional basals by grade 3, we have pulled them off the sight readers and put them into this intensive program with good success.

Systems for Success (Follett, Chicago). We have found this series of two workbooks with accompanying manuals valuable as a supplementary source of word lists, phrases, and controlled vocabulary reading sources for adolescent and adult illiterates. It is not, however, a complete literacy program for illiterates, as advertised. So far, there is no self-contained package available that can be depended upon to bring adult or adolescent illiterates (approximately third-grade level or below) to functional literacy (sixth- or seventh-grade level). One major feature of this series is its excellent vocabulary control. Words introduced are carefully reinforced in reading selections that also maintain phonic families without sounding ridiculous.

Materials for Vocabulary, Spelling, and Word-Attack Skills

Many materials listed under subsequent headings contain vocabulary and word analysis skills practices, but only those materials designed *primarily* to teach these skills are included in this section. Both research and our own observations lead us to conclude that, in general, no available published material teaches functional spelling. Some materials occasionally help children do better on spelling tests, but their performances do not seem to transfer to their regular writing. We have found spelling workbooks and kits a valuable means of improving vocabulary and word-attack skills.

Basic Goals in Spelling (Webster Division, McGraw-Hill, New York). Two to four copies of each publisher's spelling workbook plus each publisher's phonics and word-attack skills workbooks should be collected and filed according to level and skill to be used as reinforcers to learning. In this way, each child can work on a word-attack skills weakness at his own level because his teacher has an adequate supply of materials. This series covers grades 1 to 8 and is the usual fare one finds in such workbooks.

Basic Phonics Program (Reardon, Cleveland). Grades 1–middle grades. This series and *The Speech to Print Phonics* series (Harcourt, Brace & World) have proved to be the best self-contained software phonics programs that I have used in various projects throughout the country. The Reardon series can be used to supplement any beginning reading program. It supplies pictures for teaching auditory discrimination of sounds in words and alphabet words, plus an excellent series of workbooks and teacher manuals. Different sets of alphabet cards allow teachers to choose letters with or without serifs to match the typefaces of particular basal readers used in the classroom. The workbooks and teacher's manuals present each specific phonic skill in a separate lesson with regular reviews. The sequence of the skills contains traditional irrelevancies to reading, but beyond this level the skills are valid. Because each skill is clearly separated into separate lessons, teachers can use the series to remediate children's specific phonic needs. By collecting pages of exercises from workbooks of other publishers, teachers can build a file of phonic exercises cataloged by skill and coded to parallel this series. Thus, the Reardon series can become a basic phonics course and other publishers' exercises can back up each lesson when specific children need extra drills.

Breaking the Sound Barrier (Macmillan, New York). This is one of the most effective phonics programs available. A traditional phonics program integrating teacher-directed instruction and workbooks, it has the usual flaws of traditional pedagogy—slow feedback, insufficient supply of reinforcement exercises for certain skills and not enough for others, too many nonphonic skills cluttering up the program, and so forth. But along with the Reardon *Basic Phonics Program* and the Murphy-Durrell *Speech to Print Phonics,* we have still found this program better than most.

Conquest in Reading (Webster Division, McGraw-Hill, New York). This workbook is designed for middle grades through junior high school, but we have also used it successfully above grade 9. The content of this workbook appeals more to older children than *The Magic World of Dr. Spello* workbook (described below), which covers approximately the same word-attack skills. This workbook is also included in the Webster package called *Classroom Reading Clinic.*

Games for Word Analysis. Every reading classroom should have a collection of word games, "Phonics Fish," "Word Lotto," and so on. "Scrabble" and "Scrabble, Jr." are traditionals and appeal to all levels of achievers. A number of companies manufacture such games. A jobber of school supplies usually lists various manufacturers in his catalog. One set of each game per classroom is sufficient. About $20 worth of games in each reading classroom will provide a sufficient variety.

Macmillan Reading Spectrum—Spectrum of Skills (Macmillan, New York). A series of colorfully packaged programed books on various levels teaching vocabulary development, word analysis, and reading comprehension skills makes up the *Spectrum of Skills.* Pupil record books and a detailed teacher guide are also available. The programs are designed for intermediate through junior high school level and are useful with school dropouts or semiliterate adults. In addition to the *Spectrum of Skills,* there is a portable library of paperbound books designed primarily for the intermediate grades (see under Comprehension Skills listing). Teachers using the *Spectrum of Skills* felt it was too difficult for retarded reading junior high school pupils. The content is culturally distant from the socially disadvantaged blacks and Puerto Ricans.

In general, many teachers are still not comfortable with programed instruction, especially when it takes the form of programed books that supply the correct answers beside each exercise item. There is the constant complaint that pupils "cheat." The idea that a pupil who needs to see the answer should have the answer available is unacceptable to many teachers. If the constructed responses were modified so that two answers are given, only one of which is logical, the subject would be required to think through the response even though he cheated. Our experience with school dropouts shows that many of them merely copy the answer without reading the problem. It has also been our experience, however, that when we do not require the pupil to write the answer, and the stimulus-response exercise is private, he quickly tires of cheating and plays according to the rules. A further modification was successfully tried in one project involving severely retarded-reading adolescents. The answers supplied after each stimulus were blacked out. A separate tally sheet of answers was inserted in the back of the book. This method allowed the materials to be used in a self-directing manner with a mildly delayed feedback. With this modification, enough delay was maintained between stimulus and feedback to cause the subject to make a response.

The skills series will work with a small number of junior high school retarded readers. However, it is less successful with the majority of socially disadvantaged Puerto Ricans and blacks who are two years or more retarded in reading.

New Phonics Skilltexts (Merrill, Columbus, Ohio). These four paperback workbooks cover grades 1–6, offering systematic exercises in phonics with some work in dictionary and structural analysis skills. Each unit begins with listening exercises emphasizing sounds. This is followed by a hodgepodge of behavioral demands that the publisher labels "understanding." Then comes a phonics and a word structure section ending with a review. Checkout exercises are provided at regular intervals. The major weakness in this series is common to so many published workbooks—it lacks precise definition of the behaviors being taught. This leads to questionable sequences and practices. On the other hand, it provides some clever exercises and is the type of workbook that should be in every classroom in small quantities along with others to provide teachers with a variety of reinforcement exercises. By providing structured answer sheets and clipping answer keys into the back of each workbook, the Skilltexts can become self-directing materials for personalizing the instructional program.

New Webster Word Wheels (Webster Division, McGraw-Hill, New York). This kit includes 17 beginning blends wheels, 20 prefix wheels, 18 suffix wheels, and 8 vowel digraph wheels, color-coded and numbered according to difficulty. The wheels were developed to provide personalized instruction for children who need reinforcement in these word skills. This kit is also available as part of Webster's *Classroom Clinic,* which is not a clinic at all but a convenient package of miscellaneous reading materials from the Webster catalog.

Phonics We Use (Lyons and Carnahan, Chicago). Here is that old standby in a new cover. Every reading teacher has seen this series and most reading centers have used it, not because it is so good, but because it has been around for so long. Nor is it especially bad. It is, perhaps, the most typical phonics workbook available with all the flaws—illogical sequence of skills, too much of one skill and not enough of others, incorrect labeling of behaviors it is supposed to teach, instructions to pupils far above their comprehension abilities, and so forth. But it is still a useful reinforcer if the teacher does not use it as a developmental program. Instead, each exercise should be filed according to skill. (Do not rely on the publisher's skill labels because some are incorrect.) We have cut up the workbook, rewritten the instructions so that pupils can read them, mounted everything on oaktag, typed answers on the back of the oaktag, and filed each one according to skill and level. By using this series as a start, we have done the same thing to other publishers' workbooks and built a useful file of word-attack skills reinforcers by skill and level. This is a worthwhile project for volunteers and Neighborhood Youth Corpsmen.

Phonics Workbooks (Webster Division, McGraw-Hill, New York). This set of five workbooks provides more supplementary exercises in word-attack skills to be added to the teacher's file of resources.

Reading with Phonics (Lippincott, Philadelphia). This famous Hay and Wingo series is a useful supplementary series that can provide effective exercises to reinforce word-attack skills. By filing the materials according to sound and skill, along with other publishers' word-attack skills materials, a teacher can build a good supply of supplementary drills. A school can well afford volunteers and paraprofessionals building these supplementary files for every elementary grade classroom.

Remedial Reading Drills (George Wahr, Ann Arbor, Mich.). This famous word list by phonic family was designed in the 1930s by Kirk and Hegge for special education problems. The technique of isolating and blending word parts does not work well, but the exhaustive list of simple words in phonic families is invaluable. One copy per teacher is a great resource.

Speech to Print Phonics (Harcourt, Brace & World, New York). A kit of flashcards, set of 25 pupil response cards, and teacher's manual, this package is designed to teach phonics, alphabet, auditory discrimination of sounds in words, and word meanings to beginning readers. It is effective with all pupils at any level who need these skills. The technique is cleverly designed to differentiate instructional needs while teaching 25 pupils at once. The program requires 15 to 20 minutes work daily, supplementing any traditional basal reading program. Most valuable is the teacher's manual, which presents a step-by-step, integrated procedure of lessons that can be taught by the most inexperienced teacher. The manual can be purchased independently and is probably one of the best sequential programs in basic phonics on the market. It has been used successfully with adult Spanish-speaking illiterates as part of an English-language program. This is not a "how to" manual. It is a series of over 50 detailed lesson plans representing a tight phonics program.

Spelling and Writing Patterns (Follett, Chicago). Perhaps the most effectively packaged spelling program we have used is this series by Mort Botel. If we assume that nothing really teaches spelling, we can eliminate spelling achievement as a criterion for any spelling program and get down to important issues, such as word-attack skills—particularly phonics, reading, and a sense of language. As a program to develop a sense of language, sight vocabulary, writing, and word analysis, this is effective for all children, regardless of socioeconomic level. A multisensory approach, it stresses sound-symbol relationships. It is designed so that children can operate individually at their own level and rate of learning. It applies all learning to written expression, which is, in one sense, the final payoff to instruction.

Spellingtime A–Z (L. W. Singer, New York). A series of word study books from earliest phonics levels through high school, the material is attractive and interesting to socially disadvantaged retarded readers in the intermediate grades and junior high school. Like most workbooks, these lack immediate feedback. In one program with retarded-reading junior high school children, we cut out the exercises from the workbooks and mounted each page on a 10- by 12-inch sheet of oaktag. Answers were printed on the back of the oaktag, and all the oaktag cards were filed upright in boxes. The answers provided immediate feedback, and when finished with each card, the child would feel a form of closure which he did not feel when working in a 50-page book.

SRA Word Games Kit I (Science Research Associates, Chicago). This kit provides instructions for only one basic game, plus a workbook with word exercises. A number of game variations devised at MFY have since been expanded by their Materials Development staff into a supplementary manual of games that can be played with the kit. In this way, the kit becomes a tool for teaching a number of specific word-attack skills. Further work with the kit revealed that word retention was not permanent. Children tended to forget most of the words covered during a particular presentation. In one project I conducted, we developed a series of reading selections coded into the kit using the words in short reading selections. The selections have been tested on socially disadvantaged retarded readers in the inner city and have proved most effective in increasing word retention over a long period. The supplementary manual and the reading selections have made the kit a useful technique in teaching vocabulary, word-attack skills, and reading comprehension.

SRA Spelling Word Power Labs (Science Research Associates, Chicago). Four different labs are designed on multilevels for pupils to learn at their own rate according to ability. A lab consists of about 80 learning wheels grouped into color-coded levels of instruction with 10 to 12 levels for each grade. Each level contains 5 to 6 wheels with duplicate wheels of the most prevalent spelling problems. The student works in the color-coded level that matches his level of speed and ability. An added feature of the Spelling Word Lab is a presentation of phonic and word analysis elements that are directly connected to phonic problems in reading. Step-by-step, single-frame word exposure on the wheel gives the student a visual image of each word. The aspect of game playing motivated by the lab gives the child a necessary change of pace. The learning wheel device is based on a fundamental idea of programed learning, quick feedback. Some teachers reported that the wheels were difficult for elementary school children who were unable to master the mechanics of the technique. Children reading at grades 6–8 worked better with the materials, but there was no evidence of growth in spelling. The wheels did, however, aid reinforcement of phonics, structural analysis, and general vocabulary. The wheels appear to be useful with youth and may be effective with Job-Corps-type subjects as well as with intermediate and junior high school disadvantaged children.

The Magic World of Dr. Spello (Webster Division, McGraw-Hill, New York). This attractive workbook is a fast review of word-attack skills. It should be available in small quantities in every reading classroom. This workbook is also available in Webster's collection of miscellaneous reading materials called the *Classroom Reading Clinic.*

Time for Phonics (Webster Division, McGraw-Hill, New York). These workbooks cover grades K–3 with a listening-speaking-reading-writing technique for teaching phonics. Unfortunately, the series is not designed for individualized instruction. Some exercises, however, can be adapted to diagnostic teaching. A couple of copies of each workbook can be added to the teacher's repertoire of supplementary word-attack skills from all the publishers' workbooks.

Word Analysis Cards (Harcourt, Brace & World, New York). A series of 3 envelopes on three grade levels with 30 selections in each, the cards are designed for individual and/or pupil learning teams of two. They are designed to reinforce word-attack skills, to teach vocabulary, and to build concept formation. One side of each card presents a random list of words and three categories. Pupils list the three categories on a separate sheet of paper in three columns and then list each word under the appropriate category. A series of categories may be, for example, "things that roll," "animals," "things found in a garden." These cards have been used successfully in various programs with pupils ranging from grade 4 to adult level. In teams of two, pupils work out each word. The first pupil writes the word in the appropriate column. When all the words have been listed, the second pupil checks the correct answers under the appropriate categories on the back of each card as the first pupil reads his list. Pupils switch roles on a second card. The technique is largely self-directing and self-correcting. This series is one of the most successful techniques for teaching vocabulary and concept formation we have used. If the teacher desires, the exercises can involve the use of the dictionary. The techniques can be applied to special areas of vocabulary. For example, in one school dropout program involved with work training, instructors made up their own word-analysis cards based on technical vocabulary used in the program's vocational training shop.

Word Attack and *Comprehension* (Ann Arbor Publishers, Ann Arbor, Mich.). These two workbooks are programed strategies to teach children in grades 1 and 2 or remedial-reading adolescents to "bust the code" as they read to comprehend. Five behaviors are first developed: verbal fluency, recognizing visual clues, recognizing auditory clues, recognizing context clues, and following directions. When these skills are mastered, they are applied until the behaviors are shaped and used automatically. This series can be used independently or it can be plugged into the Michigan Language Program after Book 5. We have used it successfully with junior high school retarded readers as an independent program.

Materials for Comprehension

Included in the following list are materials that have been effective in teaching various specific comprehension skills to disadvantaged children and youth. Other materials included offer less teaching of comprehension as a specific skill area, but are highly motivating for disadvantaged underachievers. With many of these children, just discovering materials that they are willing to try to read is a pedagogical breakthrough. Many of the materials listed teach other skills as well, but are included under comprehension because we have used them in experimental comprehension skills centers. Some collections of literature are included in this section as comprehension skill builders. We have found certain conveniently packaged series of storybooks very successful in enticing reluctant readers from disadvantaged areas to read. Although we have not attempted to compile a list of great children's literature, we have included these special packages because they have been so successful.

Basic Goals in Reading (Webster Division, McGraw-Hill, New York). Four readers, one for each half year, grades 2 and 3, present basal words in stories designed to reinforce the words taught in Webster's *Basic Goals in Spelling*. The content is not particularly appropriate for urban disadvantaged children and the interest level is barely above the readability level, but it is a series worth having in quantities of two or three per classroom.

Better Reading Books (Science Research Associates, Chicago). These three books, covering grades 5–7, 7–9, and 9–11, respectively, present excellent reading selections— 20 per book. Each selection is followed by 20 multiple-choice vocabulary and comprehension questions. This is one of the most successful comprehension exercise books that we have used with all types of populations. By providing answer keys, individual progress folders, and structured response sheets, the books become self-directing for individualized instruction. One method we have used is to have a child read a selection each day. On the first day, he answers only the odd-numbered questions of the first selection to test immediate recall. On the second day he first answers the even-numbered questions of selection 1 (delayed recall), and then reads the second selection, answering the odd-numbered questions of selection 2. The daily pattern is first to answer questions from the previous day's reading, read a new selection, and then answer questions on the new selection.

Building Reading Power (Merrill, Columbus, Ohio). Originally designed as a junior high school programed developmental reading course by New York City Board of Education personnel, the present kit is a series of linear programs in 15 short booklets. These nonconsumable booklets are divided into three skills: "Context Clues," "Structural

Analysis," and "Comprehension Skills." In its original form as a developmental program, it was notably unsuccessful in the inner city schools. The usual problem of programed frames teaching low-level skills but using higher-level language for instructions to the learner still plagues this program. However, in this new kit form, it becomes more useful as a supplement to teacher instruction. It allows individual students to gain additional reinforcement in certain skills that have been pretaught by the teacher. It has structured response sheets and immediate feedback, two strategies that positively affect the rate of learning.

Curriculum Enrichment Series (Lyons and Carnahan, Chicago). Leo Fay has collected some of the best stories we have ever used into eight thin books. The first book is at preprimer level. The last book is at grade 6 readability. The stories are high-interest, multiethnic—these may be the most successful reading anthologies we have used in the Yeshiva University Reading Clinic. Evidently, these books were designed to supplement Lyons and Carnahan's basal reading series, but the basal reader stories do not match this enrichment series in literary quality. However, this problem occurs with all basal readers.

Curriculum Motivation Series (Lyons and Carnahan, Chicago). Designed for children slightly below average who need to be motivated to read. Leo Fay has authored a second series of high-interest, low-vocabulary readers. Colorful adventure stories with easy vocabulary, these six readers span grades 1.6 to 4.1 in reading difficulty levels. However, each book reaches about two grade levels above readability in interest level. This series is excellent for reluctant readers.

Diagnostic Reading Workbooks (Merrill, Columbus, Ohio). Another workbook series for the first six grades, this one covers most of the traditional comprehension skills with vocabulary and word attack added for good measure. Once again, it is a hodgepodge of skills lacking precision. Advertised as "high-interest material," we found its content traditional and "schoolish." But it is still valuable as another resource for reinforcing certain skills and is worthy of being one of the 6 to 12 different workbooks available in the classroom.

Dimensions in Reading Series (Science Research Associates, Chicago). Out of SRA's contracts with Job Corps comes a new series of high-interest, low-vocabulary reading kits for young adults (grade 9 through adult level) but with readability at about intermediate-grade level (publisher's claim is readability 3.5 to 7.4). First in the series is the Manpower and Natural Resources kit with an American History kit to follow. The first kit includes conservation, earth science, mineralogy, weather, and occupational skills reading materials. The content is designed to fit what Job Corps hoped would be the occupational aspirational levels of corpsmen or at least what the United States government could sell as aspirations to school dropouts. In contrast to other high-interest, low-vocabulary materials for *this population*, the kit has very little competition. As usual with SRA kits, it is entirely individualized.

Literature Sampler and Literature Sampler, Junior Edition (Xerox Educational Division, New York). A colorful kit of 144 book previews, each 2,000 words in length on 4-page cards, 10½ by 8½ inches, with illustrations, the kit provides training in comprehension skills and tempts students to read the complete books. Each selection is provided with a one-page 5½- by 8½-inch card posing "why" and "how" questions for comprehension check. Another card, 10½ by 8½ inches, presents reasons why the "best" answers are so selected. Supplementing the kit are student logs containing entry pages, reading interest profiles, preselection aids, a 289-book bibliography, 4 class readings, and quizzes. A teacher guide describes the program in detail and outlines teaching procedures. The guide is one of the finest presentations of teaching reading techniques with an outstanding guide to books for adolescents, schoolchildren on the junior high school level, and adults. Reading levels in the Sampler run from grades 5 to 11 with 12 to 24 selections at each level. The Sampler, Junior, runs from intermediate grade levels to junior high. Supplementing the kit is a sampler library consisting of one copy of each of 50 different paperback books boxed in an attractive cardboard bookcase for a miniature classroom library. Reading selections in the kit are drawn from the books in the portable library, plus 94 other books available in most libraries.

In general, the kit is too difficult for retarded-reading junior high school children. It has more use in a high school in a socially disadvantaged area as a tool for developmental rather than remedial reading or in Job Corps camps. Ungraded 7–9 youths, not more than two years retarded in reading participating in some experimental programs, enjoyed the selections from the kit that were seventh-grade level or below. None of them, however, dared to try a pocketbook from the Sampler library. The junior edition appears to be much more useful with these populations. Unfortunately, the Sampler library is available for the senior kit only. The Sampler library was implemented at a summer camp for narcotics rehabilitation with young male adults, seventeen to twenty-one years old. It met with some success there. The colorful, compact library was attractive, as were the titles included in the bookcase. The men at the camp were as willing to read the quality literature on adventure, heroism, and war as they were to read pocketbooks dealing with sex or sadism. The library may be an excellent item for Job Corps camps and adult literacy programs for those who are at a minimal junior high school reading level.

Learning Units from Random House (Random House, New York). The largest publisher of children's literature has packaged its storybooks into learning units with outstanding teacher's guides, including lesson plans and supplementary activities. So far, *Taste,* an individualized reading program to develop awareness of literary forms in the primary grades; *Elementary Guidance,* which explores personality development using famous children's books as case studies; and *People to People,* an introduction to cultural geography, are available. Others will follow. Each unit develops an integrated program around quality children's books published by Random House and its subsidiaries (Knopf and Pantheon). For example, *Elementary Guidance* provides lesson plans around such themes as, autonomy, courage, responsibility, emerging identity, and handling feelings. In the package of books that form the core of this program are such classic titles as *Wee Willow Whistle, Loney Veronica, Yertle the Turtle, A Fly Went By,* and *Cowboy Andy. People to People* is a brilliantly conceived program in which each child fills out a workform analyzing his own life—who he is, how he lives, what he eats, how he travels. Then, each child selects a book at his level from the *People to People* classroom library. Each book is about a child living in another culture—*Barto Takes the Subway* (United States), *Duee, Boy of Liberia, Golden Tombo* (Japan), and so on. Each child reads his book and fills out an identical workform for the child he has read about. Then he fills out a third workform that helps him analyze how he is the same and how he is different from the other child. Meanwhile, a wall map with pins plots the countries under study; each child's book is represented on the map. Geographically determined pupil teams made up of children reading at different levels work together on special projects related to their geographic areas. The manual provides excellent ideas for projects. Whatever weaknesses inhere in these programs tend to relate to the few books that are not necessarily the best available. However, teachers can use all these programs as a start and add other publishers' books to the classroom library.

Learning Your Language (Follett, Chicago). Harold Herber has collected excellent reading materials into 6 attractive paperback workbooks that preteach key vocabulary for each selection and help develop the major reading skills. The format is appealing and the quality of the comprehension questions is a notch above the usual fare. We have enclosed each booklet in a folder that contains structured response sheets, tests, answer keys and progress plotters. In this way, the program becomes self-directing. We have found that adolescents must be reading at least about the sixth-grade level to get by in this series.

Macmillan Reading Spectrum—Spectrum of Books (Macmillan, New York). Two sets of paperback children's classics, 30 books in each for grades 5 and 6, respectively, these packages are attractively housed in a classroom display case. There is nothing peculiarly ethnic or urban about the series—just good books. The *Spectrum of Books* is a companion to Macmillan's *Spectrum of Skills,* described in a previous section.

Miscellaneous Book Packages. The following list includes packages of books that this reviewer has used with great success in classrooms for disadvantaged children. Available at the lower levels are Harper & Row's *I Can Read* series, Random House's *Beginner Readers,* Harr Wagner's *Time Machine* series and the *Fun Forest Readers,* Holt, Rinehart and Winston's *Little Owl* series, Harper & Row's *Torchlighter,* Dell's paperback *Yearlings,* Scholastic Magazine's *Arrow Books,* and American Book's *Reading Roundtable.* In addition, Benefic Press and Garrard Press have excellent high-interest, low-vocabulary book packages.

At intermediate and junior high levels, all Harr Wagner's series, some of Dell's *Yearlings* and American Book's *Reading Roundtable,* Holt, Rinehart and Winston's *Wise Owl* series, Random House's *Step-up Books,* and Harper & Row's *Torchbearer* are excellent packages and convenient ways of ordering classroom libraries.

Teachers of disadvantaged adolescents should consider Random House's *Landmark* series and *All About Books,* Doubleday's *Zenith* series, and the paperback books referred to previously in this text (Pocket Books, Bantam, Dell, Popular Library and so forth).

New Practice Readers (Webster Division, McGraw-Hill, New York). Another dependable standard for every reading classroom, this new edition comes at seven levels, grades 2 to 8 (Books A through G). The content is of high enough interest to be used at adolescent levels. The readers preteach vocabulary and then stress seven basic comprehension skills. With structured response sheets and individual answer keys, the series can be individualized and used diagnostically.

New York, New York (Random House, New York). A series of five supplementary readers designed for urban schools, these biweekly "newspapers" are one of the few materials that truly have high interest and low vocabulary. Features and stories about children in the city are written around exciting original photographs. These are supplemented by stories and articles by leading children's writers, illustrated by Roy McKie, Jack Davis (*Mad* magazine), and other top artists. The five readers ("newspapers") represent readability levels K–1, 1–2, 2–3, 4–5, and 6–12, but the interest-level spans are much higher. The series is published for the greater New York area (New Jersey and Connecticut), but response has been so great that other cities are using the New York edition.

Reader's Digest Skill Builders (Reader's Digest, Pleasantville, N.Y.). This graded series of readers covering grades 2–6 have been the backbone of too many reading programs for years. In fact, some children have been so saturated with the series that we rarely use them in the Yeshiva University Reading Clinic. The overexposure is unfortunate, because the readers are excellent high-interest, low-vocabulary materials. Teachers are cautioned about using the early level *Skill Builders* to build comprehension skills. A close look at the drills following the selections in these readers will reveal that almost all the "comprehension" questions are really vocabulary questions. One of the best things to come out in recent years are the new low-level *Skill Builders*. These are aimed at adolescent semiliterates. The Reader's Digest staff selected those stories whose content would most likely appeal to young adults that appear in the *Skill Builders* for grades 2–4. They rebound them in thin, self-contained *Skill Builders*. This newer series is one of the very few sources of materials with grades 2–4 readability and format, but high school age content.

Reading Attainment System (Grolier Educational Corporation). This kit was designed specifically for adolescents who are underachievers—high interest low vocabulary. One hundred twenty self-directing and self-correcting reading selections with comprehension questions are supplemented by another 120 skill cards. Each skill card presents a glossary and 10 exercises in word attack skills. This kit also provides 30 record books with progress plotters. It is one of the best designed kits on the market—perhaps one of the best for disadvantaged underachievers. Selections are color coded for level. Levels range from about 3.7 to 5.0.

Reading for Meaning (Lippincott, Philadelphia). Covering grades 4–9, this series is still one of the best general reading improvement workbooks available. The drill questions following each selection are neatly divided according to skill taught. This allows teachers to use the series to teach diagnostically. Some of the content is dull, a bit old-fashioned and "schoolish," and should be revised. In spite of these drawbacks, the series is still worth having in every reading classroom. By making teacher's manuals available to pupils, using structured answer sheets and progress plotters, and filing the workbooks in corrugated cartons, we have made self-directing individualized learning kits out of the series. In one project four sets of the series were purchased, and reading selections were cut out and mounted on color-coded oaktag. Each set of questions was filed according to skill. Many children read the same selections, but each child answered only those questions that provided practice in his diagnosed skill weakness.

Reading Pacemakers and Skilpacers (Random House, New York). This is another learning unit from the Random House School and Library Service. Essentially, *Pacemakers* and *Skilpacers* are the individualized reading advocate's dream—a set of high-interest children's storybooks for grades 3–8, with the learning and teaching aids needed to offset the complaint many teachers have about the administrative impossibility of individualizing reading instruction with storybooks. 5 packages of 10 books each supply the classroom with 50 famous children's books. A child selects the book he wants to read. For each book there is a vocabulary card to preteach key vocabulary and a survey card to prepare and guide him in reading the book. When he finishes the book, the child draws two sets of question cards called "Detail" and "Comprehension," plus an "Activity" card from which he can select one or more interesting projects relevant to his book. After he records his response on his progress plotter, he checks the cards and requests a book conference with his teacher. The conference is carefully guided by a set of cards which the teacher uses to comment on and discuss the book. It covers all the information and steps a good teacher uses in a book conference. The teacher has a set of cards for each of the 50 books. Finally, based on the child's progress plotter and the guided conference, which are designed to tell the teacher quickly what each child's skill deficiencies are, the teacher uses the final component, a kit of 15 sets of color-coded, 6-page cards, each set covering one comprehension skill. The teacher pulls out the card set appropriate to the child's diagnosed need. The child uses the card set with any book at his level. The cards are designed to teach and then reinforce the skill selected by the teacher. This is all done by the pupil himself in a self-directed program. Sets of reading *Pacemakers* and *Skilpacers* are being developed for all grade levels.

Scholastic Literature Units (Scholastic Magazines, New York). Perhaps one of the best reading-literature packages—each unit includes

110 high-interest paperback books; a teacher's notebook, which is both a teaching resource and set of lesson plans; 40 student notebooks with exercises, quizzes, writing assignments, reading guides; and a corrugated enclosure for the materials. Of the 110 books, 40 are a class set of anthologies centering on the unit theme. Such titles as "Animals," "High Adventure," and "Small World" are available at grades 6–8 readability. "Courage," "Family," and "Frontiers" are available at grades 7–9 readability. In addition to the class anthology, each unit provides about 15 other books in quantities of 3, 8, or 12 for small group readings. The title selections are excellent and the teacher resource notebook can help make mediocre teachers more effective.

SRA Comprehensive Reading Series (Science Research Associates, Chicago). Here is an excellent collection of high-interest reading selections, with good workbooks, adequate teacher guides, and diagnostic checkout tests. The three readers cover the intermediate grades (publisher claims grades 2–6) and are useful with low achievers in junior high school. We have used them as comprehension skill builders, and disadvantaged children have responded well.

SRA Pilot Library (Science Research Associates, Chicago). A selection of varied short stories in paperback form, this collection is organized to meet the reading levels of intermediate and junior high school pupils in three compact libraries. These were designed to be used in conjunction with the corresponding SRA Reading Lab, but can be used adequately as a separate reading source. The selections are unchanged excerpts from books by well-known authors of children's literature. Each library contains 72 stories in separate booklet form (paperback) ranging from 24 to 32 pages in length. An individual story is graded and coded by reading level and offers a step-by-step easily controlled enrichment program that can complement the brief materials of basal reading selections. SRA offers three Pilot Libraries at overlapping reading levels. In addition to free reading experiences, the Pilot Library provides a variety of exercises for each of the 72 reading selections. An answer key permits students to score their responses on their own. The teacher handbook presents specific, but simple, procedures for attaining maximum results in this program. The libraries contain excellent selections and have been successfully used as high-interest, low-vocabulary reading materials. Some of the stories have been used with school dropouts. A number of the selections listed at difficulty rates below fifth-grade level can be used on the junior high school level. Unfortunately, as in so many storybooks, the stories were selected with middle class pupils in mind. As with SRA Reading Labs, a distillation of selections from all Pilot Libraries has been made by the Job Corps staff at the U.S. Office of Economic Opportunity under the direction of Douglas Porter.

SRA Reading for Understanding (Science Research Associates, Chicago). If we use student enthusiasm as criterion for success, this is by far the most successful kit we have used. *Reading for Understanding* comes in three kits, one each for grades 3–8, 8–12, 5–college. We have used the 3–8 kit at all levels. The extras are placement tests, student record books, and some other things that are not necessary for the kit to be used effectively. Each kit provides 400 lesson cards arranged according to difficulty level. Each card provides short, high-interest reading selections in various content areas from philosophy to sports, and from science to art. The pupil reads the selection, chooses the best implied conclusion, checks his own answer, and plots his own progress.

SRA Reading Laboratories (Science Research Associates, Chicago). The Reading Labs have been the best known and most poorly used kits in a number of programs. Of the teachers I surveyed, some had used them in MFY projects, a few had some in their schools, and almost all teachers had seen them. But only one out of fifteen teachers used them correctly; that is, as the SRA manual prescribes. The misuse was due less to creative innovation on the part of the teacher than to lack of information and refusal to study the teacher's manual. Labs IIa, b, and c for retarded intermediate grade pupils through grade 9 were the most successful in programs known to this author. Reading Lab Ic was effective with retarded-reading fourth-graders. Most of the teachers did not use the listening comprehension exercises, even though low achievers usually need much training in listening skills. SRA listening exercises, however, are too difficult and uninteresting for many of these low achievers. Until new exercises are available, SRA listening comprehension exercises are being taped and reproduced in two projects. They have been presented through an inexpensive "homemade" language laboratory that I have designed and which is described elsewhere in this Appendix.

The chief value in using SRA Reading Labs is the motivation it provides in structuring a self-teaching, self-directing learning situation with immediate feedback of results in a "nontest" situation; that is, the pupil checks himself. The labs are not sufficient for teaching word-attack skills, but by working alone, youngsters free the teacher to work with small groups or individuals. Thus, the teacher can use the labs to diagnose deficiencies in specific word-attack skills by analyzing the items wrong on the "Learn About Words" section of the Power

Builders, and then give direct instruction and supplementary reinforcement exercises to individuals as needed. It may be that SRA Reading Labs are overrated in their ability to actually teach reading. Certainly, they are weak in word-attack skills. Nevertheless, they are the best technique we have ever found for breaking down the rigid, large-group instruction technique most teachers use. We have found that the labs are our first step in getting teachers and pupils used to individualized instruction and self-direction.

Standard Test Lessons in Reading, McCall Crabbs Series (Bureau of Publications, Teachers College, Columbia University, New York). Five 78-page workbooks, with one reading selection per page and multiple choice questions, the McCall Crabbs series has been in use for over fifteen years. Each of the five books is at a progressively more difficult level. The content is not particularly modern or urban; in fact, some of the selections are just plain dull. But we have continued to use them with relative success. The publisher provides structured response sheets and answer keys. We have purchased two copies of each level per classroom. Each selection is mounted on oaktag with each book (level) assigned a different color of oaktag. Answers are printed on the back of each oaktag selection. We then have a file or kit-like arrangement that lends itself to individualized self-directed work.

Teen-age Tales (D. C. Heath, Boston). This series was designed *by adults* for teen-agers who are low achievers in reading. But like most adults, the editors unduly flatter themselves if they think that most of the stories "make it" with adolescents. A couple of sports stories appeal to early adolescents, but most of the boy-girl stories are the usual "schoolmarm" propaganda pieces that adolescents have never taken seriously. But because some of the stories are written with low vocabulary load, we have used selections from these readers when we could get the adolescent past the relatively "square" illustrations of healthy, stereotyped, handsome, middle class, super-Caucasians.

Success in Language (Follett, Chicago). Similar in format and quality to the previously described *Learning Your Language,* this series is a good example of how publishers stretch the application of their products to meet the unreasonable demands of educators who ask that one piece of material teach all the language arts, plus foster psycho-social development, moral character, and so on. If we overlook the excessive claims of the publisher and use this as high-interest reading material with good vocabulary and comprehension skills development, it is an excellent series for good readers on the junior high level.

Webster Reading Packages (Webster Division, McGraw-Hill, New York). Webster publishes packages of books that deserve special notice even though I have tried to avoid listing storybooks for disadvantaged children. One of the most successful is the paperback *Everyreaders* series. This is a collection of high-interest, low-vocabulary, well-written rewrites of classics. Inner city, disadvantaged underachievers in high school reacted so favorably to these books that they disappeared from the reading centers. The colorful "linguistic" storybooks developed for the Buchanan-Sullivan Associates *Programmed Reading* are clever stories for children written in phonic families—a very difficult thing to do well. These are good for reinforcing phonics instruction with high-interest reading selections. Webster's *Beginner Science* series and the 24-book *Classroom Science Library* are excellent buys for short, highly motivating books that will entice reluctant readers.

Materials for Work and Study Skills

It is difficult to separate the materials that should be included in this and in the previous section. In some cases the decision is almost arbitrary. For example, the Barnell Loft *Specific Skills* series contains exercise books on comprehending main ideas and details that are certainly straight comprehension skills. We listed them here, however, because we have been using these booklets in the work-study skills center described in Chapter Eleven. Also included in this section are many materials from content areas (geography, history, grammar) that we have used in reading programs as reading skill-building materials.

SRA Basic Skills Series (Science Research Associates, Chicago). Three of the most successful study skills materials are the *Organizing and Reporting Skills* kit, the *Graph and Picture Study Skills* kit, and the *Map and Globe Skills* kit. They cover achievement levels 4–8. We have used them successfully from grade 5 through adult populations. As in most kits, the program is individualized and self-directing. Extras include pupil booklets and guides. Teachers using this type of kit should be sure that children test out on standardized reading tests a year or more above the level that the kit claims to be designed for. These study skills kits fascinated low-achieving, inner city high school adolescents and have become one of the materials we use to seduce reluctant readers into a high-intensity reading program.

Barnell Loft Specific Skills (Barnell Loft, Rockville Center, N.Y.). Printed materials, which can be used individually or in small groups, are a teacher's greatest aid if he truly wishes to differentiate instruction according to needs. This Barnell Loft series offers practice in five reading skills: "Using the Context," "Getting the Facts," "Locating Information," "Following Directions," "Main Ideas." There are six levels corresponding generally to grades 2–6. The series is designed to reinforce teacher-taught skills. At each level, there is a separate paperback workbook for each skill.

In "Using the Context," two or three sentences are given, and the last sentence has one or two blanks to be filled by choosing from alternative words. The vocabulary is not difficult, consisting primarily of basic words, but the principal idea of context as a cue for definitions needs to be pretaught as well. To initiate these exercises and to get pupils to use context in their reading, pairs of students can work together. One can read the sentences and the other call out what he thinks is the appropriate word, then check the presented choice and make his selection. The first child checks the answer sheet and makes corrections. After several such sessions, each works on his own. The material is excellent at all grade levels. Structured answer sheets can be purchased from the publisher. Answer keys are provided for each booklet so that they can be totally self-correcting. This series has been most successful in some self-directing compensatory education programs that I have conducted.

Be a Better Reader (Prentice-Hall, Englewood Cliffs, N.J.). Six workbooks at progressively higher levels, grade 7 through adult, provide excellent skills development in content areas of science, social studies, literature, and math. The books are not good with remedial reading cases. Only on- or above-grade achievers seem to respond well to this series, and for this group, it may be the best available. By providing structured response sheets and easy access to correct answers, the workbooks can be made self-directing. A *Be A Better Reader-Foundations* series is now available at lower readability levels.

Better Work Habits (Scott, Foresman, Chicago). In 1933, Rachel Salisbury created this workbook of basic study skills. Thirty-four years later it still sells well, and for good reason. It is still the best sequential program of organizational, outlining, and general study skills for secondary school children. Starting with simple categorizing, it moves to excellent exercises in coordinating and subordinating ideas. Outlining is taught incidentally to relationship of concepts. Each lesson covers a specific skill. Each series of lessons moves from basic simple concepts and steps to the more complex. Teachers can make them self-directing by tearing out the exercises and mounting them on oaktag with answers on the back.

EDL Study Skills Kits (Educational Development Laboratories, Huntington, N.Y.). Seven kits in science, another seven in social studies, and seven more in reference skills cover grades 4–10 readability (3–9, according to the authors). Each kit is at approximately one grade level and presents high-interest, self-directing, individualized study skills in the respective content areas. Children respond well to this series. We have found this and the SRA Study Skills kits very effective with low-achieving junior and senior high school disadvantaged adolescents.

Follett Basic Learning Program—World History Study Lessons (Follett, Chicago). Students' low performances in content areas are not solely attributable to low ability, as many would like to contend, but are often caused by poor reading ability. Follett makes this knowledge a guideline. This nine-unit series is designed for junior high school with reading selections beginning at grade 5 readability level and ending in the last units at grade 7 readability. Each unit is developed separately and contains from 11 to 23 lessons. The curriculum emphasizes the development of Western civilization. The important feature is that the materials are geared to developing reading skills. New vocabulary in the selection and a statement of reading purpose appear before the reading passage. Various comprehension exercises follow. The word count is given so students may assess their reading speeds. Plotting the rate and the percentage correct in comprehension gives the student immediate feedback on his progress. This is the system followed throughout the series. Plotting graphs or reading individual, intensive units instead of one massive text, which often appears boring and difficult, offers a chance for steady, incremental accomplishment. This can offset the usual pervasive feeling of failure and inadequacy and can allow content to "soak in" as reading skills improve.

The teacher's guide includes material on the nature of slow learning. The usual methodology is given, as well as plans for four types of lessons—a modified developmental lesson, a report lesson, a debate lesson, and a visual-aids lesson. Lists of supplementary books and visual aids are offered. By enclosing each booklet (unit) in a self-contained folder with answers to study guides and reading exercises, and by careful use of comprehension checks and tests supplied by Follett to supplement the series, teachers can make the *World History Study Lessons* both self-directing and self-correcting.

The strengths of these materials lie in format, readability level, and methodology. The weakness lies in content. It is the same collection-of-facts world history text that asks children to remember such meaningful and profound ideas as the six steps to becoming a knight. And, of course, Asia and Africa are not considered part of world history. Someday Follett or another publisher will put good content into this format and produce an ideal history publication. Until then, teachers can combine the Follett series with some creative teaching.

Gates-Peardon Practice Exercises in Reading (Bureau of Publications, Teachers College, Columbia University, New York). Gates-Peardon exercises have been old standbys for years. They serve some very useful functions if given in small doses and used as the authors suggest—as supplements to the development of reading skills. Designated for grades 2–6, they are useful for all who need practice in reading for general comprehension, details and practice in following directions, or predicting the outcome of selections. A separate booklet for each of these four topics is provided at each grade level. One important function of these exercises is their use as practice for the many standard tests the students will take. The format corresponds closely to standard tests; for example, a brief selection followed by three or four multiple-choice questions. Another important function is their aid in developing outlining skills. The ability to analyze reading material, pull out the main idea, and then expand it with the necessary details can be performed by many students. Practice and more practice is the necessary key. Along with the Barnell Loft *Specific Skills* series, the Gates-Peardon booklets lend themselves to the self-directing, self-correcting skills approach that has proved so successful with disadvantaged youth.

It's Your World (Continental Press, Elizabethtown, Pa.). For intermediate grade level readers, this series of reading skill builders through science can be used at all grade levels through adult. Ten packages of reading materials are attractively boxed. Each package contains 5 copies of 7 reading selections on a 4-page card. Selections in each box cover one scientific theme, such as the Human Body, Transportation, Sources of Energy and Space. Each child reviews vocabulary in the attractive workbook; he then reads the selection from the package and follows this up by challenging, exciting and clever exercises in his workbooks. The workbooks provide excellent progress plotters, and answer keys are available for self-checking. Also available are rexograph masters of pre- and post-tests as well as teacher records and supplementary activities for each selection. This package is a fine example of creative, effective, individualized materials that publishers are now providing to the schools.

Learning How To Use the Dictionary (Macmillan, New York). A linear programed book for intermediate and junior high school youth, the program was designed by Behavioral Research Laboratories. It is a thorough review of dictionary skills as well as supplementary word meaning skills. Like Macmillan's *Spectrum of Skills,* feedback is provided with each stimulus frame. Masks are provided to cover the answers. With some children, the feedback must be isolated or delayed by placement on the page following the stimulus. This provides a time delay between presentation of the stimulus and checking the answer. During the delay, the subject appears to make *at least* a covert response even when his intention is to cheat. In one program with seventh- and eighth-graders, programed books like these were modified. The feedback was inked out and placed on a bulletin board or at the end of the workbook. In spite of programed instruction theory, the result was better scores on the checkout tests.

Learnings in Science (Science Research Associates, Chicago). Most reading teachers never go beyond the reading, language arts, or English section of a publisher's catalog. Often, administrative restrictions prevent them from doing so, which is too bad, because some of the best materials for getting reluctant readers into a reading program are through content areas. This series consists of four kits: *Earth's Atmosphere Lab, Weather and Climate Lab, Solar System Lab,* and *Biogeography Lab.* Extras include student record books. These laboratories are excellent teachers of study skills and comprehension, as well as content. A well-equipped reading center should have one of each.

Living Your English (D. C. Heath, Boston). For each grade level, 7–12, a textbook-workbook presents grammar lessons in the form of a personal or social situation. The directions are complex and wordy, but the workbooks offer many practice exercises for each grammatical concept. Good features of this series are the easily removable perforated worksheets that are limited to one exercise skill per page, and the individual diagnostic tests. The diagnostic tests are separate from the workbooks but are carefully numbered to correspond to each workbook lesson. The student can go through the exercises and test himself when he feels he has mastered each section. Answer sheets are available for self-correction. Some teachers may be greatly interested in the manual. It provides information on the nature of slow learners and suggestions for planning and adapting materials to their needs. It is excellent for individualizing instruction according to diagnosed needs. It is included in this section because in two projects, it has been used primarily as an interesting series of reading exercises that junior high school pupils enjoyed in programed form. Whatever value it had in teaching syntax and grammar was considered secondary to its value as interesting reading material for improving reading to follow directions.

Our Nation's History (Follett, Chicago). A series of eight soft-covered workbook-texts, attractively designed, with readabilities from about grades 5–7, each book centers on a theme that is really chronologically determined by American history. Designed for slow learners, the readers teach vocabulary and comprehension. We have used them in programs to develop study skills. This series is an excellent example of teaching reading through the content area and the best American history series available for slow learners.

RSL Reading Skills Lab (Houghton Mifflin, Boston, Mass.). Designed for grades 4–6 readability, this lab can be utilized through high school level. A smaller kit (Box A) provides diagnostic tests on three levels which test each child into Box B. The latter provides series of self-directing, self-correcting, self-teaching skill builders in six skill areas: Unlocking Strange Words, Overcoming Meaning Difficulties, Reading for Different Purposes, Using Reference Aids, Studying Informative Materials, and Reading Critically. The program must be used with subjects who read at least at grade 4 level or above. Otherwise it is too difficult to handle. Even for some children at intermediate levels, the directions are occasionally confusing. Nevertheless, this package is a valuable contribution to pedagogy.

Turner Livingston Series (Follett, Chicago). The Turner Livingston readers are designed for adolescent readers who are not particularly motivated to read. The series utilizes the problems adolescents face as they learn to live with themselves, their families, and their community; workbooks are entitled *Money Spent, The Town You Live In, The Job You Get, The Person You Are, The Friends You Make, The Family You Belong To,* and so forth. Each selection is short and is consistently followed by these exercises: Matching words to definitions; supplying words with antonyms; making true-false evaluations; isolating segments of pertinent dialogue to encourage written and oral expression; making a checklist of personal reactions to words, characters, values, events; answering questions that check basic comprehension. This material is a good example of high-interest, low-vocabulary reading selections. They are short, concise, and interesting to junior high school children and school dropouts. In general, pupil response to the reading selections has been good, but the work exercises frighten the retarded reader. In one successful project teachers separated the short reading selections from the exercises and introduced small bits of the latter.

Audio-Visual Materials

Machines are a pet peeve of many reading people who feel that perhaps Americans' infatuation with automation tends to cloud their judgment so that they overvalue the machine. Or perhaps the need for something dramatic and visible drives administrators to purchase hardware regardless of effectiveness. Whatever the reason, opposition to hardware can be as unreasonable as its defense. Machines, filmstrips, and miscellaneous hardware are excellent pace-changers in any reading program, and that is sufficient reason to include them. Some machines are valuable because they execute certain strategies unavailable in software. Included in this list are machines, filmstrips, records, tapes, and miscellaneous hardware used in various reading programs for disadvantaged and advantaged children throughout the country.

AVR Eye-span Trainer, Model 10 (Audio Visual Research, Waseca, Minn.). A hand-operated tachistoscope for individual or very small groups (two to three pupils), the trainer comes with prepared slides printed on index card stock. The eye-span trainer can be programed with numbers, words, or phrases on three levels: high school and adult, advanced, and elementary and junior high school. Blank cards are also available, but oaktag cut to size can be used if teachers wish to develop their own content. The eye-span trainer, as with most tachistoscopes, is an effective motivating device with the type of population trained in dropout projects. I have found it less useful for training eye span and speed than for reinforcing vocabulary, phonics, phrase reading, and so on. This particular inexpensive tachistoscope lends itself to teacher-made materials developed to meet individual needs. Some projects have used it successfully to preteach vocabulary needed to read specific materials on all levels.

Controlled Reader Jr.; Story Filmstrips; Comprehension Power Filmstrips; Accuracy Building Filmstrips; Spelling Filmstrips; Vocabulary Filmstrips (Educational Development Laboratories, Huntington, N.Y.). The Controlled Reader was the most effective and versatile reading machine used in any of the programs at all levels from grade 1 to Job Corps. Basically, the machine is designed to project reading material scanning from left to right at controlled speeds on a screen. Both the Story Filmstrips and the Comprehension Power Builders contain good reading selections. As expected with the population under discussion, listed grade levels for the films must be interpreted cautiously. They are listed at levels much higher than what Puerto Rican and black children in slum areas were able to handle. The Controlled Reader Jr. is a smaller version of the Controlled Reader, which is designed for full class use. Consistent with this book's stress on individualized instruction and pupil-team learning, the junior is preferable for smaller groups. It is simple enough for children to operate themselves in pupil-learning teams and sturdy enough to withstand the usual wear and tear. As a mechanical gimmick, the Controlled Reader Jr. justifies itself. Pupils do not seem to tire of it; they enjoy working the machine on their own. The machine, however, is more than a gimmick; it presents graded reading material of a high quality in an effective manner. With a little imagination the teacher can use it to teach main ideas, details, anticipatory reading, phrase reading, left-to-right progression, scanning, vocabulary, and a host of other skills.

By introducing a Speed-I-O-Scope (Graflex) or similar tachistoscopic attachment in front of the Controlled Reader Jr. lens, the same machine can be used as a tachistoscope to present words, phrases, visual memory, and visual discrimination exercises. This saves purchasing a second tachistoscope machine. Generally speaking, tachistoscopic flashes of numbers, letters, or nonsense shapes do not teach skills directly transferable to reading in the populations under discussion. Filmstrips of letters, words, and phrases are much safer investments if the goal is to teach reading subskills.

Craig Reader (Craig Research, Los Angeles). A combination reading pacer and tachistoscope, this 15-pound TV-like machine is really a sophisticated rear projection slide projector with some convenient gimmicks. It is an excellent machine, but like so much educational technology, the programs are not appropriate for low-achieving, disadvantaged readers. For on- or above-grade achievers who can handle traditional middle class content, it is a highly motivating gimmick that will impress classroom visitors.

Electro Tach No. 163B (Lafayette Instrument Corp., Lafayette, Ind.). This small box with a viewing window, toggle switch trigger, and timing dial flashes printed stimuli to a single viewer or to two children sitting close together. This is a rather expensive tachistoscope for one child at a time except for two features: First, it is fed by cards on which reading clinicians can type tailor-made sequences to meet special needs. Second, it is one of the sturdiest pieces of hardware we have ever used in the classroom. Because of these two features, the Electro Tach has been one of our favorite machines.

Eye Gate Filmstrips (Eye Gate House, Inc., Jamaica, N.Y.). Three sets of Eye Gate filmstrips have been especially useful. First is Reading Readiness Set 85, which provides 10 filmstrips covering alphabet, left-to-right sequence, auditory and visual discrimination, and other useful skills. Sets 180 and 141 were designed primarily for speech improvement but are excellent aids for improving auditory discrimination and sound-symbol relationships. Teachers are cautioned against assuming that these filmstrips are self-contained programs. They are not; they are additional aids to the teacher to be used with many other materials designed to teach these skills.

Graflex SM 400 (Graflex Corp., Rochester, N.Y.; or the Society for Visual Education, Chicago). This compact, rugged filmstrip projector is the best buy in strip projectors. It is small, inexpensive, and dependable.

Homemade Audio Listening Stations or Language Labs (No specific suppliers). One of the most effective and useful learning devices is the homemade language lab. The equipment consists of any standard tape recorder and one or more headset couplers. This author has used Koss T-4 couplers, which are small boxes with four female jacks. The T-4 plugs into the output of the tape recorder. One T-4 accommodates four inexpensive bakerlite headsets. A number of T-4s can be hooked in tandem so that a dozen or more children with headsets can be hooked into a tape recorder. A variety of exercises in auditory discrimination, dictation, listening comprehension, following directions, storytelling, and so on, can be taped and presented to some children in a classroom while the teacher works with other children. Concentration is high and noise is low. Occasionally, the teacher may talk directly through the headsets (via the tape-recorder amplifier) using the microphone, by turning the set to *record* and the output jack to *monitor*. This is an effective method of talking to hyperactive learners. Children with articulation problems can talk into the recorder and, at the same time, hear themselves through the headset. This intensified feedback is an excellent aid to treating articulation problems. A favorite technique of some teachers with whom this setup was used was to record the listening skills exercises in the SRA Labs and let children work on their own, while the teacher worked with individuals on the reading comprehension and word-attack skills.

Mirrors (No specific supplier). In the teaching of auditory discrimination of sounds in words, we have established two guidelines: (1) sounds should be taught in words or word parts rather than in isolation; (2) the kinesthetic awareness of the oral cavity as it shapes to pronounce a particular sound is valuable in mastering auditory discrimination of that sound with severely retarded readers. The mirror is a device we found effective in making pupils aware of what their mouths are doing when they enunciate a particular sound. Inexpensive mirrors can be purchased in local toy stores.

Reading Pacers—Nonprojecting (Audio Visual Research, Waseca, Minn.; Educational Development Laboratories, Huntington, N.Y.; Keystone View, Meadville, Pa.; Psychotechnics, Chicago; Reading Laboratories, New York; Science Research Associates, Chicago). The best machine for increasing reading speed is a $10 stopwatch. But to lure reluctant readers into a reading center, one each of a variety of machines that will deliver reading stimuli is worth owning *if all the other software and children's books have been purchased* and money is still left over. Which ones are worth buying?

Audio Visual Research (AVR) has a dependable Rateometer. Educational Development Labs sells a Skimmer that uses a light beam. Psychotechnics' Shadowscope does the same thing. Keystone has a mechanical rod that travels down any page at controlled speeds. Reading Laboratories has a Prep-pacer, and SRA has two models of a plastic Reading Accelerator, Model IV and the more expensive Model III. We have found these machines to be the most dependable, although none has yet been purchased for the Yeshiva University Reading Clinic. We are still trying to buy up all the software and books we need.

Tachistoscopic Attachments (Society for Visual Education, Chicago; Lafayette Instrument Corp., Lafayette, Ind.; or Graflex, Rochester, N.Y.). A number of different companies market tachistoscopes that can be used on any filmstrip or slide projector. I have found the tachistoscope to be a highly motivating device for teaching a number of skills. The Speed-I-O-Scope (Graflex and SVE) happens to be the one used in the Yeshiva Reading Center, but the brand name is not particularly important. Two projects have been using Lafayette's All Purpose Tach, which is the same as the Graflex. By masking the 35-mm opening of the standard film projector, teachers may use Educational Development Laboratories' Tach-X word-study filmstrips. Tach-X words are presented on quarter-frame exposures requiring the masking device. Thin plastic or cardboard serves as an adequate mask. Simple taping also works well. Other companies also provide filmstrips for word study. SVE markets a number of filmstrips for various word-study exercises. These filmstrips present words on a full 35-mm opening, eliminating the need to mask the frame. Tachistoscope training works best with small groups, three to ten subjects. This allows the teacher to appoint tachistoscope specialists to operate the machine on a rotating basis. The teacher can solve many behavior problems by assigning problem pupils to responsible positions as "tach operators."

Tachomatic 500 Projector (Psychotechnics, Chicago). This machine is in some respects a more expensive competitor to the EDL Controlled Reader. However, this is a case in which the competition evens off in spite of price differences. The Tachomatic 500 is very dependable mechanically. It presents strips at full-line, two or three fixations per line from 100 to 2,000 words per minute. Tachomatic's films are excellent, and there is a choice of a number of different vocabulary, discrimination, and comprehension series. Many of these are at a sufficiently low level to use for remedial training with underachievers.

The Talking Teacher (Lippincott, Philadelphia). This set of five 5-inch tapes is designed to accompany Lippincott's phonic basal series but is equally valuable independently as an introduction to sounds when the children are plugged in by headset to the source. This intensifies the input and focuses on the sounds. We have transferred these tapes to plug-in cartridges in an experimental take-home program. Twenty children took home portable cartridge tape recorders each night and listened to the tapes and followed the books. Although we suspect that the excellent results were due primarily to the novelty of the experience, we are continuing this activity. Within reason, children and parents are not particularly concerned with *how* we get them to read better as long as the children improve.

T-matic 150 (Psychotechnics, Chicago). Perhaps the easiest to use and most dependable tachistoscope is this filmstrip projector with built-in tachistoscope that provides flash settings of up to 4 seconds. The letter recognition, word and phrases filmstrips, and spelling word lists are excellent.

We Speak Through Music (Stanbow Productions, Valhalla, N.Y.). A collection of 64 songs recorded in three albums by Sisters Mary Authur and Mary Elaine, these records were designed by professional personnel for use with children who have an articulation disorder. Songbooks accompany each album. Through a planned program that uses both sensory and motor approaches, the material attempts to stabilize the sounds learned by children in school or clinic by providing the child with planned practice material in the form of songs. These songs are graded for vocabulary and consonant sound development. The material is set up on the assumption that correct speaking habits are more effectively accomplished by the memorizing of songs and verses than by the repetition of sentences and words without context. Although many other verses and songs are available as practice material, they often include sounding elements and vocabulary beyond the child's level of development. Because the child cannot cope with the vocabulary, most records hinder, instead of help, his learning progress. The *We Speak Through Music* records were effective with grades K–4. Socially disadvantaged retarded readers usually cannot hear sounds in words. These records are an excellent technique for teaching such sounds.

Index

A

Alphabet, knowledge of, 29, 72, 190
  and reading success in early grades, 159
  ways to teach, 161–65
American Library Association, 171
Auditory discrimination of sounds, 166–70
Audio-visual materials. *See* Machines in the classroom
Autonomous central processes (ACP), 78–79, 103

B

Basal readers, 186, 187, 197, 211–12, 232
  See also Materials for teaching reading
Basic Remedial Word Count Lists, by grade level, 200–07
Basic Test of Reading Comprehension (BTRC), 67–68
Beginning reading program, 181–223
  materials for, 281–87
Bender Gestalt Test, 70
Benton's *Revised Visual Retention Test*, 70
Black children, attempt at conceptual development, 150
  IQ scores and learning, 25–26
  perceptual dysfunction among first graders, 88–95
  reading disability patterns, 70–74
  reading retardation in a slum, 27–29
  See also Minority groups
Boston University Secondary Reading Clinic, 63, 67, 164, 198, 225

C

California Reading Test (CRT), 63–64, 65, 66
California Test of Mental Maturity, Short Form (CTMM), 63, 64
Child development theory, 123, 125–26
Children's books. *See* Storybooks
Cloward, Robert, 67
Code busting, 51, 181, 184–85, 189, 217, 220
College Reading Association, 183
Community action programs, 5
Compensatory education, 25, 37–38, 47, 52–53, 147
Concept learning, in preschoolers, 150–55
Content areas, reading, 249–71

D

Diagnosing reading disabilities, New York City children, 70–75
    using IQ tests, 34–35
Diagnostic Test of Word Attack Skills (DTWAS), 67, 71
Diagnostic tools, tests, 56–76
Dictionaries, picture, 198–99
Disadvantaged children, 8–12, 13–31
    language and concept development, 141, 148
    learning to read, 219–21
    perceptual dysfunctions, 87–96
    reading disabilities patterns, 70–75
Durrell Analysis of Reading Difficulty, 27, 65, 219

E

Emotionally disturbed children, learning to read, 10–11
    socially disadvantaged compared to middle class, 132–33
    See also Content areas
Ethnic groups. *See* Minority groups

F

Federal funds, 171, 215, 216, 217, 225, 239, 273, 275
First grade, beginning reading, 189–91
  reading readiness skills, 160–76
Floor plans of skills centers, 241, 243, 245
Frostig's *Developmental Test of Visual Perception*, 69, 103
  administered to first graders, 88–95
  scores of, New York City children, 70

G

Gates Reading Tests, 64, 65
Gates-McKillop Reading Diagnostic Tests, 65
Gates Readiness Test, 157
Gesell, Arnold, 40, 79, 125
Good readers, home background, 159
Grapheme. *See* Phonics

H

Hall, G. Stanley, 125
Headstart programs, 22, 122, 129, 132, 147
  See also Preschool and early childhood programs
Hebb, D. O., 78–80
Hierarchy of needs model, 40–41, 48–49, 53

I

Individualized instruction, 224–48
Information-processing model, 40–41, 42–47, 53
Initial Teaching Alphabet (i/t/a), 217–18
Intelligence, modifying, 36–38, 52–53
Intelligence tests, 32–36, 52–53, 56–57, 61–63, 64

IQ and reading readiness, 8, 9, 11, 156–57
  scores of children from blue collar homes, 16
  See also names of specific tests
International Reading Association, 183
Iowa Tests of Basic Skills, 64, 65, 156, 226

J

Junior high school, curriculum change to emphasize literacy in content
  areas, 252–55
  English program diary, 256–59
Juvenile delinquency, 15, 16, 37, 225, 226

K

Keystone Visual Survey Tests, 69
Kindergarten, effectiveness, 123–25
  reading readiness skills, 160–76
  visual perceptual training, 98

L

Language patterns, 22–25
  preschool language development program, 141–50
Lee-Clark Reading Readiness Test, 157
Learning, models of, 38–55
Learning readiness, 127, 130, 176–77, 184
  program, 132–55
Letters. *See* Alphabet
Library, classroom, 264–68
  elementary school, 219
Linguistic theory, 4
  programs, 185–86, 212–13
Literacy, 6, 16, 38

M

Machines in the classroom, 4, 166, 187, 216–17, 237, 243–44
    audio-visual materials for reading programs, 311–16
    guidelines for purchasing, 274–75
    semi-automated teacher aides, 141–43
    See also Tachistoscopes
McGuffey readers, 4
Materials for teaching reading, artificial orthographies, 217–18
    basal readers, 211–12
    linguistic programs, 212–13
    phonics, 210
    physiological readiness, 136–39
    skills centers, 240–48
    See also Appendix
Mathematics, 250–52
Metropolitan Reading Achievement Tests, 64, 65, 70, 124
Metropolitan Reading Readiness Test, 157
Michigan Speed of Reading Test, 67
Middle class children, compared to lower class children, 8–12
    family's effect on language and thought processes, 24–25
    reading disability patterns compared to disadvantaged children,
        70–75
Minority groups, effect of kindergarten on school experience, 124
    ethnic distribution of reading retardation in a slum, 27–29
    ethnic distribution of school and total population of a slum, 26
    life style, 19–22
    perceptual quotients of sample first graders by ethnicity, 91–95
    reading disabilities patterns, 70–75
    See also Black children; Disadvantaged children; Puerto Rican
        children
Mobilization for Youth, 5, 20, 67, 88, 89, 91, 96, 102, 124, 136, 138,
        145, 162, 163, 170, 186, 215, 225, 276
Models of learning, 38–55
Montessori method, 138, 142, 278
Multifactor tests of intelligence, 61–63

N

Negro. *See* Black children
New York Medical Center Institute for Developmental Studies, 145
Noall, Mabel S., 63, 67, 198

O

Operant conditioning, 141–43, 162
Optometrist and ophthalmologist consultants, 69, 119–20, 138, 176
Oral-aural vocabulary, 51–52, 188, 196, 199, 208, 219–20
    operant conditioning in oral language development, 141–43
    pattern drills in teaching deprived preschoolers, 148–50
    patterns and reading achievement, 71–72
Oral Reading Test of Functional Literacy, 67–69
Organic impairment, 95–96
Ortho-Rater, 69
Osborn, Jean, 148–50

P

Paperback books, 259–69
Perceptual development. *See* Visual perception
Perceptual dysfunction, 73–74, 75, 80–100, 101–04
Perceptual quotients of sample first graders, 90–94
Phoneme. *See* Phonics
Phonics, 181, 184, 185, 220
    for beginning readers, 190, 197, 208–11
    for reading readiness, 162–70
    materials for, 287–94
Piaget, J., 79
Pitman Initial Teaching Alphabet, 217–18
Poverty, 7, 13–31
    See also Disadvantaged children; War on Poverty
Preprimer level reading skills, 187–89

Preschool and early childhood programs, 98, 122–31
    basic visual-motor training, 105–17
    learning readiness, 132–55
    materials, 277–81
    reading readiness skills, 160–76
Primary Mental Abilities test (PMA), 63, 156
Primer to first level reading skills, 189–91
Puerto Rican children, 17
    auditory discrimination of sounds, 169
    family life style in New York, 21
    perceptually dysfunctioning first graders, 88–95
    reading disability patterns, 70–73
    reading retardation, 27–29
    significance of kindergarten, 124
    See also Minority groups

R

Reading disability patterns, 70–75
Reading grade expectancy level, predicted in IQ tests, 34–36
Reading model, 40–41, 51–52, 53
Reading program in primary grades, 181–223
Reading readiness, 9, 11, 127, 129, 153, 184
    program, 156–80
Reading retardation, 30, 37
    in a New York school district, 26–29
    perceptually dysfunctioning children, 81–98
    reading disability patterns, 70–75
    training in sense modality shifts, 139–41
    visual-motor perception program with retarded-reading second
        graders, 105–15
    See also Perceptual dysfunction
Reading specialists, 183
Reading tests, 63–69
    reading achievement scores in New York, 26–29
    reading readiness tests, 156–57
    See also names of specific tests

Report cards, for skills centers programs, 247
Retarded readers. *See* Reading retardation

S

School dropouts, 16, 216
Science, 252
Self-directed learning, skills centers program, 224–48
Skills centers floor plans, 241, 243, 245
Skills centers program, 224–48
Social studies, 252
Spache's *Diagnostic Reading Scales,* 65
Stanford Achievement Test, 64, 65
Stanford-Binet Intelligence Scale, 33, 63, 70
Storybooks, 4, 170–71, 175, 187, 208, 218–19
Syndrome model, 40–41, 49–51, 53

T

Tachistoscopes, 166, 176, 208, 237
Teacher aides, homework helper tutors, 215–16
    in perceptual training, 117
    using school dropouts, 216
    See also Machines in the classroom
Teacher roles, at skills centers, 237–40
Teacher training, institutions, 9
    sensitivity, 253
    skill specialization, 215
    to teach reading, 65, 182–83
    in use of diagnostic tests, 65
    in visual perceptual training, 101–02
Tests and testing, 32–36, 56–76
    See also Intelligence tests; Reading tests; Visual perception, tests;
        and names of specific tests
Tutoring, by older children, 215–16
Two Bridges Project, 225

U

University of Illinois Institute for Research on Exceptional Children, 148

V

Visual perceptual dysfunction. *See* Perceptual dysfunction
Visual perception, 77–100
  materials for perceptual training, 278–80
  tests, 69–70
  visual perceptual training programs for earliest developmental stage, 102–21
  See also Perceptual dysfunction
Vocabulary development, controlled, 186, 198
  preschool programs for the culturally deprived, 145–50
  reading readiness, 173–75
  materials for, 287–94
  remedial word count lists, 200–07
  sight vocabulary for grades three and four, 193

W

War on Poverty, 3, 5, 6, 7, 11, 122, 224
Wechsler Intelligence Scale for Children (WISC), 61–63
  scores of New York children, 70–71, 73–74
White children, reading retardation in a slum, 26–29
Winter Haven Lions Publications Committee Program, 137–38
Word Analysis Test, 67
Word count lists, by grade level, 200–07

Y

Yeshiva University Ferkauf Graduate School Reading Center, 63, 65, 69, 70, 72, 73, 74, 97, 138, 162, 165, 184, 186, 276